PROJECT REHABILITATION IN DEVELOPING COUNTRIES

In the past it has been common practice to abandon a development project whose performance falls below certain expectations. More recently, however, there has been a growing concern that abandoning a project wastes an existing asset, which could instead be rehabilitated. It is towards this end that *Project Rehabilitation in Developing Countries* is directed.

The book works from the assumption that once failure has been diagnosed the rehabilitation policy should be drawn from two broad categories: internal structure and operation of the project; and external factors which influence performance. Project failure often results from inadequacies in both categories. Illustrating this the book covers four related areas:

- The cause of project failure is addressed – examples of which are drawn from a wide range of countries.
- Alternative procedures and techniques are examined for use in selected projects.
- Detailed case studies demonstrate rehabilitation and recovery programmes.
- The management and institutional aspects of project rehabilitation policy are assessed.

The contributors have extensive experience in development project planning and management. The editor, **Colin Kirkpatrick**, is Professor of Development Economics at the Development and Project Planning Centre, University of Bradford. He has held numerous visiting appointments around the world and has acted as consultant to various international organizations and development agencies.

PROJECT REHABILITATION IN DEVELOPING COUNTRIES

Edited by
Colin Kirkpatrick

London and New York

First published in 1991
by Routledge
11 New Fetter Lane, London EC4P 4EE

Simultaneously published in the USA and Canada
by Routledge
a division of Routledge, Chapman and Hall Inc.
29 West 35th Street, New York, NY 10001

Typeset by NWL Editorial Services, Langport, Somerset TA10 9DG
Printed and bound in Great Britain by
Biddles Ltd, Guildford and King's Lynn

British Library Cataloguing in Publication Data
Project rehabilitation in developing countries.
1. Developing countries: foreign assistance
I. Kirkpatrick, Colin *1944–*
338.90091724

ISBN 0–415–06711–1

Library of Congress Cataloging in Publication Data
Project rehabilitation in developing countries /
edited by Colin Kirkpatrick
Includes bibliographical references and index.
ISBN 0–415–06711–1
1. Economic development projects – Africa – Evaluation.
2. Economic development projects – Africa – Management.
3. Economic development projects – Developing countries –
Evaluation.   4. Economic development projects – Developing
countries – Management.   I. Kirkpatrick, C.H. (Colin H.), 1944–   .
HC800.Z9E447   1991   90–27288
338.9′0068 – dc20   CIP

CONTENTS

v

FIGURES

TABLES

CONTRIBUTORS

Ramesh Adhikari   Research Fellow, Development and Project Planning Centre, University of Bradford.

Farhad Analoui   Lecturer, Development and Project Planning Centre, University of Bradford

George Assaf Industrial Development Officer, Regional and Country Studies Division, United Nations Industrial Development Organisation (UNIDO)

Paul Cook   Senior Lecturer, Institute for Development Policy and Management, University of Manchester

Basil Cracknell   Consultant and former Head, Evaluation Unit, Overseas Development Administration

David T. Edwards   Professor of Development Policy and Planning, Development and Project Planning Centre, University of Bradford

Mike Faber   Professor of Economics, Institute of Development Studies, University of Sussex

Tom Franks Lecturer, Development and Project Planning Centre, University of Bradford

Colin Kirkpatrick (editor) Professor of Development Economics, Development and Project Planning Centre, University of Bradford

Guy de Lusignan Deputy Director, Economic Development Institute, The World Bank

CONTRIBUTORS

Martin Minogue Director, International Development Centre, University of Manchester

David Potts Lecturer, Development and Project Planning Centre, University of Bradford

Michael Tribe Lecturer, Development and Project Planning Centre, University of Bradford

John Weiss Senior Lecturer, Development and Project Planning Centre, University of Bradford

Michael Yaffey Lecturer, Development and Project Planning Centre, University of Bradford

PREFACE

Economic growth and development depend essentially on an economy's capacity to invest and make efficient use of its resources. Over the past decade investment levels have fallen significantly in many developing countries. At the same time, there has been growing concern with the poor performance and 'failure' of existing investment projects.

The contraction in investment levels and performance has focused attention on the issue of project rehabilitation as a means of stimulating more efficient use of resources. The chapters in this volume examine this issue from a number of perspectives. Part I provides an overview of the topic. The contributions in Part II examine the lessons of project evaluation studies as providing a basis for the formulation of rehabilitation policy. In Part III, procedures and approaches to project rehabilitation are discussed. Part IV contains three chapters reviewing different aspects of experience with project rehabilitation programmes and policy. In Part V, the managerial and institutional dimensions of project rehabilitation are discussed.

It is hoped that this volume will be of interest and practical value to persons involved in the formulation and implementation of rehabilitation policy in developing countries. The chapters were originally presented at a conference on 'Project Rehabilitation in Developing Countries' held at the Development and Project Planning Centre, University of Bradford, in December 1988. Financial support for the conference was received from the Directorate General for Development of the Commission of the European Communities, the National Westminster Bank PLC and the University of Bradford Research

xiii

Support Fund. Thanks are due to these organizations for their assistance.

Finally, I should like to thank Mrs Pearl Golden who typed successive drafts with her usual efficiency, speed and good humour, and also Ramesh Adhikari and Barbara Evers for providing invaluable support in preparing the final manuscript for publication.

Colin Kirkpatrick

INTRODUCTION

EDI AND THE MANAGEMENT OF CHANGE

Guy de Lusignan*

INTRODUCTION

This material was used for an opening address on 12 December 1988, on the occasion of the University of Bradford conference on Project Rehabilitation in Developing Countries. Our concerns were, first, to set the tone on this important subject in making a few remarks within the context of The Economic Development Institute's current thrusts. Second, we wanted in very broad terms to briefly highlight the importance of the changing world economy in which we live today which makes the task of all development practitioners – whether from industrialized or developing countries – much more difficult than thirty years ago. Finally, we discussed what all this implied for EDI under its 1990–94 Strategic Plan.

PROJECT REHABILITATION

The project concept was defined specifically in the Articles of Agreement adopted at the Bretton Woods Conference in 1944 which established the International Bank for Reconstruction and Development (IBRD). What the Bank was created for was to make or guarantee loans for the purpose of specific projects of reconstruction or development. And the Bank's interpretation of the concept of project from the beginning of its operations was to broadly cover the use of resources for a specific productive purpose. Warren Baum and Stokes Tolbert define a project as a '*discrete* package of investments, policies, and institutional and other actions designed to achieve a specific development objective (or set of objectives) within a designated period'.[1] This is a much

3

broader definition of the project concept than certainly the authors of the Articles of Agreement had in mind but it is closer to the Bank experience. Another interesting definition is the one of a former EDI staff member, now retired from the World Bank, whose book on *Economic Analysis of Agricultural Projects*[2] is an EDI 'best seller' and is used widely in training institutions: a project is 'an investment activity in which financial resources are expended to create capital assets that produce benefits over an extended period of time' and it is an 'activity for which money will be spent in expectation of returns and which logically seems to lend itself to planning, financing and implementing as a unit'. We can say that over the last forty years there have been major developments and successful efforts in the planning and implementing of development projects. Economic growth rates have been higher than during any other period. And yet, despite the large and dramatic rise of public investments funds – whether under bilateral or multilateral aid – over the last twenty years, their performance has often been so disappointing in the least-developed regions such as sub-Saharan Africa and for those lower income groups of the populations in these regions. Why have projects failed, especially in the 1970s? Was it because they were poorly designed? Was it because of wrong priorities, wrong choices, or hasty decisions on very expensive projects which were studied inadequately if at all (the so-called white elephants)? Was it because planning the implementation stage of a project tended to be neglected, as well as its supervision? Was it because not enough care was given to the capacity of executing institutions? The importance of making the investment – and thus the project – sustainable was not realized until very recently. Was it because of lack of attention to the vagaries of markets and prices? Or was it also due to the mismanagement of the institutions in charge of development and project investments? Was it (or is it still) due to the overall inefficiency or rather the ineffectiveness of the public sector? To what extent did many projects and programmes fail and require drastic rehabilitation measures?

At this point, for the sake of giving an illustration of a bad case, I would like to strike a personal note. In my second year at the World Bank, I participated in the appraisal of the Madagascar Lake Alaotra Project. The main objectives of the project were to develop high-quality rice production and introduce crop

4

diversification through double-cropping of rice fields in an area in north-eastern Madagascar which was producing one-third of all marketed rice in the country. At that time (1969–70), Madagascar was not only self-sufficient in rice, she was also a rice exporter. Today she is importing rice. As a senior loan officer I chaired the negotiations of this project and presented it to the Board of Executive Directors for approval. It was considered a very good and important project with an economic rate of return of 11 per cent. Twelve years later, in a report published on the first two decades of concessionary loans by an affiliate of the Bank Group, the International Development Association (IDA),[3] I learnt that this project had made no significant contribution to the economy of Madagascar following the evaluation of the project in 1980, five years after its completion. Reasons: wrong assumptions, unrealistic goals, poor design and execution, institutional weaknesses, inadequate supervision, inadequate attention to social and cultural environment. Certainly, in the course of any project, there can be project changes due to unforeseen technical problems which may lead to unexpected financial problems – for instance, cost overruns. But, above all, there can be unanticipated socio-political problems such as poor response to the objectives of the project by the population expected to benefit from it. Worse: the government which has approved the project can show less commitment during its execution. It may realize that it lacked the managerial capacities to really achieve the project objectives. Hence the failure of the project.[4]

This interesting case raises many questions and many difficult ones. These would need more work. Let us simply say that some borrowers may think that project lending and, as is the case today, adjustment lending are being forced into the 'discrete' strait-jacket neatly described above. This allows everyone to agree in full good conscience to loans, credits, and grants given to developing countries from all sources. This is to the credit and professionalism of the excellent staff involved in these project and programme lending operations. Everyone's objectives and targets are achieved and everyone is happy, except when in a few cases – and fortunately only in a few cases – things go wrong. Then, one questions both the degree of political commitment and the institutional efficiency of the borrower. From the sources of

5

lending, one can blame the poor resources put at their disposal to supervise the project or programme, or the lack of dedication of the authorities to undertake the reforms negotiated and approved. But how many countries have said that many of the procedures, processes, and policies recommended or used result in standardized products as if these are ruled by blueprints applied all over the world? Alas, such an 'off-the-shelf' product does not work. It may be preferable to consider a product which consists of different step-by-step evolutions. What about sets of adjustment conditions that adapt themselves to changing circum-stances, to unforeseen situations, to changing parameters, to new objectives? Those who like to produce a perfect product, which does not or would not normally take account of non- economic or non-financial criteria, find this difficult to accept. And when people in a few parts of the world fight, riot, and kill because bread prices and/or mass-transport fares become dearer, we in the Western world express surprise and consternation. Such unrests had not been anticipated in the conditions set forth to restrain inflation and to put the economy and its finances in a better shape.

Actually, to be successful a project does not only require a moderate to high rate of return, it has to help strengthen borrowers' institutions and policies and to lay down solid foundations for growth and sustainability.[5] When, finally, the overall political environment does not allow sound imple-mentation of projects because of domestic and international constraints, how then can a sustainable development policy be put into place? We are concerned whether ongoing projects and policies work out or not and we are concerned about the need to give more attention and resources to supervision. Thus, we are worried that while adjustment policies remain necessary, ongoing projects and programmes require drastic rehabilitation measures. We believe that, at the end of the day, project investment is likely to become, once again, more fashionable and we are also worried that we shall not be ready for this.

A CHANGING ENVIRONMENT

As pointed out by Peter Drucker[6], we are already living in a changed world economy. Thus, we have to be prepared to be confronted by crises and to know how to change; we have to anticipate change, and rather than resist, learn to manage it – but are we capable of doing this?

In the 1970s and early 1980s, most international conferences were referring to the concept of North and South and to the need to create a new international order between them. Well, the world has since changed in the sense that it does not form two monolithic groups, but several groups among industrialized as well as developing countries; all have uneven economic performances; all are facing crises, constant competition and evolution. And, they all have to face unexpected wars or natural catastrophes. Peter Drucker is right when he writes that

> from now on any country – but also any business, especially a large one – that wants to prosper will have to accept that it is the world economy that leads and that domestic policies will succeed only if they strengthen, or at least do not impair, the country's international competitive position. This may be the most important feature – it surely is the most striking – of the changed world economy.

Countries and economies are more interdependent than ever. There is something even more daunting. The twenty-first century is near to us. What will it consist of? Who will be the superpowers – the USA and USSR? The future of the USSR lies in the success or failure of *perestroika*; the USA is faced with drastic changes. Will they be capable of managing them? In the USA, for instance, there will be a decreasing number of blue-collar workers, more than half of the labour force will be women, Blacks and Hispanics, and labour costs will become less and less important, both as a comparative cost and as a factor in competition, as a result. Robotization and high technologies will have become more sophisticated by the early 2000s. Another important visionary thought: in the US there is likely to be a shift from primarily labour-intensive industries to more 'knowledge intensive' industries. What success stories will emerge from other predominant countries/regions such as Japan and/or the Far East and the Pacific Rim. Already the dramatic performance of Japan and other 'Asian dragons' dominates this region. By the twenty-first century what will be the position of China and its outlets of Hong Kong and Taiwan? In any event, the East and the Pacific will be dominated by Japan and by China. Yet another group (worth mentioning whatever changes may occur in Eastern Europe) will be Europe and the 1993 Common Market, with the German, the French and the British forming the dynamic and maybe still quarrelsome core. Finally, what about the developing countries? Well, a few of these will closely follow the current NICs, Brazil, Mexico, India and maybe the Mediterranean countries. Will the role of the others, especially of sub-Saharan Africa, be rather limited and with little influence?

Why such a cynical and awesome view with respect to sub-Saharan Africa? A few basic facts first. After the golden years (1960–74) of sustained yet equitable growth, Africa is in a non-growth situation, despite some recent improvements in a small number of countries. The crisis has been more acute in sub-Saharan Africa following the two oil shocks, the natural disasters, the reduction in the demand for basic commodities and the closing of some developed countries' markets, the rising demand for imports and the resulting debt burden. African peoples are in distress. They are doing no more than surviving. African world records are its population growth and its dramatic deterioration of income. Africa is not a developing continent now, it is a continent under pauperization. What makes it even worse is the degradation of its ecological potential due to deforestation, drought, soil erosion, etc.

True, the situation in Africa is more complex than elsewhere. In a couple of EDI seminars, some African decision-makers have asked why are they performing so differently than their brothers from Asia and the East? A somewhat difficult question! And yet, how can one understand Africa without recalling slavery, colonialism and its legacy, ethnic strife, imposed and irrational boundaries, and the failings of the post-colonial period? Did not the former colonial powers, the technical cooperation experts, the advisers from bilateral and multilateral agencies, the consulting firms and contractors, the bankers, sometimes give the wrong advice and assist in the frenzy of newly-independent countries to industrialize in order to guarantee – so those countries said – their economic independence? Was this advice not to the detriment of agriculture and rural development? Did we advise or disagree with the right or wrong incentives and fiscal policies, without mentioning the vested interests that we all had, and still have? Why was there such an emphasis on centralization and urbanization with the resulting large and costly administrative machinery? Are the poorly performing and badly managed public or semi-public enterprises not the successors of pre-colonial enterprises?

Despite what has already been written and said on the gloomy fate of Africa, there are many of us who still believe and have hope. We believe in its rehabilitation. We say this because we believe that among present decision-makers, African intellectuals, economists, writers, historians, managers, entrepreneurs, and in Africa's next generation of technocrats, there is a will to change the structures inherited from the past and to rectify the mistakes made over these last twenty-five years. There is hope.

To quote Julius Nyerere,

> there will be pain and sacrifices especially for those of us who have grown accustomed to living in the economic South as if we were citizens of the economic North, ... we must not denigrate our traditions but adapt them to meet the demands of modern technology. ... We must cease to organise ourselves from top-down because we do not trust our people. They have demonstrated an ability to learn new techniques and to adapt.[7]

There is hope because there have been, since 1984 at the height of the drought, major efforts from many African governments to institute major economic reforms. This with a view to restoring deteriorating balances of payments and laying the foundations for a return to economic and social growth and, also, with a view to restoring agriculture and to emphasize its role as an engine of growth. Of course, there were many prices to pay for that – a financial price, policies imposition, and both political and social costs. Courageous measures were taken. There were signs of recovery and even some successes. Rigour and financial austerity were understood as being imperative. There were failures and scepticism. Are rigour, austerity and sacrifices understood by everyone? Are they explained properly, are they accepted? Are the policies of adjustment sustainable? Has the attention given to structural adjustment policies been to the detriment of solid project-oriented investments of the past? Maybe so, although the total adjustment operations financed by the Bank do not represent more than 25 per cent of its total lending operations –

project finance, therefore, still having the largest share. However, the questions just put forward are good questions. Donor agencies realize today more than before that in granting any aid, in making any loan – whether for a project or a programme of structural adjustment – the institutional and political aspects of the development process must be given due consideration. In other words, how best to manage development and sustain equitable growth. How to manage scarcity and how to manage in a much more complex and contracting economy. How to manage people in a particular cultural environment and to make sure that populations in the always painful process of change, will understand and agree to the changes, including their consequences and costs even if in the long run they will benefit from them. How to manage by influence and how to influence the external environment both domestically and internationally. And, finally, how to manage change!

INSTITUTIONAL ASPECTS OF DEVELOPMENT

The World Bank lending operations have always put emphasis on 'institution building' and, therefore, on the good implementation of projects through good, sound, and well-managed institutions. Increasingly, components of loans served to finance assistance to institutions, thereby strengthening these institutions – especially through training. In 1983, the *World Development Report*'s main topic was management in development. This topic is still a major concern of the Bank today. Suggestions have been made to intensify not only investments, but also education and even cultural change, to attempt to straighten out institutional weaknesses or to push institutions to solve their own institutional problems themselves.[8] Here, there are some inherent biases among economists in particular, who prefer to focus on the most effective ways of allocating resources. This is much easier to quantify, of course. This being so, we can all agree that the dialogue between economists, administrators, managers, and politicians is usually rather difficult. The fact of the matter is that institutional development problems in LDCs, and above all in Africa, are very complex. To strengthen institutions and to lay down a human resources development strategy requires quite a number of actions which are not easy to define and to fulfil.

What seems most important is to have a clearer vision and understanding of development objectives, of priorities, and of the choices and alternatives. This should be the function of governments with a full appreciation of the constraints and limits of both the public and private sectors. What can be the real role of the state in achieving the objectives of a well thought out and clearly spelt out economic and social policy? In short, how can 'the visionary strategic function of the State' be rehabilitated?[9] Soon after independence, African states, particularly ex-French colonies, created ministries of planning and planning commissions; planning units within industries were also created. The purpose of these bodies was to design development policies and programmes; in fact, their main task was to prepare lists of projects to be submitted to aid agencies. In addition, the Ministry of Planning was to negotiate the financing of foreign aid with the donor agencies. There was no group really able or allowed to think freely on the development strategy of the country, taking into account its economic and human potential and bearing in mind the physical, political, social and financial obstacles. In the final analysis, it was, and still is, the Ministry of Finance which made the choices considering short-term budgetary consider-ations. Frequently, however, it was the head of state who decided in the last resort. The decision-making process rested with those who controlled the finance of the state. This is still the case. What has become more and more important is the need to adapt the decision-making machinery to the increased intricacies of the international environment. A group of knowledgeable persons should be given the task of thinking of the future of their country with imagination and vision, considering the short, medium, and long-term prospects. They should anticipate possible crises, investigate various alternative scenarios, take account of the constraints of the country, and emphasize the management of changes.

One of the key aspects of any development strategy should be the acceptance of a policy of rigour and financial discipline. The reform or adjustment process, as it is called today, should not be considered on a short-term basis. It should not be seen simply as a rather tough phase to go through that will soon pass with the support of the donor community. It is completely irrational and unreasonable to believe that donors' medicine will cure no matter

11

how strong and painful the treatment is. Fortunately, many governments realize it. They realize that the adjustment process required to ensure equitable and sustainable growth will take a very long period of time. A certain momentum will have to be maintained to enable these policies and measures to continue to redress the situation. Therefore, it is imperative that the adjustment process be internalized so that governments do not feel, as is often the case, that the prescription is imposed by the IMF and the World Bank. The government has to be convinced that it has been truly involved in the preparation of the reform – that the adjustment programme is its programme. Therefore, the reforms of the institutions will be crucial. A poorly-designed, ill-prepared and loosely-implemented policy of austerity will adversely affect the overall economic and social situation of the country. Strengthening the capacity of civil servants, managers, and decision-makers to realize the implications of the reform process and to take the right steps towards carrying it through, will become absolutely necessary; hence the importance of training, and the building of training institutions in macro-management, sectoral management and strategic planning – in short, in development management. Furthermore, an administrative reform policy strongly supported by an improved management of the civil service appears all the more necessary to sustain the efforts made under the reform programme. Otherwise, how vain would be those efforts and the sacrifices that would have accompanied them.

POLITICAL ASPECTS OF DEVELOPMENT

Economists are right to address the political aspects of development when they talk about the political economy of development. One cannot deal with the development problems of a country without being fully familiar with the history of the country and of its people. The colonial and pre-colonial history of any independent state determines the development of this state regardless of any fine macroeconomic analysis. Many political scientists, particularly in the US, have tried to capture all these situations in the historical perspective of Africa. The notion of 'state' cannot really be comprehended using Western democracies as a basis for comparison.[10] Until colonialism, most African

12

territories, regardless of their ethnic boundaries, were not states: Africans were living in chiefdoms or in communities. During colonialism, political parties and trade unions, particularly in Francophone Africa, were very closely linked to corresponding groups in France and played a major role in the decolonization movement. After independence, it is interesting to note that African heads of state have always carefully watched the position of ethnic groups and tribes, being aware that tribalism may endanger the cohesion of the state and their own personal positions. Besides, how can political dimensions be disregarded when the international environment and the zones of influence of superpowers as well as of the former colonial powers all loom so heavily on the fate of African governments? When one comes to the basics, to the practice of development, one has to lay down facts as to the accountability of statesmen in the face of the debt issue, which is indeed a political issue on which some heads of state show their great art as manipulators: shifting, for instance, coalitions of support both internally and externally, playing beyond finance and economics, realizing that their superb geo-political situation make them essential to foreign powers' own geo-political strategies.

Here, two points have to be singled out: the decision-making process would be politically so much easier if there were a genuine attempt to establish the right policy coordination mechanism to ensure a better visionary strategic function. This is again very true with respect to adjustment. If sacrifices are decided in a vacuum by the highest offices of the state without wider consultation, if major reforms are decided outside or against the country itself, those reforms have no future. They may lead to rejection as they will be regarded as being against the interests of the people of the country. Conversely, one of the key institutional and political aspects of development is a firm commitment from the country, its leader, its decision-makers, and those who manage and execute programmes, projects and reforms. Quoting Arturo Israel[11] 'when there is commitment to a program, there is agreement about the objectives and the methods for achieving them and the main actors will form a coalition to support those objectives'. True, in the coalition and negotiation process, new interests may emerge, depending on the strength of the leadership. At all levels of responsibility, the commitment of one group may stimulate the behaviour of others. At all phases of the management of the project cycle or of a reform programme, commitment is the key to success.

EDI: PAST, PRESENT AND FUTURE THRUSTS

EDI is fully aware of all these aspects of development which are constantly referred to in its seminars and as a result has undergone considerable changes itself over recent years.

It was realized in the early 1980s that EDI had a much more complex mandate than it had in the 1960s and 1970s. The pervasive conditions in developing countries had to be taken into account: on the one hand, the persistent and growing demands for more rapid rates of economic growth and wider distribution of the benefits of growth, the slowing down of the amount of resources available to promote higher growth rates and, above all, the deterioration of income per capita in Africa; on the other, the continuing shortages of analytical and management skills in developing countries, although this varied in degrees and capabilities from one region to the other. EDI's programmes represented only one among many types of in-service training available. International and national aid agencies had been offering a large range of training courses. For quite some time, significant numbers of universities in the industrialized countries had been developing short courses specially designed to serve people from developing countries. But much more important, the developing countries themselves had established great numbers of higher-level training institutions.[12] These institutions have numerous potential advantages of easier access, greater relevance, and the greater possibility of using newer flexible training modes which adjust to particular needs and are intertwined with on-the-job experience. However, many of these institutions were weak, unstable and too academic, had poor staff, ineffective training materials, and poor financial arrangements.

Therefore, the normal course of action for EDI between 1985 and 1989 was to help countries to acquire and strengthen their analytical and management skills in order to contribute to more rapid economic growth and a wider distribution of benefits. Another basic assumption in EDI evolution was to take

14

into account the continuing rapid technological, political and economic change throughout the world.

EDI's programme of operations had to be flexible enough to adapt itself to the changing conditions and needs of the Third World. Its main functions were as follows:

1 training mid- and upper-level staff from the developing countries in the applications of institutional and managerial approaches, as well as in analytical techniques towards assisting or promoting more effective development decision-making;
2 exposing people to other countries' experience in the application of these techniques and approaches;
3 providing a forum for discussion among top decision- makers, the World Bank and other agencies on key issues of development;
4 assisting development of national and regional institutions engaged in higher-level training of development practition- ers, especially on an in-service basis.

Senior policy and economic and sector management seminars are the main training activities of EDI. Training of trainers forms an important aspect of technical assistance to training institutions. As for project analysis and management training, it can best be met by basic local programmes reflecting local conditions with the support of national or, in their absence, regional and sub-regional training institutions. EDI is to assist training institutions in this effort, taking the form of promoting networks of national training institutions with possible twinning arrangements between them and a more advanced training institution in the region or outside the region, or in an industri- alized country. In this regard, the exchange and strengthening of faculty members, the development of consulting services, and the exchange of training materials are examples of joint efforts. This forms the backbone of any major institution-building programme. However, EDI economic and sector management training include modules closely linked to the economic and social benefits of projects. EDI also believes very strongly in the role of special programmes helping to improve the capabilities of developing countries in economic analysis of projects, and are concerned that such programmes should have an impact on training institutions.

15

The combination of policy seminars at the senior level and at the level immediately below (target groups usually benefiting from the economic and sector management seminars) has reflected the interest of many countries involved in policy and institutional reforms. They have become very valuable tools to stimulate reflection on alternative ways to cope with economic difficulties. The seminars have strengthened government capacity to continue the dialogue with international financial agencies and they have spread the understanding necessary to improve the effectiveness of the implementation of the reforms. In brief, EDI certainly helps the 'internalization' process in those countries which are undertaking major adjustment programmes. It also helps in assisting their efforts to expand their capacity in analysing issues and policies related to their investment efforts in response to the changed policies and incentives.

When the impact of EDI's first Five-Year Plan was evaluated in 1986, it was concluded that if effectively pursued it would enable EDI to achieve a highly functional system by the late 1980s which would disseminate development experience among countries and convey it to those for whom it would be the most valuable. First, EDI ought to function as a valued point of support for many regional and sectoral networks of higher-level training programmes and policy think-tanks, with a particular ability to help maintain a practical focus and to catalyse cooperation from relevant partners outside their region or sector; second, EDI should become a well-respected promoter and producer – in collaboration with partner institutions – of high quality training materials for seminars and workshops addressed to development leaders and managers; third, EDI should pursue its role as an acknowledged leader in the pedagogical design of training and interchange of ideas among policy-makers, policy analysts and development managers. It was also concluded that EDI seminars, and particularly senior policy seminars, had a two-way stream effect: they enabled member countries' officials to convey views in an informal and non-confrontational environment beneficial to a better mutual understanding with the Bank; and Bank representatives, on most occasions acting as resource persons in our seminars, would feed back in the regional offices of the Bank in Washington.

Of course, the experience acquired over these five years – the successes, the mistakes, the failures, the ambitious goals for EDI ten years from now – was taken due consideration of when preparing the EDI Strategic Plan for 1990–4.

EDI's central purpose will be to mobilize the knowledge and experience accumulated by the World Bank to help strengthen development decision-making and management in its member countries. The key questions to ask are what to mobilize, to whom should it be addressed and how to convey it? What seminars to offer? Whom to invite? The EDI's audience will continue to be mid-career and senior officials of the World Bank member countries and EDI partner institutions. The core themes of EDI will be those which reflect the experience accumulated by the World Bank and its borrowers:

1 how to improve the quality of macroeconomic management, especially the degree of flexibility of countries to respond to internal shocks;
2 how to make the management of the public sector more efficient;
3 how to render poverty reduction efforts more effective, in particular, the protection of the poor during macroeconomic adjustment.

From a regional point of view, the high priority assigned to sub-Saharan Africa under the first plan of 1985–9 will be retained, with 51 per cent of EDI's total yearly operations taking place there (seminars and assistance to institutions). Asia will receive 21 per cent with a strong preponderance for China and with emphasis on the institutionally weak least-developed countries, e.g., Indochina, Bangladesh and the South Pacific islands; there will be 16 per cent for Latin America and the Caribbean, and 11 per cent for the Arab countries (the Middle East and North Africa) and Europe. These figures do not include the non-regional courses and world-wide seminars. Finally, EDI intends to follow three functional thrusts to convey the fruits of the World Bank and its borrowers' development experience:

1 assisting development of training capacity in developing countries;
2 organizing inter-country exchange of experiences;
3 producing educational publications and documentation.

These functions are actually consistent with what EDI has tried to achieve to date. We believe that EDI policy seminars are very important for improving the dialogue and understanding and cooperation among countries in terms of regional, sub-regional and inter-regional cooperation. The first objective is even more important because no cooperation and inter-country exchange of experience can be effective without enhancement of managerial skills and without seriously considering how to train the next generation of leaders and policy-makers; and without the means to improve the capacity of those in charge right now, no rehabilitation of any nature – macro, sectoral, or institutional – is possible. Mid-career training capacity building is, therefore, essential. The last function is the foundation and the intellectual cement of the others. In order to build up local capacities and institutions, it is as essential to develop publishable training materials, including case studies.

In conclusion, this introduction has covered many subjects and many issues close to the day-to-day problems in our respective jobs. The subject of managing change should form the basis of further research which might be useful to trainers and managers of training institutions. This could help the training capacity of developing countries' training institutions and agencies and would be consistent with project and policy rehabilitation programmes which, in any event, should include a training component.

NOTES

* The findings, interpretations, and conclusions expressed here are entirely those of the author and should not be attributed in any manner to the World Bank, to its affiliated organizations, or to members of its Board of Executive Directors or the countries they represent.
1 See Warren C. Baum and Stokes M. Tolbert, *Investing in Development: Lessons of World Bank Experience*, New York: Oxford University Press for the World Bank, 1985.
2 See J. Price Gittinger, *The Economic Analysis of Agricultural Projects*, 2nd edn, London and Baltimore: Johns Hopkins University Press for the Economic Development Institute, 1982.
3 World Bank, *IDA in Retrospect*, Oxford: Oxford University Press for the World Bank, 1982.
4 A rehabilitation project has since been approved by the Bank group and is under way.

5 *Sustainability of Projects: Final Review of Experience*, Operations Evaluation Department, World Bank, 14 June, 1985 (restricted distribution).

6 See Peter F. Drucker, 'The changed world economy', *Foreign Affairs*, 1986.

7 It is also worthy to note ECA Executive Secretary, Abebayo Adedeji (in an article in the *Journal of Modern African Studies*, March 1985) who wrote: 'within the cluster of internal causes of Africa's external indebtedness, the following can be identified: ... a policy of excessive dependence on external resources for financing development ... , poor economic management coupled with misuse of resources and wastage of public funds. ... The inadequacy of policies and institutions for monitoring the contracting of external debts, their utilization and servicing (poor debt management) and ... lack of trained personnel to administer resource policies ...'

8 See Arturo Israel, *Institutional Development-Incentives to Performance*, Baltimore: Johns Hopkins University Press for the World Bank, 1987.

9 See Xavier de la Renaudiere's note for EDI seminar series on Development Management of Institutional Development Process and Structural Adjustment, 1987.

10 See John Lonsdale, 'Political accountability in African history', in Patrick Chabal (ed.) *Political Domination in Africa*, Cambridge: Cambridge University Press, 1985.

11 See Arturo Israel, op. cit.

12 See 'Management training and research for African development', *EDI Policy Seminar Report Series*, no. 5, Washington, DC, January 1987.

Part I

OVERVIEW

1

PROJECT REHABILITATION
An introduction to the issues
Ramesh Adhikari and Colin Kirkpatrick

INTRODUCTION

For many Third World countries the 1980s was a 'lost decade' when, confronted by a serious deterioration in the international economic environment, investment and economic growth rates fell well below the levels achieved in the preceding decade. The resumption of sustained long-run growth will require a reversal of the declining trend in investment experienced in the 1980s, but in the shorter term, a more efficient utilization of the existing capital assets could contribute to an improvement in growth performance. Thus, in recent years there has been a significant shift in the focus of development policy in the majority of developing countries, from stimulating new production capacity to encouraging more efficient use of resources, with increasing interest being shown in the contribution that 'rehabilitation' of existing productive assets might make towards generating economic recovery.

The growth performance of an economy depends on both the level and productivity of investment. Numerous studies have demonstrated the existence of a long-term structural relationship between growth and investment: for example, a recent empirical estimate of this relationship, using average growth and investment rates for 1973–87 for 125 developing countries, showed that on average a 1 percentage point increase in the ratio of investment to GDP would, other things being equal, raise the overall growth rate by about 0.1 per cent (IMF 1988: 76). It is also well established empirically that the efficiency with which inputs are utilized – total factor productivity – contributes to output growth. Chenery (1986), for example, estimated that for a group

23

of typical developing countries, total factor productivity accounted for as much as 20 per cent of output growth.

Investment rates in developing countries fell sharply during the 1980s. In a sample of 30 developing countries, average total investment increased from 18 per cent of GDP in the early 1970s to a peak of 23 per cent in 1978–82, and then declined to around 18.5 per cent of GDP in 1985–7 (Pfefferman and Madarassy 1989). In most developing countries the public sector plays a more significant role as an investor than it does in industrial countries, reflecting a greater need for infrastructure development. Public sector investment in infrastructure is often complementary to private investment, acting as a catalyst to private sector capital formation (Blejer and Khan 1984). For the early 1980s, public sector investment as a percentage of total investment averaged 43 per cent in developing countries, as compared to 30 per cent in industrial countries (World Bank 1988: table 2.3). The most recent data indicate that public investment levels have fallen significantly, with the share of public investment as a percentage of GDP declining from around 10 per cent in 1980 to 8.3 per cent in 1987 (Pfefferman and Madarassy 1989: table 9a).

The results of the fall in investment rates are seen clearly in Table 1.1. As the table shows, there was a marked slowdown in growth during the 1980s, across regions and income levels, with the single exception of the Asian economies. The decline was particularly pronounced in the highly-indebted countries and in sub-Saharan Africa. In the latter region, per capita income growth was negative for most years, resulting in an absolute decline in living standards during the 1980s.

The resumption of rapid economic growth in the developing countries will be dependent upon raising the overall level of investment, and an increasing number of economies have implemented policies aimed at raising the level of aggregate domestic savings (World Bank 1989a). But the impact of these measures will only emerge in the medium to long term, and in the interim, a more efficient utilization of the existing capital stock can contribute to an immediate improvement in output performance. Consequently, there has been a growing concern on the part of policy-makers with improving the productivity of existing assets, particularly in the public sector. The focus of

Table 1.1 Average annual growth rate of GDP in
developing countries (%)

Country group	1965–80	1980–7
Low income economies (excluding China and India)	5.5	1.7
China and India	5.3	8.5
Middle-income economies	6.2	2.8
Lower middle-income	5.7	2.1
Upper middle-income	6.7	3.4
High-income economies	3.7	2.6
OECD countries	3.6	2.7
Others [1]	8.1	–2.6
Regional Aggregates (low and middle income)		
East Asia	7.2	8.0
Europe, M. East and N. Africa	6.2	n/a
Latin America and Caribbean	6.0	1.4
South Asia	3.8	4.8
Sub-Saharan Africa	5.1	0.4
Memorandum items:		
Seventeen highly indebted	6.1	1.1
Highest growth rate [2]	15.2	13.0
Lowest growth rate [2]	0.1	–6.1

Source: World Bank (1989), as given in Easterly (1989).
Notes: Averages are weighted.
[1] Countries classified by UN or otherwise regarded by their authorities as developing.
[2] For an individual country.

investment policy has shifted therefore from new investment activity to the more effective use of the available capital stock. A senior World Bank official explained these changing priorities as follows:

we are acutely conscious of an environment of much greater resource scarcity. ... Because of that resource scarcity, we recognise that our support for public sector investments has to be much more concerned with the efficiency and the use of the capacity once created, and we have to be more sensitive to the ability of the country to finance those investments out of its own resources.

as you will see from the statistics, the percentage of lending directed towards specific investments has declined, and rather sharply, from 60 per cent to about 40 per cent [1980 to 1984]. ... One of the reasons for the drop in that percentage is that the Bank has already shifted more attention towards rehabilitation and maintenance operations. This is particularly evident in sub-Saharan Africa, where it clearly made no sense to continue to add to productive capacity when the existing capacity could not be utilized and was not being maintained. Rehabilitation and maintenance will remain a prominent feature of our investment-related operations in the years ahead.

(Wood 1986: 93–4)

The pattern of lending of the international development banks reflects the shift in interest towards improving the performance of the existing capital stock. Since 1982 the European Investment Bank has been financing rehabilitation projects in the African, Caribbean and Pacific (ACP) countries, and the proportion of its financing on rehabilitating capital investment amounts to about a quarter of total EIB financing to ACP countries (EIB 1986, quoted in UNIDO 1988). The World Bank has provided about US$3.8 billion* for more than fifty industrial sector rehabilitation programmes during 1980–8 (World Bank 1989c: xi). More than 70 per cent of this lending was in the period 1986–8, and reflects the shift away from 'greenfield' projects geared to creating new capacity towards physical rehabilitation projects, which dealt mainly with modernizing public enterprises.

The current interest in improving project performance is reflected in the contents of this volume, and in the subsequent chapters various aspects of project rehabilitation policy in developing countries are examined in detail. The remainder of this chapter is given over to providing an overview of the topic and a discussion of a number of thematic issues.

THE CASE FOR PROJECT REHABILITATION

The recent interest in project rehabilitation as a means of improving productivity reinforces a longer standing and more

---

* The US billion (1,000 million) is used throughout this volume.

general concern with the performance of public sector investments. It is widely held that the public sector in many developing countries was over-extended during the 1960s and 1970s, and as a result: 'In many countries the expansion of the public sector has stretched its managerial capacity to the point where serious inefficiencies result' (World Bank 1983: 46); and: 'Over the years, inefficiency has flourished in many state enterprises, its overt consequences masked by the ready availability of budgetary support (IMF, 1986: 16).

It is now generally accepted that the size of the public sector *per se* does not have a significant bearing on the performance of the sector or the economy as a whole. What matters is the effectiveness with which resources allocated to the public sector are utilized. Definitive conclusions about the micro-level efficiency of public investments are difficult to reach. For public enterprises which are producing a marketed output, it may be possible to compare financial and productivity performance with private sector enterprises, although it is often difficult to compare like with like, because either the public and private enterprises operate under different market conditions, or the publicly-owned enterprise is required to pursue different operational criteria. Where it has been possible to compare performance of public and private enterprises in developing countries, there is no systematic evidence that public enterprises are less efficient than private firms (Millward 1988). This is not to deny that many public enterprises are capable of achieving significant improvements in efficiency, but it does caution against broad generalizations about 'poor' public enterprise performance.

For public projects which are not producing a marketed output, evidence on performance is commonly drawn from evaluation studies. There is a large body of knowledge on project performance (much of which is unfortunately not easily accessible) which has accrued from the evaluation reports formally carried out on donor-funded projects.

In its *Project Performance Results for 1987*, the World Bank (1989b) reports on the evaluation of a total of 187 projects undertaken between 1972 and 1986. A number of different measures of performance were used. For half of the sample (96) a project economic rate of return was calculated at project appraisal stage and was recalculated upon project completion. In the case of projects for which economic rates of return (ERR) were not appropriate – such as in human resources, technical assistance, institution-building – the performance assessment was based on guidelines as to the accomplishment of project objectives and achievements.

Almost three-quarters (72 per cent) of the 1987 cohort of projects were judged to have achieved satisfactory results. Performance shortfalls were concentrated in the sub-Saharan Africa region which accounted for 45 per cent of all unsatisfactory project outcomes. The average re-estimated ERR for the projects so evaluated was 15 per cent, as compared to the appraisal ERR average of 26 per cent. Factors contributing to the slippage in performance include time and cost overruns, poor project design and overestimate of the prices of project output. Disaggregation of the overall ERR average reveals sizeable variations across sectors and regions, with sub-Saharan Africa experiencing a 20 per cent divergence between *ex ante* and *ex post* performance.

A serious weakness of most evaluation reports is that typically they are prepared when the donor agency's disbursement obligations are completed. They give no indication, therefore, of the sustainability of projects after the initial period when the donor is involved. Indeed, World Bank (1985) reported that 'among the projects reviewed there was little evidence of attention given to features in project design which explicitly attempted to enhance the postcompletion sustainability of project activities'. In recognition of this limitation of earlier evaluation reports, the World Bank's Annual Project Reviews now include an assessment of sustainability. Based on subjective judgements as to the likelihood of the project continuing to operate effectively up to the predicted completion date, about half the projects reviewed in World Bank (1989b) were judged 'likely' to sustain their benefits.

The evidence on project performance is broadly consistent therefore with that of public enterprises. The overall performance indicators suggest that in aggregate, projects have produced acceptable returns and that the claims of widespread 'project failure' are not supported by the empirical evidence. At the same time it is recognized that there has been considerable variation in performance at the individual project level, which suggests that there is scope for significant improvements in the performance of particular projects.

WHAT IS PROJECT REHABILITATION POLICY?

Project rehabilitation policy is intended to improve the economic performance of existing projects. Depending upon the diagnosis of the causes of the project's currently unsatisfactory level of performance, rehabilitation policies will be selected from two broad categories. The first are directed at changing the internal structure and operations of the project, the second are those that are intended to change the external factors which influence project performance. In many instances project 'failure' can be related to both internal and external factors and a combination of rehabilitation measures will be employed. (UNIDO 1988).

'Restructuring' is a closely related but distinct policy option and is used to describe measures that are intended to encourage the reallocation of productive resources in response to changes in demand patterns, relative prices and technology. Restructuring takes place when an enterprise or project shifts to a product mix or cost structure that increases its competitiveness. As with rehabilitation, policy to assist restructuring can be directed at both the external environment or the internal organization of the project (World Bank 1989c).

In practice, it will be difficult to maintain the distinction between rehabilitation and restructuring policy. Changes in market conditions and technology typically make it inappropriate to aim at recreating the original project, and the selected policy programme is likely to contain elements of both rehabilitation and restructuring. The term 'project rehabilitation policy', therefore, is used henceforth to refer to any set of policy measures intended to improve the performance of an existing project.

PROJECT FAILURE AND THE NEED FOR REHABILITATION

The need for rehabilitation arises from the perceived 'failure' of projects. A project is deemed to have failed if it is unsuccessful in achieving the predetermined performance targets. Project failure can be the result of a variety of internal and external factors, and the design of an effective rehabilitation programme requires the analyst to identify the relative importance of these different influences on project performance.

Chapter 2, by Basil Cracknell, draws on a large sample of

29

project evaluation reports and presents the main lessons regarding the causes of project failure. A common finding is that consideration is seldom given by donors to the sustainability of projects in the post 'hand-over' period. Inadequate financial and human resources for maintenance of the project result in project failure. Interestingly, Cracknell's review of rehabilitation project evaluations finds that inadequate maintenance is often a cause of such projects themselves failing. Cracknell concludes that if rehabilitation projects are to be more successful than the original investments, greater attention must be given to the managerial, institutional and social aspects of rehabilitated projects.

Weaknesses in project design are an important cause of project failure, and Chapter 3 by David Edwards identifies the impact of poor project design on agricultural project performance. The study shows that there is considerable scope for 'designing out' many of the problems which projects encounter during the implementation stage. Identified problems are related to their underlying causes and to possible means of reducing their incidence which can be applied at the time of project preparation. The strengthening of project design can make a significant contribution to the success of agricultural and rural rehabilitation projects.

Further evidence on project performance and the need for a rehabilitation strategy is provided in Chapter 4 by David Potts, which investigates the performance of export-oriented estate agriculture in Tanzania over the last twenty years. The causes of the decline in estate agriculture are identified to include inadequate labour supply, declining prices, poor marketing, limited access to foreign exchange, and organizational weaknesses. The chapter goes on to examine the measures needed to rehabilitate the estate sector, emphasizing the need for a new approach to the organization of estate production which recognizes the changes that have occurred in the policies and resource availability situation in Tanzania.

PLANNING AND APPRAISAL OF REHABILITATION PROJECTS

The analytical approach to the identification, planning and appraisal of rehabilitation projects is likely to differ significantly from the procedures applied to new projects. Two major differences in rehabilitation policy are: macro-level analysis to identify and remove policy-related obstacles to performance, and micro-level analysis to identify internal constraints and policy prescriptions. Moreover, the standard financial and economic procedures for project appraisal may not be appropriate in assessing rehabilitation project proposals.

Chapter 5, by George Assaf, explains the UNIDO diagnostic approach which is aimed at identifying projects for rehabilitation and outlining the policies and measures for improvements. UNIDO rehabilitation studies adopt a three dimensional 'top-down' approach. The 'top-down' approach starts with an examination of the macro-economic level, descends through the sector, sub-sector and branch levels, and finally arrives at the enterprise (plant) level. Assaf shares the concern that the concept of industrial rehabilitation should be broadened beyond merely thinking in terms of benefits to individual plants, and should be interpreted as securing optimal use of existing capacities and resources through upgrading and transformation for future overall industrial growth. Project rehabilitation should be combined with a restructuring of the industrial sector as a whole to ensure growth dynamism, domestic integration and the provision of support industries and services. At the project level, a rehabilitation programme may include restructuring of capital, organization and management, procurement and marketing; or in some extreme cases it may require plant closures. Industrial 'rehabilitation' in this broad sense is similar therefore to industrial 'restructuring', as discussed earlier.

Chapter 6, by Michael Yaffey, explores the financial analysis of rehabilitation projects especially from the viewpoint of the development banker. Applying the incremental approach, it considers the consequences of agreeing versus refusing rehabilitation finance. It distinguishes between a foreign investor whose stake in a country may be limited to one or two projects and a local development finance institution which has an entire portfolio of similarly affected projects to consider. Whilst successful rehabilitation may call for a portfolio approach, if funds are insufficient for this, an ambivalent or hesitating response to individual requests may be the result.

In Chapter 7 Michael Tribe explores the economic appraisal of rehabilitation projects. He is concerned not only with the microeconomic principles on which such appraisal is based (taking for granted the application of 'social opportunity cost' resource valuation) but also with the interface between microeconomic and macroeconomic issues where rehabilitation is proposed in the context of 'economic recovery' or 'structural adjustment' programmes. Taking the objective as rehabilitation only of 'sound' projects, and mindful of the extent to which appraisal methods and data can be 'fixed' in order to give the superficial semblance of 'soundness' to 'unsound' project proposals, he recommends:

1 abandonment of the 'sunk cost' doctrine and its replacement by the logically consistent application of opportunity cost principles;
2 the use of the incremental project worth criterion as a test of acceptability, and
3 the additional requirement that 'with' project worth (with inclusion of existing assets as a cost based on systematic valuation principles) should be acceptable.

In the context of structural adjustment programmes, Tribe reminds us that many investment decisions (including many rehabilitations) are not of a 'marginal' nature and in this context decision-makers have a need for clear decision rules relating to intersectoral and intrasectoral investment priorities.

PROJECT REHABILITATION: POLICY AND EXPERIENCE

There is general agreement with the notion that good policies cannot make a bad project good, but poor policies can make good projects bad. The existence of the right policy environment is an important determinant, therefore, of successful project rehabilitation.

Chapter 8, by Mike Faber, places project rehabilitation in the broader context of macro- and sector-level policy. He argues that many rehabilitation projects are likely to occur as part of externally negotiated programmes of policy reform and the success of the rehabilitation project will be bound up with the implementation of the structural adjustment programme. The interrelationships between project and economy-level rehabilitation programmes are explored using the example of the Ashanti Gold Mine in Ghana.

The link between macroeconomic adjustment programmes and micro-level rehabilitation measures is discussed by John Weiss in Chapter 9 in the context of the manufacturing sector in sub-Saharan Africa. The successful rehabilitation of manufacturing may not be possible through supply side measures alone, but will also require market rehabilitation. The concept of market rehabilitation can have several different dimensions. At the project level it implies the need for enterprises to adapt to a more competitive environment in terms of the availability of goods. At the industry level, market rehabilitation implies that demand growth will be adequate to cover the full capacity sales of enterprises in the industry.

The contribution by Paul Cook and Martin Minogue (Chapter 10) argues that rehabilitation policy needs to be viewed in the context of broader socio-political and administrative considerations. Using the examples of public enterprise rehabilitation programmes in India, Pakistan and Thailand, the authors argue that such an analysis engages closely with the policy implementation process in developing countries. It provides a framework for exploring policy ineffectiveness or failure and offers an analytical structure for considering what policy changes can be realistically prescribed, adopted and carried through.

REHABILITATION: MANAGEMENT AND INSTITUTIONAL ASPECTS

A common failing of project analysis has been to emphasize financial and economic appraisal at the expense of managerial and institutional strengthening for project implementation. Many project failures are due not to production or technology, but to institutional weaknesses.

Chapter 11, by Tom Franks, emphasizes the symbiotic relationship between the 'hardware' (physical assets), 'liveware' (human resources) and 'software' (organization and management) in the rehabilitation process. Improvements in the physical assets of the project must be matched by institutional changes if the rehabilitation programme is to succeed. Institutional improvements will typically involve changes for the individual agents, within the system, and changes to organizational procedures. There will often be resistance within the project organization to such changes and consideration will need to be given to how these barriers to change are to be overcome during the rehabilitation process.

Farhad Analoui, Chapter 12, emphasizes the importance of the managerial dimension in project rehabilitation. Successful rehabilitation will require the introduction of a management style that can operate the project in relation to a changing economic and socio-political environment. The replacement of a 'prescriptive' management style with a 'preventative' management philosophy can contribute significantly to the success of the project rehabilitation process.

CONCLUSION

For many developing countries the 1980s has been a decade of economic decline. As a result of the deterioration in the external environment, particularly after the debt crisis in 1982, many economies were confronted by a decline in the external finance available to meet the difference between domestic savings and domestic investment. Domestic savings failed to increase to match the reduction in external resources, and adjustment required a decline in domestic investment. Adjustment typically fell disproportionately on public sector investment.

Sustained economic recovery will require both an increased level of external resource flows to the developing countries, and an increase in domestic savings levels. The prospects of an immediate and significant improvement in either of these flows are limited. For the immediate future, therefore, recovery will depend heavily on improving the output performance of the existing capital stock.

Project rehabilitation is likely therefore to continue to be an important strategy for most developing countries in the 1990s. The challenge is to ensure that the lessons to be learnt from project 'failures' in the past are fully assimilated in the design of project rehabilitation procedures and practices.

REFERENCES

Blejer, M. and Khan, M. (1984) 'Government policy and private investment in developing countries', *IMF Staff Papers*, vol. 31.

Chenery, H.B. (1986) 'Growth and transformation', in H. Chenery, S. Robinson and M. Synquin (eds) *Industrialization and Growth: A Comparative Study*, London: Oxford University Press.

Easterly, W.R. (1989) 'Policy distortions, size of government and growth', PPR Working Paper no. 344, World Bank, December.

European Investment Bank (1986) *Annual Report*, Luxembourg.

International Monetary Fund (1986) *World Economic Outlook*, Washington, DC.

—— (1988) *World Economic Outlook*. Washington, DC.

Millward, R. (1988) 'Measured sources of inefficiency in the performance of private and public enterprises in LDCs', in P. Cook and C. Kirkpatrick (eds) *Privatisation in Less Developed Countries*, Brighton: Wheatsheaf Books.

Pfefferman, G.P. and Madarassy, A. (1989) 'Trends in private investment in thirty developing countries', *International Finance Corporation Discussion Paper no. 6.*, Washington, DC.

United Nations Industrial Development Organization (1988) *UNIDO Policy on Industrial Rehabilitation*, Vienna, February.

Wood, D.J. (1986) 'The World Bank of tomorrow: policies and operations' in *Recovery in the Developing World: The London Symposium on the World Bank's Role*, Washington, DC: The World Bank

World Bank (1983) *World Development Report*. London and New York: Oxford University Press for the World Bank

—— (1985) *Tenth Annual Review of Project Performance Audit Results*, Operations Evaluation Department, World Bank, Washington, DC.

—— (1988) *World Development Report*, London: Oxford University Press for the World Bank.

—— (1989a) *World Development Report*, London: Oxford University Press for the World Bank.

—— (1989b) *Project Performance Results for 1987*, Operations Evaluation Department, World Bank, Washington, DC.

—— (1989c) *Industrial Restructuring: Policy and Practice*, Industry Development Division, World Bank, Washington, DC (March).

Part II

PROJECT FAILURE AND THE NEED FOR REHABILITATION

2

PROJECT REHABILITATION
Lessons from evaluation findings
Basil Cracknell

INTRODUCTION

This chapter is an attempt to glean from a cross-section of evaluation reports (most of them syntheses of findings covering many projects and programmes) the main lessons with regard to:

- under-utilization of existing capital investments, with special reference to inadequate maintenance as a factor leading to a growing emphasis on rehabilitation;
- findings related to a small sample of the relatively few rehabilitation projects as such that have been the subject of evaluations;
- possible ways of improving the sustainability of projects (i.e. their survival once the donor's inputs have ceased).

A total of twenty evaluation reports has been analysed (see references), emanating from some of the major bilateral and multilateral donors.

EVALUATION FINDINGS RELATING TO UNDER-UTILIZATION AND INADEQUATE MAINTENANCE

A common finding of many evaluation reports is that often very little consideration is given at the project planning/design stage to the eventual 'hand-over' problems. It is almost as though the project planners thought that sustainability would follow automatically once a project had been implemented, and that it did not need to be consciously thought about beforehand. Yet as a major evaluation of European Development Fund (EDF) projects in Africa the EEC (1978) pointed out:

39

A project lasting 3 to 5 years cannot bring about a fundamental change in the capacity of the communities concerned to generate the finance needed to meet the capital costs and operating costs of their own supervisory structures.

Whilst the donor is on the scene there is an assured supply of funds for goods and services, and it seems that very little provision is made to cover the hand-over. Admittedly, special conditions are often introduced requiring the recipient government to take over the funding of recurrent costs in a planned manner, but the common experience of such donors as the Overseas Development Administration (ODA 1985a) and the World Bank (World Bank 1981, 1982) is that such conditions are seldom honoured.

In extreme cases this failure to ensure efficient hand-over can threaten the very survival of the project. When EEC funding of an animal health project in the Central African Republic came to an end, the supervisory staff were forced to live on the generosity of the villagers because the Ministry of Agriculture had not made provision for their salaries (EEC 1978). The survival of EEC-funded animal health protection groups in Chad was found to be in jeopardy because no budgetary provision had been made for working capital for the purchase of veterinary products (EEC 1978). Sometimes over-optimistic plans were made for hand-over to take place over too short a period. A Federal Republic of Germany evaluation report commented that too little attention was paid to the timing of the German withdrawal, and often the date for hand-over had to be postponed 'because of inadequate counter-part contributions (e.g., buildings) and an insufficient number of qualified local staff' (FRG 1986). A Nepalese contributor to an ADB Seminar (ADB 1984) commented that a five-year perspective was often far too short, and he suggested that fifteen years would be more appropriate. The EDF evaluation already quoted (EEC 1978) also considered that the Commission's five year lifespan of project planning was too short to ensure smooth hand-over. The US Agency for International Development some years ago adopted ten years as the lifespan for project planning, following a detailed evaluation of recurrent costs (USAID 1982).

One of the basic reasons why short time-horizons inhibit efficient hand-over is that training of skilled personnel, acquiring management experience, and building effective institutions – all vital components of sustainability – are necessarily long-term operations. As a World Bank evaluation report on a project in Niger comments: 'building institutional capacities for road maintenance is far more difficult than building roads' (World Bank 1984). George Honadle, in a contribution to the Asian Development Bank Seminar in 1984 (ADB 1984) emphasized the crucial importance of a long-term planning horizon – at least in relation to rural development projects. 'A local manager cannot build long-term local institutions when the project budget is devoted to the short-term installation of physical infrastructure.' Often the donors themselves have pursued policies that have led to 'enclavement' (World Bank 1984), i.e., the creation of expatriate-led management structures that work in isolation from the local administrative arrangements. A classic case of this was the International Bank for Reconstruction and Development's Maradi Project in Niger where the IBRD even ignored the appeals of the Niger government in insisting upon the estab-lishment of its own enclave administration (World Bank 1984). The evaluation concluded: 'The failure to articulate clear institutional objectives for the post-project period, and to incorporate a plan of action in the design of Maradi I and II, leaves a very difficult institutional (and financial) problem currently unsolved.'

In recent years, the problems arising from inadequate maintenance and servicing have loomed larger and larger, as the 'stock' of new capital projects continues to grow, and almost every evaluation report adds fresh evidence to the already huge pile. There is now a growing awareness of the high economic cost of poor maintenance. The German synthesis (FRG 1986) estimated that the total cost of a road, assuming it to be used for fourteen years, increases by 125 per cent over the originally estimated costs if the necessary maintenance work is not carried out. An evaluation of a large EDF Rural Development Project in Sierra Leone, commenting on the poor conditions of the roads, estimated that: 'if the roads are left without maintenance for more than 2 or 3 years they will no longer be good for motor traffic, especially in the hilly southern parts of the region'. An evaluation of the Iringa Rural Development Project in Tanzania (SEDES 1986) noted that timber bridges only have a life of three to five years if not repaired regularly. A USAID evaluation report (USAID 1982) quoting a World Bank investigation, stated that the stream of returns to road maintenance is of the order of two to five times that of new construction, proving that maintenance and rehabilitation are likely to be far more cost-effective than new construction. A World Bank evaluation of a highway project in Tanzania (World Bank 1984), estimated that the lack of maintenance and the poor condition of the roads reduced vehicle life by 50 per cent.

These references to the economic costs of poor maintenance open up the wider question of how rehabilitation projects should be appraised and evaluated in economic terms. This is an aspect of the subject which has been discussed more fully elsewhere, but at least some of the evaluation report studies have significant comments to make about the economic concepts involved. One in particular relates to the economics of assessing the benefits of a railway rehabilitation project in Malawi (ODA 1981). The original economic appraisal had been only a partial analysis and had therefore grossly overestimated the potential benefits. The evaluators commented:

> In order to make a proper assessment as to whether the line should remain open or not the total discounted costs of using the railway should be compared with the total discounted costs of the next best alternative which in this case would be by road.

The evaluation also pin-pointed mistakes that had been made in estimating the benefits of rehabilitating lengths of track which in the absence of rehabilitation would have required a drop in train speed. These examples illustrate the point that rehabilitation projects raise issues in economic appraisal and evaluation which are rather different from those that arise with new projects.

Poor original project design is also an important factor leading to subsequent deterioration and premature need for rehabilitation. Some roads, particularly in Africa, have been built to accommodate vehicles with limited axle loads, and as the heavier lorries come into use, they have caused serious damage (the main spine road through eastern Botswana is an example of a major road built to inadequate axle loading standards). Some countries attempt to ensure that axle limit restrictions are enforced, and some donors have funded sector credits that are aimed at assisting developing country governments to pursue effective transport sector policies, e.g. International Development

Association (IDA) projects in Kenya and Ethiopia (World Bank 1982). However an evaluation by the Transport and Road Research Laboratory of a major road in Kenya found that even though the road was carrying heavier traffic than it was originally designed for, it had not deteriorated badly because the original construction had been good and quality standards had been adhered to (ODA 1984). It follows of course that if roads are not built according to proper quality standards, pavement failure can occur earlier than it would otherwise do.

Evaluators have found that the quality of maintenance tends to decline the more the responsibility for it is switched from the local level to the government level. The main reason is that the Public Works Department is often chronically starved of the necessary funds since governments often fail to attach adequate funding to maintenance work. However, when local people are responsible, and their own livelihoods are at risk, they will raise the necessary money and also provide their own labour if this is appropriate. This was one of the main findings of a major evaluation of irrigation projects by USAID (USAID 1983). They found, for example, that in Thailand as irrigation budgets expanded (i.e. the responsibility shifted from local people to the regional or central government level) the percentage of the total budget devoted to operation and maintenance declined from 7 per cent to 2 per cent. As to drainage projects, it is even more difficult to ensure proper maintenance because the price of failure is less obvious and less immediate. Where a country is passing through a financial crisis, as with Tanzania in recent years, evaluations have shown that the Public Works Department virtually ceases to carry out any maintenance at all. This was true at Iringa (SEDES 1986) and for the Tanzanian Highways generally (World Bank 1984). The World Bank found that after 20 years of effort, and 100 man-years of technical assistance, the Tanzanian Roads Department had only 16 crews operational out of the strength of 100, and there was a 68 per cent vacancy rate at the upper skill levels. The roads were still in a very bad state despite the huge sums poured into the sector.

The problems of undue dependence upon the Public Works Department for maintenance are so great that some evaluations have found that great efforts are being made, as in connection with Bangladesh Grain Storage (ODA 1985a), to find some alternative to PWD funding – particularly ways of raising revenues locally so that basic maintenance can be carried out on time. The evaluators found that:

> There was virtually a complete lack of maintenance of buildings and infrastructure. Such maintenance is the responsibility of the PWD, and it is infrequent. The PWD is responsible for the maintenance of most government buildings and has very little budget for Ministry of Food maintenance.

Where possible it has been found advantageous to enlist the help of local communities in maintenance, e.g. in rural roads. IDA has assisted in the setting up of bodies to organize the local funding of maintenance activities, e.g. in Kenya and Rwanda (World Bank 1982). A good example of IDA involvement in road maintenance relates to a project in Niger dating from as far back as 1968. Under this project a road maintenance organization was set up which (by special arrangement with the Ministry of Finance) had its own budget to stock spare parts for road equipment. In 1976 another IDA project funded training for regravelling brigades for road maintenance. Through a special District Roads Improvement and Maintenance Programme, started in 1974, over 1,500 km of minimum-access all-weather roads have been improved and maintained in Niger, often using heavily labour-intensive methods (over 5,000 labourers being employed).

Shortage of funds is such a key factor that great interest has centred in recent years on the search for new systems of user-charging and cost-recovery. Some success has been achieved in this direction, but in the irrigation area for example, where this would seem to be a very likely panacea, problems have arisen because of reluctance to impose an extra burden on the poorer farmers, especially if supplies may at times be erratic. There is also the familiar problem of charging for what people have traditionally assumed to be a 'free good'. Once again, the key may be in fixing the responsibility at as local a level as possible. A good example of this was the Koinadugu Project in Sierra Leone where, in contrast to the disastrously bad maintenance of the roads, the wells were all well maintained because: 'the wells are considered to be the property of the village and not of the Government'. However, with the larger water and irrigation projects this transferring of the responsibility for maintenance to local people may not be feasible, and in these cases it usually falls to regional or government institutions to carry out the maintenance, and they generally have difficulty in introducing charges. A classic case was the IDA Mahaweli Ganga project in Sri Lanka. The IDA had agreed with the government that user charges (for operating and maintenance) would be imposed, but then there was a change of government and the incoming government refused to implement these arrangements. No charges were collected for the period 1970 to 1977. Charges were then introduced, but by 1977 collections had amounted to less than 1 per cent of the total operating and maintenance costs. This illustrates the difficulty donors have in persuading developing country governments to introduce user charges on public services (World Bank 1982).

Lack of funds is not the only reason for bad maintenance. Often there can be horrendous delays in obtaining spare parts. A fairly typical example relates to the Iringa project, Tanzania, where a spare part for a road grader was ordered in January 1984 and did not arrive until April 1985 (SEDES 1986), during the whole of which time it was out of action. Sometimes the problem is lack of foreign exchange, often a main cause of shortages of fuel for vehicles. The moral is clear: the less the dependence upon imported components the better. In other words, the problems of sustainability need to be considered early on, during the planning stage, rather than being left until after the project has been completed. This point was well brought home in the ODA synthesis report on grain storage (ODA 1985a). The present writer participated in the African component of this synthesis and had personal experience of grain storage establishments working at far less than full capacity because of shortage of fuel for vehicles, spare parts for equipment, and even money for the purchase of grain for research purposes; and well-trained staff were rendered almost redundant for the same reasons, even unable to keep abreast of technical developments for lack of money for books and journals. This was the situation in Zambia and Malawi and it should have been foreseen and steps taken to ensure sustainability, e.g. through a modest follow-on programme. An IBRD evaluation of 26 large irrigation projects (World Bank 1981) reported that in 14 of them no provision at all had been made for proper maintenance as part of the appraisal. The need for maintenance workshops has been almost totally ignored. The time to plan for maintenance is at the project design stage because it usually takes a long time for skills to be acquired, for institutional arrangements to be made for generating recurrent revenue, and for maintenance manuals to be drawn up.

Sometimes maintenance is poor because it is not clear who is responsible for it. Good staff houses were built in some of the more remote parts of Iringa Province, Tanzania, but no-one had decided who was responsible for maintenance and their survival was very much at risk (SEDES 1986).

Another factor affecting maintenance is the tendency for donors to supply inappropriate equipment and technologies. Any number of examples of this could be quoted from evaluation reports, but one will have to suffice. It relates to a small irrigation project in Jordan where some relatively sophisticated engines were supplied which were entirely unfamiliar to the people in that part of the country. The evaluation report (ODA 1974) describes how:

> Engines were out of commission for long periods. All five engines are at present idle at the power station. Engine No. 1 has a seized piston; engine No. 2a had the cylinder block broken by a con-rod at 3,300 hours; engine No. 2b has broken pistons; engine No. 3 awaits the spares required for a general overhaul, and engine No 4 also has a broken cylinder block. The fifth engine lies gutted following an unknown failure. These events have led to the four generating sets and aluminium covers being locally known as the 'blue coffins'.

Unfortunately the Third World is littered with 'coffins' of this sort, simply because it was easier to supply the machines in the first place than to ensure that they could be adequately maintained. Another similar mistake was made on this project when a relatively sophisticated automated system of control was chosen instead of a simple well-head diesel system that could be operated by unskilled labour.

> At Wadi Dhuleil the automatic control system for pumps never fully worked. For a short period it was possible to start the pumps from the power station but the flow metering devices never worked. The automatic recording station presently stands empty with all dials at zero: a monument indicating a

LESSONS FROM EVALUATION FINDINGS

failure to appreciate the realities of the technical status of the
operating agency.

This was written in 1974, and one might easily assume that the
lessons have now been learned and such mistakes are no longer
made today. But unfortunately that is not the case. The writer
visited a water supply project in Botswana in 1988 where a
computerized control system had been installed which was well
beyond the capacity of the local staff to maintain, and the
expatriate manager was reconciled to the fact that as soon as he
left they would have to revert to manual control.

It sometimes happens that whole industries, or complete
public sectors, become so run down that major rehabilitation
programmes have to be implemented, and many of these have
yielded excellent economic returns. Examples that come to mind
are the assistance given by ODA to the rehabilitation of the
railways in Bangladesh, including the strengthening of the major
bridges; the rehabilitation of the Indian Railways by IDA, and the
rehabilitation of public tree-crop production in Indonesia, again
by IDA. The IDA's brief review of its rehabilitation of 12,000
hectares of an abandoned rubber estate in Sumatra (World Bank
1982) is worth quoting as an example of the very encouraging
results that can flow from this kind of major rehabilitation
activity:

Consultants financed by IDA surveyed the estate and found
it still suitable for rubber and oil-palm production. At the
government's request, IDA staff prepared a project which, when
implemented, enabled the government to successfully
rehabilitate the estate through extensive new plantings, better
husbandry standards for existing plantings, construction of a
palm mill and rubber factory, and the improvement of existing
processing facilities. Management was organised and
strengthened, with technical assistance provided for a wide
range of specialisations. The estate is now highly productive,
with sound management and organisation. Financial results
have exceeded expectations. Net real income from rubber
expressed in 1981 prices rose from a loss of $80,000 in 1971
to a profit of $4.8 million in 1981, and net income from palm
oil increased from a loss of $18,000 in 1971 to a profit of $3.0
million in 1981. Considering the estate's situation when IDA

47

began its work, there is little doubt about its critical role in assisting tree-crop rehabilitation in Indonesia.

The donors themselves are not altogether free of blame. There is no doubt that they have often preferred new investments to rehabilitation projects, as an AID Policy Paper on the subject admits (USAID 1982), and often the procedures for the supply of spare parts have been protracted and cumbersome. In the early 1980s however, the situation was much improved as all the main donors recognized the importance of orienting project design and project agreements towards effective and practicable maintenance, including training needs and provision for recurrent funds. In 1982 the Development Assistance Committee (DAC) introduced new *Guidelines on Aid for Maintenance* (DAC 1982), to supplement the existing *Guidelines on Local and Recurrent Cost Financing*. Donors agreed to contribute to recurrent cost financing 'in the context of firm but realistic phase-out agreements with aid recipients'. In recent years there has been a growing recognition that in some developing countries virtually the whole of the aid effort needs to be directed more towards effective maintenance and rehabilitation than to new projects. The Swedish aid agency, SIDA, for instance is reputed to be giving absolute priority to rehabilitation and recurrent costs projects in at least some sectors. Hopefully this switch in emphasis will reduce the incidence of project relapse due to lack of recurrent costs. It will be interesting to see the evaluations of these new types of projects when they become available.

EVALUATIONS OF REHABILITATION PROJECTS

As yet the stock of evaluations of rehabilitation/recurrent costs projects, compared with those for new investments, is very small. However, three such evaluation reports have been reviewed for this paper, comprising the Rahad Irrigation Project in the Sudan (World Bank 1984), Bangladesh Grain Storage (ODA 1985a) and the Mbeya Hospital Project in Tanzania (ODA 1983); in addition there are some synthesis evaluations which also cover rehabilitation projects, such as those by USAID (1982) and IFAD (1986). The general conclusion is that rehabilitation projects tend to be very effective ones, both in terms of the economic rate of return and also of their use of human resources and their institution-building aspects. The AID report lists the advantages of rehabilitation projects (in the irrigation field) as follows: (i) they tend to have lower costs; (ii) they generally yield quicker returns; (iii) they generally utilize the better soils rather than the more marginal ones, which often tends to be the case with new investments, and (iv) they have the advantage that the local population is familiar with the project and the technologies used.

Taking all the evaluation evidence together, the main lessons, regarding the effectiveness of rehabilitation projects as such, are as follows:

1   A rehabilitation project should not be simply a replica of the original one because in the time interval since it was first established circumstances may have changed markedly. It was a major criticism of the IBRD's Rahad Project in the Sudan that it replicated all the weaknesses (as well as the successes of course) of the Gezira Project (World Bank 1984).

2   Rehabilitation projects often tend to overemphasize physical construction aspects, whereas managerial, institutional and social aspects tend to be disregarded (USAID 1983).

3   Rehabilitation projects often tend to be conceived on a large scale, and often involve incorporating small elements into the larger concept. This often results in a loss of social cohesion at the local level. Too few governments have seriously tried to incorporate the small-scale traditional systems into the larger ones. IFAD have built on this experience in the design of the Special Programme for sub-Saharan Africa (IFAD 1986) and have introduced five pointers incorporating the main conclusions listed in this section.

4   Maintenance is still important with rehabilitation projects, and is often a cause of such projects themselves failing. USAID found that rehabilitated watercourses in Pakistan's Punjab reverted to their previous state of neglect within one to three years if they were not properly maintained. Rehabilitated roads in Tanzania's Iringa Province soon reverted if not maintained, and that could mean anything from two to five operations per annum. The evaluators considered that there were too many components of the project for adequate maintenance: they were spread over too wide an area 'like salt on an omelette' (SEDES 1986). They recommended a 'Concerted Action Zone Programme' to ensure that the key

rehabilitated roads received proper maintenance.

5   Sometimes the recipient government prefers a new investment to a rehabilitation project. ODA had quite a problem persuading the Tanzanian government that the rehabilitation of the Mbeya Hospital was more cost-effective than building a new one (ODA 1983). In the event the ODA were proved right and the rehabilitation project was a success; however, within a few years there were already alarming signs that maintenance was again being seriously neglected and proper provision for recurrent costs was not being made.

IMPROVEMENTS SUGGESTED BY EVALUATORS

It is not the main purpose of this chapter to propose specific ways of improving the present situation, but rather to synthesize what is already known about the problem. However, a number of useful suggestions were put forward by the evaluators, and since they emerge directly from their analyses of the situation they should be taken into account. They can be summarized as follows:

1   Sustainability needs to be built into project design (FRG 1986).
2   More short-term experts should be employed for post-completion follow-up (FRG 1986).
3   The readiness of the target population to make voluntary communal contributions towards maintenance should be explored. To quote the conclusions of the FRG evaluation 'The readiness of the target population to make voluntary communal contributions should be more strongly taken into account in the future than to date, because this motivation deepens, stabilises and secures the success of the project.'
4   Ways of raising revenue, in addition to 3 above, should be explored, e.g. user fees should be considered wherever possible (ADB 1984).
5   More training and technical assistance are needed to help institutions set up their own maintenance units whenever they decide to do this (e.g. to lessen their dependence upon the PWD) (ODA 1984).
6   There needs to be more effective long-term financial planning to cover recurrent costs years before they will be required: 'until budgets and schedules reflect a commitment to long term organisational learning, the common mismatch between

rhetoric and resources will remain and sustainable development will continue to be elusive' (ADB 1984).

7 Donors should consider extending the project period beyond the point when project structures are completed (i.e. to enable monitoring to take place during the phasing-in of effective maintenance) (ADB 1984; ODA 1985a). A contributor to the Asian Development Bank (1984) seminar, after describing a laboratory in an East Asian country which had been handed over as a fully functioning unit but had quickly deteriorated, commented: 'Employing a short-term expert to monitor whether the advice on maintenance, servicing and repairs, is acted upon, would no doubt be advantageous – at least in the short term.'

8 Wherever possible local people should be given a vital role in initiating, defining, implementing and maintaining, development programmes, as in sharing the benefits which accrue from them – this is the key to what is being called 'People-centred Development' (ACP/EEC 1986).

9 Aid donors need, in the words of the DAC *Guidelines* (1982) 'to address policy and institutional weaknesses that undermine the ability of developing countries to mobilise sufficient technical and financial resources to make full use of existing public facilities and productive capacity'. In other words, institutional strengthening for rehabilitation and maintenance is an urgent need.

10 As far as possible existing institutions should be used in preference to the creation of new ones. 'In many cases it is better to adapt the technological level of innovations to existing capacities and adjust the institutional framework accordingly' (IFAD 1986).

11 To ensure local commitment it might be better to make more use of aid in the form of a 'matching grant' (i.e. whatever the individual or local group are prepared to spend on a project will be matched by an equivalent amount in aid) (EEC 1978).

CONCLUSION

This chapter has turned out to be as much about inadequate maintenance as about rehabilitation. However that is not really surprising since the current emphasis on rehabilitation is itself

51

largely a response to the growing disillusionment with new projects that so quickly deteriorate (for a number of reasons, with inadequate maintenance being among the more important). Moreover, as this chapter has shown, rehabilitation projects are themselves likely to be the victims of inadequate maintenance. Rehabilitation is in fact no sure panacea for what are deep-seated problems of financial and human management. These problems need to be tackled at their roots if rehabilitation projects are to prove any more successful in the long run than new investments have been.

REFERENCES

African, Caribbean and Pacific States/European Economic Community, (1986) *Towards 2000: People-Centred Development*, Report prepared by Mr C. Jackson for ACP/EEC Joint Assembly, 1986–7, Brussels: EEC.

Asian Development Bank (1984) *Rural Development in Asia and the Pacific*, vol. 1, Papers and Proceedings of the ADB Regional Seminar on Rural Development, vols I and II, Manila, Philippines: ADB.

Development Assistance Committee (1982) *Guidelines on Aid for Maintenance and Strengthening of Existing Services and Facilities* (Addendum to DAC *Guidelines on Local and Recurrent Cost Financing*, 1979), Paris: OECD.

European Economic Community (1978) *Integrated Rural Development Projects Carried out in Black Africa with EDF Aid: Evaluation and Outlook for the Future*, H. Dupriez, Brussels, EEC.

Federal Republic of Germany (1986) *Learning from Mistakes: Nine Years of Evaluating Project Reality, Findings and Conclusions*, Ministry of Economic Cooperation, Bonn.

International Fund of Agricultural Development (1986) *Rural Development and the Peasant Farmer*, A Statement by Bahman Mansuri, Director, Africa Division, IFAD, at EDF Seminar 'Rural development: how can we make it work?', Brussels.

Overseas Development Administration (1974) *Wadi Dhuleil Jordan: An ex-post evaluation*, London.

—— (1981) *An evaluation of ODA financed projects to assist Malawi Railways*, London.

—— (1983) *A review of ODA's experience with hospital projects'*, London.

—— (1984) *The evaluation of aid projects and programmes*, London.

—— (1985a) *An evaluation of the UK/Bangladesh grain storage rehabilitation project'*, London.

—— (1985b) *Major issues in grain storage: an overview of evaluations*, London.

SEDES (1986) 'Evaluation of the Iringa region (Tanzania) Agricultural development project, phase II, interim report'.

US Agency for International Development (1982) *Aid Policy Paper: Recurrent Costs*, Washington, DC.

—— (1983) *Irrigation in AID's Experience: A Consideration Based on Evaluations*, Washington, D.C.

World Bank (1981) *Water Management in Bank Supported Irrigation Project Systems: An Analysis of Past Experience*, Washington, DC.

—— (1982) *IDA in Retrospect*, Oxford: Oxford University Press for the World Bank.

—— (1984) *Institutional Development in Africa: A Review of World Bank Project Experiences*, two vols, Washington, DC.

3

IMPROVING AGRICULTURAL PROJECTS DESIGN

David T. Edwards

INTRODUCTION

Design problems represent by far the most important single reason for the unsatisfactory performance of agricultural projects. If planners are to avoid repeating past errors and to reduce the need for rehabilitation measures, it is important to understand the nature of such problems and to explore means of improving project design.

The study on which this chapter is based was undertaken by the Food and Agriculture Organisation Investment Centre[1]. It had the objectives of: identifying problems which occurred in the implementation of a selection of development projects prepared by the FAO Investment Centre; assessing the extent to which the problems may reasonably be attributed to errors in the process of designing the projects prior to implementation; seeking to establish the underlying causes; and examining some alternative approaches to project preparation and analysis which could contribute to a higher project success rate, and consequently to a reduced need for rehabilitation in a project's later life.

First, this chapter refers to the nature of the projects examined and to their performance. After listing the nature of the problems encountered in implementing the projects, the chapter outlines how project design can be improved. Finally, it presents the main conclusions and operational implications of the study.

THE PROJECTS AND THEIR PERFORMANCE

The study covered a total of 75 projects – distributed between regions and project type – from amongst those planned between

54

1970 and 1980 by the FAO Investment Centre.[2] The total investment costs at the time of appraisal were estimated to be US $2.25 billion. Funding was provided mainly by the International Development Association (IDA) and the International Bank for Reconstruction and Development (IBRD), with a few projects being financed by the International Fund for Agricultural Development (IFAD) and the Asian Development Bank (ADB).

The performance of the projects was compared with the targets for cost, time to completion, and the economic rate of return (ERR). The results may be summarized as follows:

1 Forty-nine per cent of the projects had cost over-runs of over 10 per cent above the appraisal estimate while, conversely, 19 per cent incurred costs of less than 90 per cent of those estimates;
2 Twenty-five per cent of the projects equalled or exceeded forecast projected economic rates of returns (ERRs), 33 per cent achieved recalculated ERRs of below 10 per cent, while for 16 per cent of the projects the ERR was less than 5 per cent; major design changes were introduced into 13 per cent of the projects at time of appraisal, and into 34 per cent during implementation.

At first sight these statistics suggest a rather poor performance of projects. Very few projects actually succeeded in achieving their original goals within the allotted time. Out of the fifty-two projects for which economic rates of return have been recalculated, there were only four which, without major adjustments during implementation, could be considered as 'on-target' in the terms of: (a) costs falling within 10 per cent of the appraisal estimate, (b) disbursements completed with a time overrun of no more than six months, and (c) an ERR of over 10 per cent.

But this is too negative an interpretation of results. The figures also show that only 15 per cent of the projects for which data exist attained economic rates of return of less than 5 per cent, which may be a reasonable estimate of the long-term opportunity cost of capital. Moreover, fewer than 20 per cent of the projects ran into cost overruns of over 25 per cent, part of which could be attributed to unpredictably high rates of inflation during the period. It could be reasonably claimed that this record is quite good, given the circumstances under which these projects were prepared and implemented – the unprecedented rise in rates of inflation and other side-effects of two oil crises, the extent to which entirely new types of projects were being experimented with, and the steep increase in resource transfer targets and resultant constraints in absorptive capacity.

THE NATURE OF THE PROBLEMS ENCOUNTERED IN THE IMPLEMENTATION OF THE PROJECTS

An attempt was also made at identifying both the nature of the problems encountered by the sample projects during their implementation and the severity of their incidence. These were grouped for the purposes of a preliminary assessment into eight major categories as shown in Table 3.1. The incidence/severity score attributable to each problem is exhibited in Figure 3.1.[3]

In spite of some reservations about the methodology, the study concluded that the resulting figures provide a reasonable and credible assessment of the nature and incidence of project implementation problems and that the grouping of problem types into major categories indicates the main sources of difficulties into which the projects had run. The relatively close inverse correlation between the problem severity ratings of projects and their economic rates of return tended to confirm the validity of the assessment.

An important aspect of the context in which projects operated and which had a critical impact on project performance is the macroeconomic policy regime. Until recently projects were conventionally designed to function within a given domestic policy environment. Many of the projects covered by the study were, in fact, prepared and implemented during a period when the domestic policy environment was characterized by overvalued exchange rates, high rates of inflation, subsidized urban food prices, and a rapid growth in the role and scale of public sector and parastatal institutions.

In addition to the national factors affecting the performance of projects, international factors can also be the reason for project failure. The behaviour of international markets in particular, has a profound impact on the viability of most agricultural projects. While recognizing the crucial importance of the macroeconomic environment and the international dimension of the framework

Table 3.1 Problems in project implementation

Problem type	Problem category
Too many or unbalanced components	Conceptual
Too big	
Schedule too tight	
Non-sustainable	
Inflexible	
Production shortfall	Technical
Poor engineering	
Under-estimated costs	Financial/economic
Counterpart and recurrent budget shortage	
Low output prices or market problems	
Inequitable benefit distribution	Social
Slow adoption	
Bad management or staffing	Institutional
Unsuitable organizational structure	
Insufficient or ineffective technical assistance	
Procurement difficulties	
Land acquisition difficulties	
Poor monitoring and evaluation	
Natural disaster	Environmental
Resource degradation	
Turmoil or war	Political
Insufficient government commitment	
Minor problem types other than the above	Other

Source: Food and Agriculture Organisation (1990).

to the performance of projects, this chapter examines how the approach to project decision can be improved by providing flexibility to cover all causes of uncertainty and by employing practices geared to the elements of projects which can be influenced and controlled.

APPROACHES TO IMPROVING PROJECT DESIGN

The review of post-evaluation material indicates several possible approaches to reducing the incidence of the most serious problems

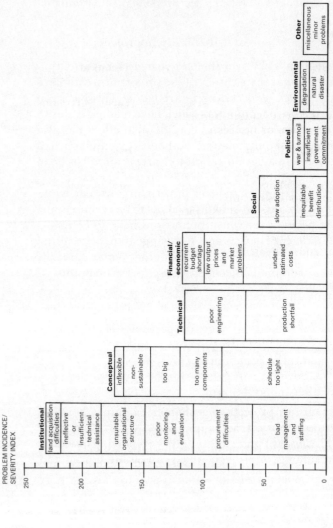

Figure 3.1 Problem categories and types: selected projects planned by the Food and Agriculture Organisation Investment Centre

Source: Food and Agriculture Organisation (1990).

Notes: Problem types are classified by primary category. Height of box indicates incidence/severity score attributable to each problem type.

which adversely affect project performance. The strategy proposed for improving project design involves: (a) incorporating greater flexibility in projects, (b) adjusting project preparation techniques, (c) improving operational approaches to project formulation, and (d) effecting various changes in the project preparation environment.

Incorporating greater flexibility in projects

There has been a tendency over the past years to focus attention on improving the apparent accuracy of the projections, estimates and analyses on which project designs are based. This has been encouraged by the use of computers which have made it easier to handle large numbers of figures. A considerable effort has also gone into refining economic analysis methodologies and much of the training offered in agricultural project preparation has been focused on improving the application of such techniques.

Past experience, of complex and 'soft' projects, in particular, is that *ex ante* projections of costs and benefits tend not to be very accurate. The longer the period over which predictions have to be made, the greater the danger of inaccuracy. What appears to be required is to design these projects in such a way that they can – within generally agreed and clearly defined objectives – adapt themselves to:

1 Improvements in information.
2 Findings of monitoring work.
3 Perceptions of emerging new opportunities/comparative advantages.
4 Changing political or economic circumstances.
5 Unpredictable events, particularly, for the agricultural sector, those of weather-induced origin.

This implies 'loosening' design, and deliberately devolving more responsibility for decisions on the allocation of resources and changes in policy, to the management of the project.

Various approaches to building increased flexibility into project design have been tried but would appear to warrant more frequent application. These include:

1 Use of 'programme loans' and 'funds', from which finance can be drawn to pay for a range of activities which are not tightly pre-specified but are consistent with the general objectives of the project and meet agreed approval criteria.

59

2   Adoption of annual operating planning (AOP) arrangements. Such plans would be subject to approval by the financing institutions, as represented by supervision missions.
3   Provision for in-depth mid-term reviews, aimed at providing for 'course corrections' to projects with relatively long disbursement periods.
4   Commitment in principle to sustain financing for a thoroughly appraised programme over a long period, but with actual funding commitments being made for a series of short-term tranches or time-slices, each conditional upon a 'short-cut' appraisal.

While all of these approaches imply a need for less accurate long-term projections of costs according to component, they place other demands on project preparation. In particular, they require:

1   A very clear definition of project objectives.
2   A clear outline of project management arrangements and procedures, especially for monitoring and responding to the findings of monitoring mechanisms;
3   Careful preparation and processing of AOPs.
4   Careful definition of criteria for approval of releases from funds.
5   Prior proof of the inherent viability of an array of specimen investment proposals, potentially subject to project financing.
6   An analysis of a range of possible outcomes, and of the extent of risk that some objectives may not be met: a critical review of the main potential sources of such risks would be essential.

It is also clear that any of the above approaches will place greater demands both on project management skills and on supervision and this may explain why some financing institutions show little apparent enthusiasm for incorporating greater flexibility in projects. The extent to which the additional supervision input could be financed through the projects as 'project implementation assistance' rather than from the administrative budgets of the financing institutions, would appear to warrant exploration.

Adjusting project preparation techniques

Whether a move towards a more flexible approach to project preparation proves to be feasible will ultimately depend on the willingness of the leading financing agencies to adjust their appraisal methodologies, and to introduce changes into the legal documentation covering their loans to permit the shifting of expenditures between categories.

As indicated earlier, most of the problems examined are susceptible, to a greater or lesser degree, to reduction through improved project preparation techniques. There appear, however, to be three principal areas of potential improvement which, if pursued, would contribute most significantly to better projects. There is a particular need to give more weight to analyses of the institutional, technical, and social feasibility of projects, matching these with some reduction in the effort put into economic analysis. The common feature of the three suggested approaches is that they are aimed at adding greater pragmatism to a process which has too often become somewhat detached from reality and has been conducted in a rather automatic manner. What is being advocated is a more focused and rigorous analysis of those aspects of project design, which the FAO study suggests most frequently contribute to a failure to meet targets and ultimately to achieving the project goals. Tightening up these areas of analysis would not be incompatible with the moves towards introducing the greater flexibility previously suggested.

Current analytical work

The principal problem is that most analyses are currently directed towards presenting a quantitative proof of a project's feasibility, with most effort being put into various forms of cost–benefit analysis rather than towards contributing to improvements in the underlying concept and design of the project. Typically, a project preparation report contains several models to demonstrate the financial impact of the project on the ultimate beneficiaries – usually farmers – and an analysis of the effect of the project on the economy. When these analyses are carried out correctly, and on the basis of well-founded cost and benefit streams, there can be no doubt as to their value as contributions to judgements on

61

the feasibility of projects. In practice, however, established methodologies are frequently applied wrongly, the terms in which the analyses are carried out may be of little relevance (for example, a financial rate of return is probably no guide to the future behaviour of a subsistence farmer), and the cost and benefit streams on which the calculations are based are seldom accurate enough to support detailed quantitative analysis. Even when the methodologies are correctly applied, little weight can be placed on the results of an economic analysis when there is a high probability of significant flaws in the underlying projections of costs, implementation schedules, and output, attributable to project interventions. What must be of concern is that, even though the weaknesses of these analyses are widely accepted, the outcome of such cost–benefit analyses continues to carry disproportionate weight in decisions on a project's feasibility.

There would seem to be considerable room for providing decision-makers with a much more informative basis on which to arrive at judgements on the feasibility of projects. Economists have sought to address the need for incorporating social as well as economic considerations in cost–benefit analysis through weighting techniques, but it might be advantageous in re-examining approaches to project justification to give greater attention to methods which implicitly leave the weighting of the various considerations to the decision-making bodies. This would imply that project feasibility studies should include not so much a proof of feasibility expressed largely in economic terms, though this is important, but rather a broad and systematic review of benefits (and any negative side effects) in terms of their consistency with national, political, economic, social, nutritional or environmental objectives. The decision-maker should also be provided with the means of assessing the chances of achieving – or not achieving – the forecast benefits. This implies a need to identify the major critical assumptions/parameters on which the design of the project is based (and on which benefits are most sensitive) and to review explicitly the degree of confidence (or conversely risk) associated with each. For instance, rather than have distributional effects represented as a weight in the analysis, a qualitative assessment of the extent to which a project improves or exacerbates the income distribution situation would be more informative.

It must also be obvious that analytical work is of greatest value if it leads to the incorporation, in the design of a project, of measures to address the weaknesses and problems on which it sheds light. If it is accepted that usually the identification of a project must be based largely upon subjective judgements, then the analyses carried out during preparation have the objective of confirming, refuting, or leading to a modification of, the initial 'hypotheses'. Project preparation is essentially an iterative process which permits the introduction of modifications in the light of emerging information and the conclusions which may be drawn from analytical work. Full advantage must be taken of this feature.

Institutional issues

It has been shown that institutional problems represented the most serious category of difficulties experienced by the projects under review (see Figure 3.1).

Several of the problem types, classified for the purposes of the discussion as in the 'conceptual' category, also clearly have important institutional implications.

For a project to be institutionally feasible there must be a matching between the tasks to be carried out, the time-frame over which they are to be implemented, and the institutional capability to execute them. If projects have failed to meet their targets in terms of timely task implementation, it is because the magnitude of the management implications of carrying out the task has been underestimated, the managerial capabilities have been over-stated, or because of a combination of both causes. The frequent inclusion of unduly high disbursement targets for the first year of a project provides the clearest evidence of the need to make a methodical assessment of scheduling implications and of the demands on management implied by each important project 'task'. As a corollary, it is clearly also necessary to be much more specific in identifying the exact nature of institutional weaknesses which need to be overcome if task implementation is to be feasible, and to examine the comparative benefits of different approaches to overcoming these. Superficiality in diagnosing areas of institutional weakness which would have a bearing on project implementation is all too common, and the subsequent recommendations for institutional strengthening are often couched in amateurish terms, which take little advantage of the accumulated experience of the management sciences. The mere provision of a modification in organizational structures, the creation of a coordinating committee and the inclusion of an input of expatriate technical assistance – although frequently advocated – does not guarantee that the institutional problems will be overcome.

Task analysis

As one step towards improving the realism of scheduling and the appreciation of the magnitude of demands on management/ staff/skills, it would seem useful to introduce some form of 'task analysis'. This could, in the case of complex projects with significant interdependence between components, involve the application of formal scheduling techniques, such as network analysis or critical path analysis, which would not only identify the time-frame required to carry out a given set of actions and the optimum sequencing but could also prove useful to project management. Alternatively, less formal techniques could be adopted to confirm or refute the implicit judgements on which estimates now tend to be based. Such techniques could simply involve identifying the key tasks implied by each of the project's main components, placing these in an operational sequence (for instance on a bar chart), estimating the likely time required for each step, listing demands on management staff or skills in potentially short supply, and noting other potential constraints/risks. From such an exercise it would be possible to derive a reasonably accurate expenditure profile for each component over time, an assessment of the demands on management and staff, requirements for coordination with other components or activities lying outside the project (e.g. passage of enabling legislation, approval of budget, etc.) and the needs for any particular skills.

Skill gap analysis

If a logical sequence is followed, the next step involves reconciling the demands implied by such an analysis with institutional capabilities. If these do not match, either the scope of the tasks must be reduced (for example, by dropping peripheral components with heavy demands on management) or the institution must be reinforced to the point at which it can be realistically expected to cope with demands.

According to the review of project implementation problems, the most serious institutional problems are not so much of a structural nature as of a staffing origin. It would seem reasonable, therefore, to direct greater attention in project design towards assessing staff capabilities and the options for improving these, where necessary. A first step in making such an assessment, is to complete a skills gap analysis, on the basis of which well-founded training programmes can be developed. (The currently recommended techniques for such an analysis, however, have been found unduly cumbersome and time-consuming, and thought must go into means of simplifying them.)

Manuals

Most project preparation reports tend to give some attention to the structural aspects of institutions, usually including an organogram, a list of functions and an estimate of staff requirements (whether or not this is supported by a skills gap analysis), and generally more than adequate provision is made for the means to work (buildings, vehicles, equipment and allowances). It is unusual, however, for such reports to address what might be termed 'institutional dynamics' – that is, how the institution and its component elements will operate. An integral part of the institutional design of a project must – at least if there have been any significant structural or staffing changes – be the preparation of a manual which clearly sets out the functions of different units and posts (including terms of reference for technical assistance staff) as well as the operating procedures to be followed within the institution. In the absence of such a manual, a new organization (or one which has undergone significant changes) will not have an adequate basis for operation, at least in the initial years of a project, and much of its limited staff skills will not be efficiently deployed.

Technical and social issues

One of the more disturbing findings of the review of problem incidence was the relatively high severity ratings attached to technical misjudgements, both on engineering matters and on crop and livestock performance. Although slow rate of adoption has been classified as a social problem, it frequently also has its origins in the weakness or inappropriateness of the technologies being promoted and hence it may conveniently be addressed alongside means of overcoming technical problems.

Several lessons, which though apparently obvious, are often disregarded in practice. They have been confirmed by the study:

1 A high standard of resource and topographical surveys is essential for the accurate design of engineering projects. Although this is bound to require heavier manpower inputs, these must be thoroughly field-checked if serious and costly engineering mistakes are to be avoided.

2 If there are no successful precedents for applying a new or improved technology under farmer conditions in or near a project area, any project which depends significantly for its success on the application of that technology – however promising it may seem on the research station or in farm models – should be of a modest or pilot scale. Such pilot projects should, if they are to provide replicable results, test promising technologies under 'real life' conditions and must be given time to achieve results before being superseded by larger projects.

3 The feasibility of projects must not depend on the future uptake of the findings expected to emerge from research activities being undertaken concurrently with project implementation. The gestation period required for investments in research – to generate results which could be applicable on a significant scale – is simply too long.

4 Projects to assist independent farmers in rainfed areas, with low population pressure on the land resources, or, where climatic risks are relatively high, are unlikely to be feasible if they depend on the application of significantly more intensive farming practices than those currently being applied – except in the case of irrigation in low rainfall areas.

The relatively high frequency with which production targets – whether for crops, fish or livestock – fail to be met could probably be significantly reduced if the experience of the lessons listed above was acted on. But in general, what seems to be required is more rigorous analysis of the underlying assumptions on which output forecasts are based, provided that it can be shown that this would significantly improve the quality of the predictions. It is not enough to show that it would be in the farmers' interest to adopt a given technical change; it must also be shown that the wherewithal (services, inputs, credit) needed for this will be readily available.

For crops, increases in production are the product of increases in yield per unit areas, and changes in the area over which such yields are obtained. While yield may respond significantly to changes in technology it is also affected by a range of environmental, biological, and managerial factors, which contribute to variability in yield attainment between seasons and between farmers. In communities of independent producers, average yields will be affected by the extent to which farmers adopt – in whole or in part – the recommended technology, and by the rate of adoption in the community as a whole.

Thus predictions of increased farm output represent the outcome of an interrelated group of judgements not simply on technical issues but also on farmer behaviour. Conventional project preparation practice involves the construction of a series of crop, livestock or farm models, claimed to be representative of various agro-ecological situations, to illustrate the impact on production and farm incomes of investments and related changes in farming technology. Judgements are made on farmer uptake rates and on this basis the models are aggregated to provide the key inputs into the cost and benefit streams from which the assessments of a project's economic viability are derived. The models are conventionally analysed to calculate a financial rate of return and a net return per man day of family labour (in the case of small farmers), and are used to demonstrate that, if credit is involved, the borrower has the means to repay his debt. Tests of sensitivity to changes in the relative levels of costs and benefits are normally carried out both at the level of the model and on the aggregate totals.

The approach outlined has the merit of simplicity and may be quite adequate for predicting agricultural output under relatively stable environmental conditions (e.g. in irrigation projects with reliable water supplies) and where there are recorded precedents for the adoption of analogous innovations from which credible forecasts of adoption rates can be derived. In other circumstances, particularly when the viability of a project is heavily dependent on incremental farm output from small farmers in rainfed areas, some selective deepening of the analysis would appear to be necessary if a proper appreciation of the probable results is to be provided.

There appear to be two principal areas on which such extended analyses should focus: on gaining a better appreciation of the range or probability of yield variations between farmers and between seasons/years in the 'with' or 'without' project situations, and on developing a better understanding of the factors affecting farmers' decisions on adoption. These are, of course, interrelated in the sense that aversion to risk (particularly risks associated with yield variability, but also perceived risks associated with markets, investment exposure, borrowing) is often one of the main factors inducing farmer reluctance to adopt innovations.

Yield variability assessment

Understandably, this commonly receives relatively limited attention because a comprehensive probability analysis places demands not only on reliable time series data, on yields and on the factors contributing to variation (which are seldom available), but also on sophisticated statistical analysis skills. However, even where it is not feasible to complete a statistical analysis of yield frequency distributions and probabilities, a qualitative assessment of yield prospects would be valuable in focusing attention on the underlying causes of risks, and ensuring that these are given due weight in the design of the project and the assessment of its feasibility.[4]

Adoption rate assessment

The production of more realistic estimates of adoption rates requires a better understanding of how the farmers would perceive the innovations proposed for promotion under the project, and how their behaviour could be influenced by various stimuli (e.g. extension services, availability of inputs, credit, subsidies, guaranteed prices, security of tenure, etc.).[5]

Improving operational approaches to project formulation

Raising government commitment

Although it is frequently claimed that commitment to a project can be enhanced by greater substantive government involvement in its preparation, a relatively low frequency is ascribed to 'lack of government commitment' as a source of project problems – and usually such diminished commitment has been attributable to domestic political concerns or to disagreements on policy issues between the government and the financing institutions.

Undoubtedly when a project preparation document is written outside the country to which it refers, it is likely to reflect thinking which has evolved within the responsible mission since its departure from the country and after it reached a preliminary understanding on the project concept with the borrower. If such changes are significant, or if a report betrays misunderstandings of technical issues, economic issues, or of national policies, it will clearly tend to contribute to a reduced commitment to the project. Under such circumstances, a thorough joint review of final preparation reports would offer one of the best means of strengthening government understanding and commitment to a project's goals. More use of this mechanism – of post-preparation seminars within the country and occasionally of involving senior government officials in headquarters reviews of draft documents – would appear to offer an attractive means of increasing government commitment to projects.

Building national project preparation capacities

This is not to imply that there is not room for developing greater indigenous project preparation capacities in borrower countries and, indeed, given the importance of the project as a vehicle for mobilizing external finance, it is surprising that so few countries have yet succeeded in creating the necessary institutions. Amongst the reasons for this could be the focus given to the training of individuals (who quickly become upwardly mobile) rather than to the broader aspects of institutional development, but it may also be that the heavy emphasis assigned in most training activities to economic analysis fails to equip people with the wider range of skills required for project identification and preparation work. The discrete nature of projects and the relative ease with which their preparation can be contracted out may also contribute to a low priority being accorded to developing national capacity for such work. Where political conditions permit durable institutional arrangements for project preparation to be built up, this can only be done with a strong and sustained commitment by both the government concerned and by the various financing institutions with which it is working. Recruitment and training plans need to be drawn up to address the long-term staffing needs of the institution, and inputs of technical assistance need to be carefully orchestrated to fill gaps rather than to substitute for locally available staff.

Increasing beneficiary participation

In most countries there are few ready means of consulting systematically with the many small farmers who ultimately make up the typical beneficiaries of agricultural and rural development projects, and their views on priorities and the feasibility of different development options can only be assessed through the application of rapid rural appraisal techniques. Much has been done in recent years to improve these techniques, and there appears to be room for deliberately increasing their use in project identification work.

While the substantive involvement of beneficiaries in project preparation is a laudable but seldom very practical objective, particularly given the time-frame in which project preparation must take place, the feasibility of projects often depends on the development of arrangements for securing the genuine involvement of beneficiaries in planning and decision-making during project implementation. If workable arrangements for this are to be developed, it requires a heavy investment in designing and field testing models at the time of project preparation, an exercise which can also contribute to a deeper understanding on the part of the preparation team of the practical options for development. Several attempts have been made in recent years to combine the testing of participative or consultative mechanisms (to be applied during project implementation) with the generation of data on which to base project design assumptions. It would seem opportune to distil the lessons of the experience.

The project preparation environment

Although some of the activities set out previously can be carried out by a reallocation of staff time between tasks, or simply by using existing time commitments more efficiently and focusing systematically on essentials, most of the suggested approaches to improving the standards of project preparation require that some more time be assigned for the work. It is also likely that if the additional analyses were to be made they would lead to more cautious assessments of investment requirements and hence to fewer and certainly smaller projects. As long as the major financing institutions give greater weight in the evaluation of their performance and that of their staff to the number and size of loans advanced, rather than to the ultimate results of the investments made, any proposal which increases administrative costs contributing to delays in meeting loan processing target dates or which reduces the size of justifiable loan commitments is not likely to attract the necessary management and financial support. The serious consideration currently being given to 'de-linking' resource transfer concerns, from commitments to specific projects, could do much to reduce the dangers of over-dimensioning. However, as long as emphasis is given to speed in preparing projects and the very tight manpower allocations prevail, this will tend to inhibit the introduction of any improvements in project preparation techniques. The effects will continue to be to:

1   preclude work necessary for investigations and analyses to improve the planning of projects;
2   reduce the thoroughness with which alternative options are reviewed prior to the 'firming up' of most aspects of project design;
3   make it difficult to carry the government and, still more, the beneficiaries along with a rapidly evolving project concept; and
4   restrict the range of disciplines that can be represented in the project preparation team thereby precluding specialized treatment of all major components.

Even if these restrictions were to be relieved, however, there are other aspects of the project preparation environment which tend to have an adverse effect on project quality and ultimately contribute to a disappointing performance. The most serious is the almost irresistible pressure for optimism on project feasibility which makes it nearly impossible to abort a project once it has been conceived and has found a place in a project pipeline. This is a complex problem which appears to have its origins not only in the importance attached within both governments and the financing institutions to achieving agreed lending targets, but also in the perceptions of the individuals involved in the processing of projects that it is in their interest to ensure a successful outcome. Sometimes the very process of project preparation tends to generate, amongst those most closely involved, an enthusiasm and commitment to a successful result that leads to an underestimation of the difficulties and risks associated with the project.

CONCLUSIONS AND OPERATIONAL IMPLICATIONS

The study on which this chapter is based, has shown that there is considerable room for 'designing out' many of the problems which agricultural development projects encounter during their implementation. Other problems stem from the inherent uncertainties associated with any long-term projections of human and economic behaviour, and from exogenous factors which may have a significant bearing on project performance.

In order to focus attention on those aspects of project performance which are susceptible to improvement at the design stage, it is necessary to relate identified problems to their underlying causes and to possible means of reducing their incidence which have to be applied at the time of project preparation.[6] The approach adopted calls for a more rigorous analysis of those variables which experience suggests have the greatest impact on project performance levels.

As long as project preparation is largely financed out of the limited administrative and technical assistance budgets of the financing institutions, even if it is held to be a country responsibility, some desirable investigations and analyses will have to be foregone. Not all the recommendations, however, call for a net increase in manpower allocations for project preparation. By deliberately building more flexibility into project design, for instance, some of the costly investigations conventionally

72

required during project preparation may be avoided at this stage. Similarly, there is room for shifting resources away from detailed economic analysis towards studies which increase the degree of confidence which can be placed in the cost and benefit streams on which the assessments of economic viability are based. In the same way, the systematic application of rapid rural appraisal techniques could do much to improve the efficiency of field studies as well as the level of confidence to be placed in the findings. If used judiciously, computers should also reduce the manpower needed for all quantitative analytical work.

In short, the need is not for the blanket allocation of extra resources for the preparation of agricultural development projects, but rather to ensure that the project preparation work which is undertaken is more accurately focused on those aspects of project design which past experience suggests have a critical bearing on project performance. The strengthening of the design of the project, and its redesign where justified in response to changing conditions and goals during its implementation, can make a major contribution to reducing the need for the rehabilitation of agricultural and rural projects.

NOTES

1 Appreciation is expressed to the FAO Investment Centre for its generous agreement for the publication of this paper, based on the Centre's Study: FAO, *The Design of Agricultural Investment Projects: Lessons from Experience* (Investment Centre Technical Paper, no. 6, FAO, Rome, 1990, p. 59, plus Appendices).

2 As with all studies, there are limitations and inadequacies in this study. The preoccupation is with 'failure' and its causes, rather than with success. The sample of projects cannot be claimed to be truly representative and involves only projects which had been fully implemented; therefore, they were designed some years ago and the approach to design may have improved in recent years.

3 A subjective assessment was made of the severity with which each project under review was affected by each problem type and a score had been attributed as follows:

problem not evident	0
problem slight	1
problem significant	2
problem very serious	3

4 A short note on simple methodologies for yield variability predictions and their presentation is given in Annex 2, FAO (1990).
5 A fuller discussion of systematic but relatively simple approaches to improving the prediction of adoption rates is given in Annex 3, FAO (1990).
6 See the checklist in FAO (1990) for a systematic review of these relationships.

4

REHABILITATION OF EXPORT-ORIENTED ESTATE AGRICULTURE IN TANZANIA

David Potts

INTRODUCTION

This chapter investigates the performance of export-oriented estate agriculture in Tanzania over the last twenty years and tries to assess potential rehabilitation strategies for the future. It is divided into three parts. The first part examines the causes of the decline of estate agriculture and contrasts this decline with the relative resilience of smallholder production. The second part examines the rehabilitation strategies under the Structural Adjustment Programme (SAP) and more recently under the Economic Recovery Programme (ERP) and indicates some potential problems. The final section examines some of the issues facing future investment in large-scale agriculture and indicates various possible alternatives to the rehabilitation strategies pursued under previous programmes.

STAGNATION AND DECLINE IN TANZANIA ESTATE AGRICULTURE

The evidence

Investment in estate agriculture in mainland Tanzania started in the German colonial period, first with rubber as the major crop and later with sisal. Following the First World War, Tanganyika was placed under British jurisdiction as a League of Nations mandate. Under British rule sisal continued to be the main estate crop, and commercial farming of arabica coffee, flue-cured tobacco and tea developed, continuing to expand well into the

Table 4.1 Production of crops with significant estate production, Tanzania 1971–88 ('000 tonnes)

Year	1971–3	1974–6	1977–9	1980–2	1983–5	1986–8
Sisal	164.5	130.1	92.8	73.5	38.9	32.2
Sugar	93.9	100.3	111.8	120.9	115.1	103.0
Tea	11.4	13.1	17.1	16.4	16.5	14.5
Flue-cured tobacco	9.4	12.5	14.4	12.7	9.8	12.7
Mild arabica coffee	36.1	36.1	35.7	41.3	36.7	34.1
Index (1977–9 = 100)						
Sisal	177.3	140.3	100.0	79.2	41.9	34.7
Sugar	84.0	89.7	100.0	108.1	103.0	92.1
Tea	66.4	76.4	100.0	95.9	96.3	84.6
Flue-cured tobacco	65.4	86.6	100.0	88.2	67.7	88.2
Mild arabica coffee	101.0	101.1	100.0	115.6	102.8	95.4

Sources: Potts, D. (1989); Project Preparation and Monitoring Bureau – *Coffee Expansion Programme*; Marketing Development Bureau – 1981, 1986 various; *Hali ya Uchumi wa Taifa Katika Mwaka 1987*.

Notes: 1 For coffee and tea years are crop years, i.e. 1970/1 appears as 1971, etc.
2 Index for coffee for 1986–8 based on 1986 and 1987 only.

post-independence period. However, large-scale farms never dominated the agricultural sector in Tanganyika in the same way that they did in Kenya, partly because of the much smaller settler population. Large-scale farms have only been important in growing sisal, sugar, tea, flue-cured tobacco and mild arabica coffee. In the late 1960s nearly all sisal and most sugar and tea were produced on estates as well as about one-half of the flue-cured tobacco and one-third of the mild arabica coffee. Cultivation of cash crops by smallholders expanded rapidly in the 1950s and into the 1960s and they became the dominant producers of cashew nuts, cotton, and eventually coffee and tobacco.

In the period from 1970/1 to 1986/7 production of sisal declined continuously at a rate of just over 11 per cent per year while production of sugar, tea, flue-cured tobacco and mild arabica coffee stagnated. Sugar and tea output showed slight upward trends of 1.0 per cent and 2.3 per cent respectively, but with considerable fluctuations. In the case of tea the period 1970–7 showed a growth of 7.8 per cent and the period 1977–87 showed a slight downward trend of 2.2 per cent. Production trends for tobacco and coffee moved slightly upward but these trends are not statistically significant[1]. A summary of the production performance of these crops is given in Table 4.1.

The overall impression of stagnation for most crops and collapse for sisal disguises significant variations between producers. In order to understand what happened to the estate sector it is necessary to look more closely at these variations in performance to identify some common features. In this chapter attention is concentrated on the sisal, tea, and coffee industries, all of which are export industries with output prices dependent on the combined effect of world market prices and exchange rate policy.

At the time of independence the sisal industry was the single most important source of foreign exchange earnings with a peak production of 230,000 tonnes in 1964. In 1967, following the Arusha Declaration, a number of sisal estates were nationalized. A second round of nationalization followed in 1973 which brought about half the industry under public ownership. After a period of institutional change, all public sector estates were brought under the Tanzania Sisal Authority (TSA). TSA was also given sole rights to market sisal.

In 1973 four major private sector growers controlled twenty-two estates and about 75 per cent of private sector output. The most important private sector companies were the Amboni Group and Ralli Estates. Ralli Estates operated more or less as a private sector company although 50 per cent of the Ralli shares were held by TSA. Most of the other private sector growers were single estates rather than multi-estate companies and by the early 1980s most single estate growers had ceased production.

The collapse of sisal production was far more catastrophic for the public sector companies and the other private sector growers than it was for the Amboni Group. By 1986 production by Amboni was still 46 per cent of the 1969 level while for the other producers it was less than 10 per cent. In seeking to explain the collapse of sisal production it is also important to explain the relative success of the Amboni Group.

In the period from 1976/7 to 1987/8 tea production in Tanzania stagnated following a period of rapid expansion. Although there was some nationalization of tea estates, it was not very extensive and was either due to nationalization of companies that also owned sisal estates or it occurred in areas where the government wanted to promote smallholder production. Tanzania Tea Authority (TTA) was primarily concerned with the development of smallholder tea and did not have any responsibility for marketing private sector tea.

Smallholder tea production fluctuated around a slightly rising trend. Brooke Bond (BBT) and Mufindi Tea Company (a TTA subsidiary from 1976 to 1985) recorded significant production increases, while the other major private sector producer, George Williamson (GWT), showed a slight increase followed by a serious decline in the last few years. The small private sector producers and the other nationalized estates recorded substantial declines in output. In general the larger producers with links to foreign companies did better. There were also regional variations: for example, production in the Usambaras and in Kagera Region fell while production in the Southern Highlands rose.

There is no significant trend at all in overall coffee production but, when the figures are broken down, the absence of trend conceals a drastic fall in the production of coffee estates which is compensated by a significant rise in production by smallholders in the Southern Zone. The collapse in the production of coffee estates is almost as great as that of the sisal industry, particularly in the case of those estates nationalized in 1973 and initially handed over to primary societies belonging to the Kilimanjaro Native Cooperative Union (KNCU).

In the case of the coffee industry the private sector estates were, and still are, predominantly owned by individuals rather than companies grouping estates together. For the coffee industry it is necessary to ask why the coffee estates fared so much worse than the smallholders and why the nationalized estates performed particularly badly.

Indices showing the production performance of different producer categories in the sisal, tea and coffee sub-sectors are given in Table 4.2.[2]

The causes

A number of issues are commonly raised when discussing the decline or stagnation of estate agriculture in Tanzania. The relevance of each will be discussed in turn.

Labour supply problems

Most estate agriculture in Tanzania was established on the basis of migrant labour. This was particularly the case in Northern Tanzania where very few of the labourers on the estates were indigenous to the areas in which the estates were located. The migrant labourers came from the south and west of Tanzania and from Northern Mozambique and Burundi. Labour recruitment agencies tended to treat certain regions as 'labour reserves', a factor which contributed to the lack of development in these regions [3].

The situation changed following independence and particularly in the 1970s after villagization in Tanzania, the allocation of land to Burundian refugees, and independence in Mozambique. People from areas traditionally regarded as labour reserves were encouraged to develop their own areas and in some cases were actively discouraged from migrant labour. These circumstances led to an ageing labour force as the younger generation were no longer prepared to accept the conditions of work on the estates. Particular problems were experienced with harvesting work (sisal cutting, tea plucking, coffee picking). In

Table 4.2 Production indices by producer for sisal, mild arabica coffee and tea, Tanzania 1971–88 (Index: 1977–9 = 100)

Year	1971–3	1974–6	1977–9	1980–2	1983–5	1986–8
Sisal						
TSA estates	175.5	142.4	100.0	76.8	32.7	27.1
Amboni Group	127.4	110.1	100.0	89.9	70.5	62.4
Other private sector	229.2	165.5	100.0	73.3	31.7	28.0
Tea						
TTA smallholder factories			100.0	87.9	96.9	95.6
TTA and TSA Estates			100.0	75.4	57.7	33.7
TTA subsidiary			100.0	111.9	107.4	109.8
Brooke Bond			100.0	107.7	115.9	128.4
George Williamson			100.0	110.4	94.5	60.4
Other private sector			100.0	81.8	61.0	46.2
Mild arabica coffee						
Estates	146.5	103.5	100.0	82.1	63.2	41.5
Smallholders	88.8	100.4	100.0	124.7	113.5	110.0

Sources: Tanzania Sisal Authority; Tanzania Tea authority; Tanzania Coffee Marketing Board; Marketing Development Bureau –
Annual Reviews of Tea and Coffee

Notes: 1 For coffee and tea years are crop years, i.e. 1970/1 appears as 1971, etc.
2 Index for coffee for 1986–8 based on 1986 and 1987 only.

the case of coffee picking the labour supply was also affected by the move to universal primary education which reduced the availability of child labour.

The change in the circumstances of migrant labour availability was not matched by a change in approach by employers. Wages for agricultural labourers tended to follow the statutory minimum wage for rural areas irrespective of the relative shortage of different categories of labourers. No attempt was made to change the wage structure to attract a more settled permanent labour force [4]. The problem was exacerbated by a drastic decline in the real value of the rural minimum wage from 1975/6 onwards. In the early 1980s it also became very difficult for rural workers to secure food at official prices. By 1985/6 the real value of the rural minimum wage had fallen to less than one-third of its value in 1974/5.

By the mid-1980s casual wage rates on smallholder farms were considerably above the rural minimum wage and many estate workers supplemented their earnings by working for small farmers in nearby villages or by establishing their own plots, either in, or close to, the estates. Absenteeism became a major problem and on many sisal estates workers on piece-rates would only report for work on 10 to 15 days a month. From about 1977 onwards large areas of mature sisal were left uncut. From 1982 to 1986 it is estimated that more than half the total leaf potential was left uncut during a period of declining leaf potential [5].

Labour shortages were particularly severe in the sisal industry and in the north of Tanzania. Food security provides part of the explanation. The percentage of estate workers of migrant origin is significantly higher in the north. These workers depend to a greater extent on purchased food than do workers with access to their own land. In addition the bimodal rainfall pattern of the north is more prone to periodic drought than the monomodal pattern of the south-west because the rainy periods are shorter and therefore their timing is more critical. Drought-related food shortages occurred in the north but not in the south-west and estate workers in the north were exposed to high unofficial prices for basic foods.

Estate workers also faced a deterioration in estate housing. Under conditions of poor or negative profitability, funds for the maintenance of buildings were not available and on many estates houses fell into disrepair.

Prices and marketing

The three crops under scrutiny share a common dependence on the combination of world market prices and the exchange rate. Falling world prices is often given as an explanation for the collapse of the sisal industry, but the trend decline in sisal prices for the period 1970–87 is 2.4 per cent per annum, the same as for the tea industry, although the trend for sisal is less statistically significant. The downward trend in world coffee prices is less than 0.4 per cent per annum and is not statistically significant [6].

Fluctuations in the world prices for the three crops are probably more important than any declining trend. Sisal prices reached record levels in 1973–4, tea in 1977 and 1984 and coffee in 1976–7, but these prices did not lead to significant investment in primary production.

For the first half of the 1970s the rate of inflation in Tanzania was broadly in line with the international rate. From 1978 onwards the rate of inflation in Tanzania exceeded the international rate. The divergence between Tanzanian and international inflation rates was not reflected in movements in the exchange rate and so the decline in the real value of export prices externally was reinforced by the rapid increase in local costs. The real value of export prices measured in terms of shillings declined almost continuously from 1974 to 1985 for sisal, from 1977 to 1982 for tea, and from 1977 to 1985 for coffee. The sisal industry was particularly badly hit because of the timing of world price movements in relation to movements of local costs.

The average quality of production also declined in this period, partly due to lack of investment in processing equipment. The decline in quality was more marked for coffee and sisal than it was for tea, being particularly marked for smaller estates.

The change to single channel marketing of sisal imposed additional burdens on producers. TSA was set up at a time when production was well over 100,000 tonnes and the scale of the organization was related to this level of production. It proved very difficult to reduce TSA overheads in line with the fall in production and consequently the level of deductions increased as a proportion of the export price.

There were no intermediaries between the tea estates and the world market. A proportion of the output of each grower was allocated for the local Tanzania Tea Blenders on a basis agreed with Tanzania Tea Growers Association (TTGA) and prices were usually related to world market prices. In the early 1980s, prices for tea sold locally were higher than the world market price and local consumers were helping to offset the effect of the decline in real prices.

The Coffee Authority of Tanzania (CAT) was established in 1976 following the dissolution of the cooperative unions. CAT took over the primary marketing functions of the unions as well as export marketing on behalf of the growers. The primary marketing function was returned to the unions in 1984 while export marketing continued under the auspices of the successor to CAT which was renamed Tanzania Coffee Marketing Board (TCMB). Coffee growers are paid a producer price in three stages. The first payment is paid on delivery of the crop. The government announces advance producer prices which are not necessarily directly related to world prices. Coffee is hulled and then auctioned by TCMB and if the auction prices are good enough an interim payment is made to growers about six months later. When all the coffee for a season is sold a final payment to growers is made after deduction of TCMB expenses.

The system of producer prices adopted has led to an indirect subsidy from the more efficient coffee growers to growers in areas with low yields and high collection costs. Under this system some inputs have been provided free with the cost deducted on a per kilo basis to estimate the producer price. Growers with high yields pay more per hectare for the same quantity of inputs. Coffee estates would normally expect higher than average yields and therefore have received lower prices than they might have done under a different system. The problem has been compounded by a narrowing of the quality differential in prices from which estates would otherwise expect to benefit.

Export-oriented estates suffered from a drastic fall in the real value of the prices of their output over the period 1977 to 1985. This fall was more sustained for sisal and coffee than for tea and was compounded by marketing arrangements that did not favour the producer. The result was a severe erosion of profitability that did not allow investment in the replacement of worn out equipment, proper maintenance of fixed assets or adherence to routine schedules for replanting and infilling. The problem of replanting was more severe in the sisal industry because the industry works on a 10- to 12-year replanting cycle. Tea and coffee estates work on a 25- to 30-year cycle and the bushes can last much longer if necessary. A collapse of profitability therefore undermines the physical basis of a sisal estate much faster.

Foreign exchange availability

From the late 1970s Tanzania entered a period of critical shortage of foreign exchange. From 1978 onwards the value of exports was less than half that of imports. This was a contributing factor to the continued decline of the estates as well as a consequence of that decline.

Estate production of sisal, tea and coffee is dependent on foreign exchange. Sisal and tea are semi-industrial crops and the first stage of processing must be undertaken within fairly easy reach of the crop. Sisal and tea estates require spare parts and replacements to keep the factories operating, and efficient leaf transport systems usually based on either lorries or tractors with trailers. Sisal also requires heavy land clearing equipment for rotational replanting. Coffee estates do not have such large requirements for transport or processing, but the condition of the pulperies affects the quality of the coffee.

Tea and coffee estates rely heavily on fertilizer to achieve good yields and most estates use herbicides if they are available. Coffee is vulnerable to pests and diseases and considerable use is made of pesticides and fungicides. All the estates rely on diesel for vehicle operation.

Reliable estimates of the direct and indirect foreign exchange requirements of sisal, tea and coffee estates vary [7] but it is reasonable to assume that, for normal operation, sisal and tea estates require about 20–25 per cent of foreign exchange earnings with coffee estates requiring about 15–20 per cent. At low levels of production these percentages become much higher, and for coffee the figure is very sensitive to yields because of the extensive use of chemical inputs.

The foreign exchange shortage made it very difficult for the estates to keep processing and transport facilities in good condition. Shortages of diesel and insufficient or untimely supply of inputs exacerbated the problem. The result was a steady deterioration in processing facilities, periodic and sometimes permanent closures of some factories and frequent interruptions to production.

Nationalization and institutional change

The estate sector of all three crops was affected by the nationalizations of 1967 and 1973. The impact was greatest on the sisal industry and least on the tea industry, although the estate sector was only a relatively small part of the total coffee industry.

The first round of nationalization of the sisal industry led to the establishment of the Tanzania Sisal Corporation (TSC). The estates nationalized in the second round were put under TSA which also took over all marketing of sisal. Eventually TSC and TSA were merged and the estates were organized into three zones under the head office. In 1981 the zones were reorganized into five subsidiary estate companies. These companies were semi-autonomous but the process of transfer of assets was never completed and they remained financially dependent on TSA headquarters. More recently some of the most run down estates have been sold back to the private sector and management of the remaining estates has been recentralized. For most of the period under examination, TSA had both an executive chairman and a general manager as well as general managers for each of the subsidiary companies.

The performance of TSA was the subject of considerable criticism from both the private sector and the parent ministry. The management structure contained an inherent conflict between the executive chairman and the general manager. The subsidiaries were never able to become financially autonomous and so conflict also extended between the subsidiaries and headquarters. TSA made some substantial investments in sisal spinning capacity and diversification which absorbed a great deal of the surplus earned during the period of very high sisal prices at a time when sisal production was already beginning to fall. Subsequent failure to maintain replanting schedules or to improve the terms and conditions of estate workers meant that the spinners were never able to secure enough fibre.

Investment in sisal spinning and domestic capacity for bag manufacture was based on the view that the market for sisal fibre was threatened by synthetic substitutes. In fact sisal production fell so rapidly that the market was never a serious problem. In the end Kenyan producers took up part of the market abandoned by Tanzania. From 1970 to 1972 Kenyan production was only 24 per cent of Tanzanian production. By 1985 the Kenyans were producing 58 per cent more sisal than Tanzania.

Nationalization and single-channel marketing led to a lack of confidence by the private sector reflected in a replanting record that was even worse than that of TSA. Only the Amboni Group were able to maintain adequate levels of replanting. By 1981 most of the rest of the private sector had ceased to replant at all.

Nationalization also had an effect on the motivation of management and technical workers on the estates. The real value of their salaries declined even faster than the wages of production workers. The value of fringe benefits (housing and access to transport) deteriorated with lack of maintenance and estate management became progressively disillusioned.

Reorganization of the public sector also affected sisal research in which Tanzania was the leading country during the 1960s, financed largely through Tanzania Sisal Growers Association (TSGA). The research station at Mlingano became part of Tanzania Agricultural Research Organization (TARO) and sisal research was effectively discontinued. Accidental replanting of a rogue hybrid by the Amboni Group in the early 1980s caused serious loss of output which might have been prevented by more active research.

Nationalization had little effect on the majority of private sector tea estates. The smallholder-oriented factories of TTA were developed with World Bank assistance and, despite some technical problems, production levels have been maintained. Two estates in the Usambaras were nationalized and experienced similar problems to the sisal estates. The decline of these estates was similar to that of the private sector estates in the same area and can probably be related to more general problems rather than to nationalization *per se*. Mufindi Tea Company prospered during its period of nationalization, completing a new factory and embarking on a programme of green leaf expansion.

It is significant that the private sector tea growers retained their own association in which TTA participated. This helped to avoid the conflicts between public and private sector that were observed in the sisal industry. No major organizational changes occurred and the tea industry was united on most issues.

Nationalization affected the marketing of coffee and production on the nationalized estates. The private sector retained their own growers' association which helped them to secure some of their input requirements but could not change the marketing system.

Although some nationalized coffee estates were put under CAT and the National Agriculture and Food Corporation (NAFCO), the most important group of nationalized estates were those handed over to KNCU in 1973. Following the dissolution of the Cooperative Unions in 1976 these estates were handed over to the regional administration until 1984 when they were handed back to KNCU. There were three changes of ownership in eleven years in which the problems of transfer of title deeds to land and physical assets were never resolved. It was therefore very difficult for even the most profitable of the estates to secure loans for working capital or replacement of equipment.

Survival responses in an adverse environment

Estate agriculture faced an increasingly adverse environment in Tanzania in the late 1970s and early 1980s. The real value of prices was declining, estate labour was discouraged, foreign exchange was difficult to obtain and for some crops rapid institutional change was disruptive. Taxation policy on some imported inputs and transport equipment and on the incomes of management and technical workers also was not conducive to the development of the estate sector. The government itself had an ambiguous attitude towards the estates. Estate labour was viewed as a degrading occupation, but the estates were an important source of foreign exchange.

Many estates closed down, particularly in the sisal industry. Although some degree of rationalization was probably necessary in view of the long-term market prospects of the sisal industry, the closures were not planned. In Tanga Region large areas of some sisal estates were taken over by squatters, often including workers from the estates.

The first response of producers was to cut down on maintenance expenditure and reinvestment including replanting. This led to a fall in sisal leaf potential that could not be reversed until 1989. On coffee and tea estates, gaps where bushes had died were not filled. Some areas were abandoned to grow wild without pruning. The strategy of reduced maintenance and reinvestment started with the smallest estates with the lowest reserves and gradually spread to some of the larger producers. Those that were able to tackle the problems of availability of labour and foreign exchange and reduced profitability survived best.

Labour availability was more of a problem in the north than in the southern highlands. The obvious solution was to pay higher wages to the categories of labour in short supply, but many estates were not sufficiently profitable to pay higher wages and did not want to step out of line with rates determined on the basis of industry-wide agreements. The problems of estate workers were not just related to wage levels. Supplies of basic foods and other essentials also became increasingly scarce.

Those estates with access to surplus land cultivated maize or allocated land to workers for this purpose. The latter approach was taken by most sisal estates. On TSA estates immature sisal was intercropped with maize. On some coffee estates stumped coffee was intercropped with beans. These efforts were supplemented with attempts to secure permits for the purchase of essential commodities in which the bigger and more influential estates were more likely to be successful. World Food Programme assistance was secured for TSA to supply food at subsidized rates to their workers with the proceeds used to construct improved housing. The scheme was eventually extended on a more limited basis to the private sector sisal estates.

The Amboni Group attempted to tackle the problem of labour shortages in a systematic way by instituting a scheme for sisal cutters called 'Mkato Bora' (excellent or special cutter). Cutters who agreed to a strict regime of work discipline, attendance and productivity were paid at rates above the nationally agreed rate and were also given incentive goods and priority allocation of scarce commodities. The scheme, which was designed to increase labour productivity rather than to recruit labour, was successful for a time and was extended to other categories of workers. The major problem was that the level of discipline and productivity required was more than many workers were able to accept and depended on a nutritional and health status that was difficult to sustain.

The Amboni Group were also pioneers in the introduction of Hybrid 11648, a variety that gave improved yields and was easier to cut. Their efforts to improve revenue rather than to cut costs contributed to their relatively good production performance.

Some tea estates tried to increase revenue by introducing sprinkler irrigation in the dry season. This improves yields throughout the year and reduces seasonal peaks of production, allowing more intensive use of factory capacity. Improvement in the condition of the tea bushes also attracts pluckers who are paid piece rates and find it is easier to pluck bushes in good condition. Recently some private sector estates have attempted to resolve labour shortages by using specially adapted shears. This is thought to have an adverse effect on the quality of tea, but is preferable to abandoning areas for lack of pluckers.

TSA attempted to improve profitability by diversification into sisal spinning and livestock. These enterprises used the funds generated by the estates in the 1970s and did not alleviate their deteriorating financial position in later years. Amboni also invested in livestock and spinning on a smaller scale and with more success.

Many coffee estates were mixed enterprises including dairy cattle as a second activity. The declining profitability of coffee led to concentration on other activities including uprooting coffee and planting maize on some of the KNCU estates.

Foreign exchange requirements for equipment and spares can be reduced to some extent by better maintenance and repair. Both TSA and Amboni invested in central workshops for the repair of processing and earth moving equipment, but TSA were unable to secure qualified engineers to work on their estates. Amboni, a Swiss-based company, localized nearly all estate management positions but had great difficulty in attracting local engineers and the majority of their estate engineers were expatriates.

Most inputs and many spare parts are imported and vehicles and machines must eventually be replaced. By 1985 most producers that survived were receiving some form of foreign exchange support either directly or indirectly. TSA were supported by government development budget funds for replanting which included earth moving equipment and tractors. Some private sector sisal and tea estates received Dutch or Norwegian import support. Coffee inputs were obtained through the EEC-funded Coffee Development Programme (CDP) and through bilateral import support programmes.

REHABILITATION AND EXPANSION – PAST PROPOSALS AND MEASURES

The export crop packages

By the early 1980s Tanzania was experiencing serious economic problems, partly caused by the war with Uganda and unfavourable commodity prices, but also associated with some of the policies pursued by the government in the 1970s. In an attempt to secure external support the government launched a three-year Structural Adjustment Programme (SAP) in 1982. One of the major objectives of SAP was to improve the performance of traditional agricultural export crops. This was to be achieved by the implementation of 'Export Crop Packages' – a set of policy proposals, projects and import support programmes to be drawn up by the Ministry of Agriculture (Ministry of Economic Affairs and Planning 1982).

Although SAP was supposed to run from 1982 to 1984, work on the Export Crop Packages did not start until late 1983 and the main report was not completed until April 1984. It was impossible to plan to the original schedule and some of the original targets were physically impossible to achieve because of the gestation period involved in planting perennial crops. Nevertheless, an attempt was made to define resource requirements and policy measures and later to elaborate these into individual crop programmes and projects. Programmes for the sisal and tea industries were completed in 1984. Initially no detailed work was undertaken on coffee due to the existence of the Coffee Development Programme, but eventually some work was undertaken on the nationalized coffee estates in 1985/6. A Coffee Expansion Programme was finally prepared in 1987/8 under the Economic Recovery Programme (ERP).

The shilling was devalued by 10 per cent in 1982, 20 per cent in 1983 and by 26 per cent in 1984. It was announced that export industries were to receive 10 per cent retention of foreign exchange earnings for the purchase of inputs and spare parts. The cooperative unions were reintroduced, and extension officers under crop parastatals were returned to the Ministry of Agriculture. Previous attitudes to the role of the private sector in commercial agriculture were modified and private sector investment was welcomed within the framework of the Agricultural

Policy of Tanzania (Ministry of Agriculture and Livestock 1983). The government actively supported private sector estates in their attempts to secure import support and external funding for rehabilitation. Single channel marketing of sisal was discontinued and the TSGA was eventually reformed as the Tanzania Sisal Growers, Spinners and Marketing Association (TSGSMA). A Human Resources Deployment Act was passed to try to reverse the influx of people to urban centres and to relieve rural labour shortages.

Despite the policy measures taken, the production of most export-oriented estates continued to decline. The devaluations were not sufficient to restore the profitability of the estates to a level that would allow for major rehabilitation and in 1985 there was no devaluation. Foreign exchange retentions were not enough for the needs of the producers and, in the case of coffee, were not in practice made available.

Some micro-level policy proposals were not implemented. The proposed reform of TSA never took place. Proposals to introduce productivity-related incentive schemes and improved wage levels for estate workers were delayed. A number of the most run down TSA estates were sold to the private sector but a proposal that redevelopment of sisal on these estates should be restricted because of eventual market limitations was not implemented.

A number of project proposals were developed under SAP, but only Mufindi Tea Company in the public sector and Brooke Bond and Amboni in the private sector were able to secure adequate funding for reinvestment. Development budget funds allocated to TSA for replanting and to Bulwa Tea Estate for factory rehabilitation, were well below what was required to prevent further decline. Part of the problem was the substantial divergence between financial and economic profitability. In many cases financial profitability was moderate to marginal with fairly optimistic assumptions about implementation performance, and incremental profitability was sometimes derived from the improvement over a 'without project' situation that implied continued financial losses.[8] A relatively small shortfall in performance would lead to financial problems and it was difficult for enterprises that were already insolvent to secure normal commercial funding.

Rehabilitation under the Economic Recovery Programme

In 1986, following agreement with the IMF, Tanzania launched the ERP. This programme follows a major and continuing exchange rate adjustment and a much tighter monetary policy intended to contain inflation. Agreement with the IMF has given greater access to funding from bilateral and multilateral agencies and the foreign exchange constraint on financially viable export projects is effectively removed, although the capacity to generate such projects remains a constraint. The shift towards encouragement of private sector investment continues and is reflected in a number of joint venture projects either agreed or under negotiation.

Implementation of some joint venture proposals has been delayed over issues relating to the degree of national control over the project and the production and marketing of the crop in question. Should private sector investors be allowed to cure and export their own coffee when there is enough curing capacity already and when coffee marketing is subject to international quotas? Should rehabilitation of a nationalized sisal estate company be undertaken by expatriate management independently of the existing TSA organization? These questions relate to long-term policy on the purpose and degree of government intervention in the production and marketing of export crops. From the point of view of production, the relatively *laissez-faire* approach taken to the tea industry appears to be more successful.

The measures taken in the ERP will lead to a significant improvement in the profitability of the export crops. Despite generally unfavourable export prices for all three crops, the shilling value of export crop price indicators by 1987 rose in real terms by more than 60 per cent for tea and coffee and by over 100 per cent for sisal over the 1985 level. In 1987 sisal production increased by 10 per cent, only the second increase in any year since 1969. For tea, improvements in performance did not start to take place until 1988/9 at which time there was still no indication of improvement in coffee production. World tea prices were particularly low in 1987 and the coffee crop in 1986/7 was affected by very late delivery of inputs. It takes a long time for the effect of exchange rate changes to have a positive impact on coffee growers because of the three stage system of payment. The first effect coffee growers experience is the increase in the price of inputs and its impact on working capital requirements.

Production of tree crops cannot respond immediately to major policy changes and producers face constraints of inadequate input supplies and imperfect credit institutions.

There are already indications that the measures taken under ERP will lead to a significant increase in private sector investment in estate agriculture. This will be reflected in substantial output growth in five to ten years time. If such growth occurs in the traditional tea and coffee growing areas there will be considerable localized pressure on land availability and substantial increases in wage labour requirements. The sisal industry may eventually face problems in marketing the increased output leading to downward pressure on prices. The implications of these possible effects need to be given careful consideration.

ISSUES FOR FUTURE INVESTMENT IN ESTATE AGRICULTURE

Tanzanian estate agriculture has been less resilient than smallholder agriculture to the adverse changes in the economic environment that occurred in the 1970s and 1980s. This was partly due to an ambivalent attitude by the government towards the growth of estate production which was associated with the detrimental effects of migratory labour and foreign control over Tanzanian resources. Estate agriculture is also more dependent on imported equipment and inputs and is therefore more vulnerable to foreign exchange shortages. The record of nationalized estates is not very good, partly because of inadequate resources and partly because of poor motivation of management and workers related to lack of autonomy over pay and conditions.

Future rehabilitation proposals must consider the reasons for the original decline and whether these are primarily to do with an adverse policy environment or whether there are other reasons relevant to the direction of rehabilitation measures. These questions are examined in relation to the causes outlined above.

Labour supply

The problems of estate labour supply are partly due to a deterioration in wages and conditions that can be reversed with the improved profitability derived from exchange rate changes.

Food availability has also been a problem, but this seems to have been solved for the time being. Some problems are more intractable. The estates in northern Tanzania are still heavily dependent on migrant workers who come from regions that have significant economic potential. The migrant labour system is disruptive to development efforts in these regions and potentially damaging to the social and nutritional status of the families left behind. If migrant labour is undesirable, future estate development must depend on the settlement of migrant labourers or recruitment of workers locally. In either case a change in the status of estate labour is essential. A change in status and attitudes depends on improvement in both social conditions and wages. Investment in housing and social facilities is therefore important in rehabilitation projects.

Greater use of local labour could require modification of the existing task-based systems for permanent labour. The Tanzanian village system makes the organized recruitment of labour possible during slack periods in smallholder agriculture. Work could be subcontracted to the villages and there would be no need for individuals to stick to the standard tasks. Some producers have already tried this with mixed results. The main drawback is that peak labour requirements for smallholders and estates tend to coincide. Sisal is an exception because harvesting can be done in the dry season if there is enough water to run the decorticator. The possibilities of this system are nevertheless limited if estates want to maintain a steady level of production.

Improvement in wages is problematic in the cases of tea and sisal where there is evidence of a decline in the real value of world prices. Once exchange rate adjustment has been made, wage improvements can only be derived from increases in productivity or distributional changes from capital to labour. The latter possibility is limited by the need for a level of profitability that allows for the maintenance and normal replacement of assets.

The major bottlenecks to increased productivity in the sisal industry are cutting and stacking. There is no indication that cutting can be mechanized. Improved wages for sisal cutters can only be derived from changes in work organization or from transfer of the benefits of productivity improvements elsewhere. A possible source of improvement is in the introduction of mobile decorticators to reduce leaf transport costs. This would allow changes in the organization of production because it would not be necessary to stack the leaves for subsequent transport.

The best prospects for improved productivity in the tea industry lie in increased yields through irrigation and improved planting material. The use of shears and tea plucking machines may affect the quality of tea produced.

The major problem for coffee estates is the control of pests and diseases. Like tea, coffee responds to irrigation and proper fertilization. These improvements would only restore productivity to levels already achieved on some estates in previous years.

Prices and marketing

There is evidence of a declining trend in world prices for sisal and tea. A long-term decline in the market size for sisal is due to competition from synthetics and changes in baling technology. Other uses for sisal, particularly in the manufacture of paper, would only be economically viable at prices well below those prevailing at present. There is potential for market expansion in Eastern Europe and some developing countries and it might be possible to regain some of the market lost to synthetics, but it is unlikely that sisal prices will increase. Future development of the industry therefore depends on increased productivity and reduced costs.

The market for tea has been growing slower than production and the result has been a fall in prices. Tanzania is not a major producer of tea and Tanzanian production is unlikely to affect world prices. In the long term it is likely that shortage of land suitable for tea will lead to a recovery of tea prices. A similar argument applies to coffee.

Marketing of sisal has been reformed, but the rehabilitation of the industry is taking place in a manner which may eventually lead to competition for a declining market. Reduced capacity utilization with the present fixed decorticator technology has a serious effect on profitability. Rehabilitation of the industry on the same lines as before could therefore lead to serious marketing problems. The technological alternative of using mobile decorticators could involve smallholder outgrowers which would require the introduction of a system for marketing sisal leaf.

A serious issue for tea marketing could arise if factories currently based on estate production were to take in significant quantities of smallholder green leaf. The current system of fixed producer prices for smallholders has discouraged private sector factories from taking smallholder green leaf because it has not been profitable at the world prices prevailing for most of the 1980s. Future smallholder production for private tea factories would require a system like that used for coffee with a fixed first payment and subsequent payments based on 'made tea' prices received on the world market and from the local blenders.

Rehabilitation of estate coffee would require the separate auction of coffee from the larger estates or groups of smaller estates to allow growers to receive the full benefit from the quality of beans produced. The issue of allocation of sales under the quota system would have to be resolved for independent marketing of coffee by private sector growers to take place.

Foreign exchange

Estates are very vulnerable to a lack of foreign exchange for the purchase of equipment and inputs. Retention schemes for sisal and tea producers have been introduced but it is not the most efficient way to ensure the availability of the relevant items. It is difficult to estimate the percentage actually required by each producer and to ensure that the retentions are actually made available. The requirements of a producer embarking on a major rehabilitation with a low current output are much higher than the requirement for normal annual production.

For coffee estates the position is more complicated because they export their coffee indirectly through TCMB. If a retention is made should TCMB act on behalf of the interests of all coffee growers? What happens when views on priorities differ? How are competing claims for the same fund resolved?

When estates are operating efficiently their net foreign exchange earnings per unit of area are usually higher than smallholders because their yields are higher. On the other hand their foreign exchange earnings per unit of foreign exchange used are lower because their methods of production are capital and input intensive. The importance of the criteria depends on the relative scarcity of the resources in question. In areas where land is not scarce, a well-developed smallholder production system may be more economically efficient than an estate system.

Alternative organizations

Sisal has always been grown on estates in Tanzania because the fixed decorticator requires a large volume of leaf and the low proportion of fibre in the leaf makes transport over long distances uneconomical. Past attempts to introduce smallholder sisal in Tanzania have failed for technical, organizational, and logistical reasons. Most Brazilian sisal is grown by smallholders and decorticated in the field, but the fibre quality and decortication efficiency are lower than for estate grown sisal. An in-field decorticator has now been developed in Kenya that may be able to produce sisal of a comparable quality to that produced by the the fixed decorticator. A future sisal industry could involve a central factory with mobile decorticators processing leaf grown by smallholders. This would allow more variation in the area of sisal farms and more ability to respond to changes in market conditions.

Smallholder tea development in Tanzania has been constrained by pricing policy, leaf transport problems and inability to match factory capacity to green leaf supply. Smallholder tea has been much more successful in Kenya, partly because the returns to the farmers have been directly related to the performance of the factories (i.e. the quality and quantity of 'made tea' produced). Under the new exchange rate regime now operating in Tanzania and with a modified system of payment, smallholder development could take place either alongside or instead of estates with factories owned either privately or publicly or by cooperatives. The approach could be applied to rehabilitation wherever potential for smallholder tea exists, and estate rehabilitation could be accompanied by the development of smallholder tea so that the factory would be less dependent on estate labour.

Primary processing of coffee does not have to be done on a large-scale so the issue of outgrowers is not very relevant to most private coffee estates. The issue does arise for the KNCU estates because they are owned by the primary cooperative societies and, if the estate pulperies were rehabilitated, they could be used as central pulperies for smallholders.

A more fundamental issue raised by the KNCU estates and some of the tea and sisal estates in and around the Usambaras, is that they occupy land in areas of land shortage. There is an obvious contradiction with the labour shortages of the estates which might be resolved if the wages and conditions on the estates were sufficient to attract local people. An alternative solution is to redistribute land. Some of the coffee estates have deteriorated to a level where yields are lower than on surrounding smallholder farms. If funds for estate rehabilitation were not available it would be more economical to redistribute the land to the members of the primary societies.

A similar issue relates to some of the nationalized sisal estates which have far more land than they are likely to need for sisal. Some of this land could be redistributed or, with mobile decorticator technology, sisal estates could be developed as cooperatives with mixed sisal and food crops.

In the Usambaras some tea estates have been forced to abandon some areas for lack of pluckers. A possible solution is to redistribute or to rent land to smallholders with inadequate holdings.

In the long run it is important that estate agriculture should adapt to changing circumstances. The old style of estate based on poorly paid migrant labour has a limited future. The estates that have survived best are those that have been able to improve productivity based on a relatively settled labour force with adequate housing and social facilities. This essentially means that the estate becomes more like an industry and labourers become proletarianized.

The alternative is an outgrower system which can have processing facilities owned by a private company, a cooperative or a parastatal. The cooperative option would appear to be most in line with the stated political objectives of Tanzania, but resource considerations may necessitate the first approach. A combination of the two is a possible compromise that gives the outgrowers a stake in their factory.

Tanzanian estate agriculture has been neglected for a long time and there has been little attempt to consider the various options available for future development. Rehabilitation of estates under the ERP provides an opportunity for those planning and managing the estates to develop different approaches to the organization of production that are more appropriate to the current circumstances, policies and resource availability of Tanzania.

NOTES

1 Semi-logarithmic trends were applied to calculate annual growth rates. Details are given in Potts (1989).
2 These were derived from Tables 2, 3 and 4 in Potts (1989).
3 'During the colonial period, coffee and missionaries brought income and education to Kilimanjaro, while recruitment agencies maintained Kigoma as a backward labour reserve for the plantation sector' Raikes 1986: 107.
4 The reluctance of estate employers to use wage increases as a means of attracting labour has a long history. See Bolton (1985), pp. 119–26.
5 PPMB (1986) p. 98.
6 The world price trends were derived from data in Table 8 in Potts (1989).
7 MDB (1986a) refer to their study of import requirements for major crops which indicates 67 per cent, 21 per cent and 29 per cent of export earnings for sisal, tea and coffee respectively. The figure for sisal is a reflection of the very low level of production and poor state of repair of the industry at the time the estimate was made and is much higher than would be required under normal operation.
8 A review of studies undertaken by PPMB and some other agencies in the period 1982–6 gives the following results for estate rehabilitation projects:

| Industry | Date | IRR at market prices | | IRR at shadow prices (%) |
		With the project (%)	Incremental (%)	
Sisal (public)	1984/5	5–12	9–15	26–34
	1982/3		<10	16–28
Sisal (private)	1983		25	44
Tea (public)	1981/2		6	17
	1982/3	12	18	31
	1982/3		19	39
	1984/5	7	15	38
Coffee	1985/6	4–53	7–18	14–32

REFERENCES

Bolton, D. (1985) *Nationalization: A Road to Socialism?*, London: Zed Press.

Government of Tanzania, Marketing Development Bureau (1981) *Price Policy Recommendations for the 1982–3 Agricultural Price Review*.

—— Marketing Development Bureau (1986a) *Annual Review of Agriculture*.

—— Marketing Development Bureau (1986b) *Annual Review of Sugar Cane*.

—— Marketing Development Bureau (1986c) *Annual Review of Coffee*.

—— Marketing Development Bureau (1986d) *Annual Review of Tea*.

—— Marketing Development Bureau (1986e) *Annual Review of Tobacco*.

—— Ministry of Agriculture and Livestock Development (1983) *The Agricultural Policy of Tanzania*.

—— Ministry of Finance, Planning and Economic Affairs (1988) *Hali ya Uchumi wa Taifa Katika Mwaka 1987*.

—— Ministry of Economic Affairs and Planning (1982) *Structural A ustment Programme*.

—— Project Preparation and Monitoring Bureau (1984a) *Export Crop Packages – A Framework for Action*.

—— Project Preparation and Monitoring Bureau (1984b) *National Sisal Programme*.

—— Project Preparation and Monitoring Bureau (1984c) *National Tea Programme*.

—— Project Preparation and Monitoring Bureau (1988) *Coffee Expansion Programme*.

Potts, D. (1989) *Rehabilitation of Export-oriented Agriculture in Tanzania – Same Again or Something Different?*, mimeo, Development and Project Planning Centre, University of Bradford.

Raikes, P. (1986) 'Eating the carrot and wielding the stick: the agricultural sector in Tanzania', in J. Boesen and K.J. Havnevik, *Tanzania – Crisis and Struggle for Survival*, Uppsala, Scandinavian Institute of African Studies.

Part III

PLANNING AND APPRAISAL OF REHABILITATION PROJECTS

5

UNIDO STUDIES ON INDUSTRIAL REHABILITATION IN AFRICA

George Assaf

INTRODUCTION

As part of the Industrial Development Decade for Africa, UNIDO is paying increasing attention to the problem of industrial rehabilitation. Through its integrated, multidisciplinary rehabilitation programme, UNIDO offers support:

1 at the macro-industrial policy level, in order to remove major obstacles to the viable development of industry;
2 at the sub-sectoral level that encompasses a number of enterprises engaged in similar and interrelated lines of production; and
3 at the level of a specific enterprise and in productive plants, in order to cope with critical bottlenecks identified by requesting governments.

As part of this programme, the Regional and Country Studies Branch is conducting diagnostic studies to determine the major problems of African manufacturing and the potential for regenerating the sector. The diagnostic studies aim to outline policies and measures that may lead to overall improvements and to identify individual plants for rehabilitation assistance.

To date, three in-depth rehabilitation studies on Angola, Liberia and Zambia have been completed. Two additional reports on Tanzania and Morocco are being finalized. The reports are the result of an intensive, month-long field mission to each of the countries by an experienced team of experts which includes economists, industrial engineers and management specialists.

Each study analyses the performance of manufacturing industry in the overall economic and institutional framework and

103

within the context of changing external economic conditions. They assess major constraints and resulting inefficiency of production faced by industry in terms of availability of financial resources including foreign exchange, technology, material inputs and human skills, markets, and industrial structure and relevant infrastructure. In addition to estimating resource requirements for selected industrial plant rehabilitation, expected results from such rehabilitation are assessed. Finally, the studies provide recommendations for both the short term and long term. These recommendations seek to rectify shortcomings – whether technical, financial, organizational, or market-oriented – in the overall performance of the plants and the environment in which they operate.

Prior to the missions, an overview was prepared of the manufacturing industry in all African countries (UNIDO 1988a). These country profiles provide brief background information on key economic characteristics, trends and problems, rehabilitation needs, and prospects for manufacturing within the framework of overall economic policy. This provides a basis for identifying those countries with the greatest need and potential for rehabilitation.

This chapter outlines the approach and scope of the diagnostic surveys and highlights the substantive issues relating to industrial rehabilitation in sub-Saharan Africa. It also presents a brief summary of our findings and recommendations with regard to Angola, Liberia and Zambia (UNIDO 1988b).

THE AFRICAN ECONOMIC SITUATION

It is obvious that compared to other continents or developing countries Africa is in dire straits. Of the major developing country regions, sub-Saharan Africa has the lowest provision of basic needs, the highest population growth, and the lowest efficiency of investment. Per capita GNP growth rates continue to stagnate or to decline in most countries. Most per capita incomes are desperately low – less than US$300 in Zaire, Mali, Ethiopia, Mozambique, and Malawi – and in many cases are lower than they were twenty years ago. The per capita income of the region as a whole today is lower than in 1970. Of the thirty-three countries listed in UNIDO's *Industry and Development – Global Report 1988/89* with a per capita income of less than US$400, more than two-thirds are African (UNIDO 1988c).

Agriculture, the major source of livelihood in the great majority of African countries, has not been able to provide the region's fast-growing populations with essential food supplies. For most countries, agricultural products are also the principal source of foreign exchange, yet agricultural export earnings have dropped dramatically. Revenue from other raw materials has also dropped appreciably. Prices for ferrous and non-ferrous metals, for example, decreased by 20 per cent during the 1980–6 period, and the price of crude oil dropped by 50 per cent. African exports to other world regions declined from US$60.5 billion in 1985 to US$50 billion in 1986, a drop of 14 per cent. The European Community, traditionally the region's main trading partner, reduced its imports from the region by 24 per cent in 1986.

With respect to the manufacturing sector, manufacturing growth rates in African countries generally resembled those of other developing countries until the early 1980s. Africa's share in world manufacturing value added (MVA) rose from 0.7 per cent in 1970 to 1 per cent in 1982. Since then, however, industrial performance in Africa as a whole has deteriorated relative to other developing regions.

Africa also has the lowest average rates of capacity utilization. Utilization rates well below 50 per cent are not uncommon. In the mid-1980s, for example, the rate was 33 per cent in Sudan (private sector), 36 per cent in Liberia, under 35 per cent in Sierra Leone, 25 per cent in Tanzania, and between 30 and 50 per cent in Zambia (selected major industries). In Mali, a 20 per cent utilization rate is common in most factories. Much of the installed industrial capacity is idle or underutilized as a result of poor investment choices, falling incomes, bad management, and the lack of foreign exchange needed to purchase raw materials and spare parts.

Africa owes much of its plight to circumstances beyond its control. The world economic crisis of the mid-1970s, characterized by the steep rise in oil prices and the severe fall in the prices of primary export products, exposed the weak and vulnerable structure of African manufacturing industries. Although most African countries are heavily dependent on raw material exports, export earnings show few signs of increasing as prices remain depressed. Meanwhile, prices of imports have continued to rise, causing Africa's terms of trade to fall disastrously during the 1980s: whereas the terms of trade index stood at 109 in 1981 (1980 = 100), it had fallen to 60 in 1987.

The unfavourable external economic environment – particularly the slump of commodity prices in world markets – coupled with a large external debt have had disastrous effects on the balance of payments problems of sub-Saharan Africa. In addition to the fall in commodity prices, the introduction of substitute and synthetic materials has depressed the demand for Africa's staple products, traditionally its main source for foreign exchange. At the same time, debt has accumulated – much of it incurred to meet the fall in export receipts. Total external debt of sub-Saharan African countries grew from US$45.5 billion in 1982 to approximately US$120 billion in 1987. The sub-Saharan debt service ratio increased from 8.4 per cent to 10.8 per cent over the same period; in individual countries the ratio is often more than 30 per cent of annual export earnings. Moreover, capital flows have been drying up. The resulting shortage of foreign exchange has prevented the import of other raw materials and essential equipment and spare parts for industry. The lack of such imports has already led to widespread breakdowns in machinery and low capacity utilization rates. The picture is bleak indeed.

THE NEED FOR REHABILITATION

The underlying causes of the present situation in Africa are both macroeconomic and microeconomic in nature. Being highly dependent on imports (both raw materials, components and equipment), industry in Africa has been seriously affected by the need to reduce imports as a result of balance-of-payments crises in individual countries. Furthermore, during the early stages of industrialization, projects were often based on unrealistic assumptions of domestic market demand growth, availability of local raw material, export prospects and the development of a supportive national infrastructure. Therefore, many infant industries have tended to remain weak and financially vulnerable. Macroeconomic policies and specific pricing, trade and industrial policies have in many cases distorted product markets and production conditions. At the microeconomic level, in many instances investments have also been made on the basis of project concepts that were technologically too complex to be sustained over the long term without significant foreign assistance. In many projects, insufficient support in the form of training and other essential auxiliary inputs tended to drastically affect productivity. In other cases, especially in the food processing industry, expected raw material supplies to manufacturing proved to be insufficient, irregular or even non-existent.

The principal objective of UNIDO's industrial rehabilitation programme, therefore, is to contribute to improving industrial capacity utilization and productivity in African countries. But how do we go about this most effectively? How can we be assured that we have covered all the bases?

The 'top-down' approach

Manufacturing industries which overcome or master specific internal problems may not escape the obstacles imposed by the government's fiscal and monetary policies and economic policies in general. It is therefore very important to include such problems as price policy, import and export tariffs, foreign exchange and tax policies as rehabilitation issues.

It is for this reason that we have adopted a 'top-down' approach in the rehabilitation surveys. This approach starts with an examination of the macroeconomic level, descends through the sector, sub-sector and branch levels, and finally arrives at the plant level.

There is an inherent danger in assessing the need for rehabilitation by taking a 'bottom-up' approach. There is always the possibility of misinterpretation at any one individual level, but more importantly, the lower the level looked at the easier it is to be misled. The problem is that it is always possible to leave out an important variable. It could be that a plant is performing poorly because of external government policies – this has nothing to do with technological or managerial reasons. Lack of access to foreign exchange and imported raw materials has effectively closed many plants in Africa. The 'top-down' approach, therefore, is more relevant for signalling the need for rehabilitation in Africa. It is also more appropriate for determining the real reasons for low capacity utilization.

The resulting significant and increasing underutilization of industrial production capacities is the greatest single problem facing African manufacturing today, and one of the major factors hindering Africa's economic recovery. Some plants have been forced to shut down entirely, or operate on a partial basis. If this trend could be reversed, greater utilization of installed capacities and improved productivity would be a powerful – and the most economical – means of restoring economic growth.

Until now, most rehabilitation work in Africa has not been systematic or comprehensive. Rather, it has been viewed as either the treatment of a plant's technical problems – without an analysis of the real causes or their ramifications – or as a macroeconomic issue only. In the first case, technical assistance activities have often been carried out in isolation, separate from issues such as financial requirements, market possibilities, or the availability of raw materials and intermediate inputs. This approach has frequently resulted in rehabilitation projects and government requests that were too narrowly focused. Often, corresponding international cooperation has been on the basis of such narrowly-defined project concepts. Thus, there is the serious risk of only 'patching a leak', with the possibility of another leak developing elsewhere.

The UNIDO surveys attempt to move away from this approach – which at times amounts to little more than 'plant-level tinkering' – toward an approach aimed at providing a broader diagnosis and recommending a wider range of action. Manufacturing industries do not exist in isolation. They are surrounded by an ever-changing environment. The plant needs to be viewed in this total environment. In addition to technology and engineering, aspects such as organization and management, finance, product range, sources of raw material and spare parts, local and foreign market conditions, and fiscal and monetary policies should also be taken into account.

The surveys thus seek to assist African governments in linking the macro, branch level and project issues in making decisions for rehabilitation and upgrading production. Our approach is also expected to increase the rate of survival of the particular plants or sub-sectors in which rehabilitation projects are undertaken.

Industrial rehabilitation considerations

Industrial rehabilitation must be a dynamic, forward-looking concept. To restore industry back to what it was may not be sufficient. The world and economic conditions change rapidly. To ignore these conditions might lead the industry back to pre-rehabilitation conditions – which were at times very depressed. After all, inability to cope with changes in external conditions may have been the cause of the industry's poor performance in the first place.

The concept of industrial rehabilitation should be broadened beyond merely thinking in terms of benefits to individual plants – rather, it should be interpreted as securing optimal use of existing capacities and resources, through upgrading and transformation, for future general industrial growth. The true challenge, then, is to identify which enterprises are best suited for rehabilitation – that is, where scarce foreign exchange and other resources would be most efficiently used to upgrade production and company performance with the largest possible effect on overall growth. The second task is to combine the plant rehabilitation process with a restructuring programme of the industrial sector as a whole to ensure growth dynamism, domestic integration and the provision of support industries and services. Such a programme will entail investment in new capacities in industry, infrastructure, services and commodity production. The third parallel task involves suggesting modifications to the policy and administrative framework to facilitate and stimulate domestic and international efforts towards the industrial regeneration objective.

Towards this end, in some particular and extreme cases, 'industrial rehabilitation' may boil down to recommendations for plant closures. In such cases it is recognized that there are important social and political implications to be considered. The established meaning of the concept of rehabilitation may block such actions because it restricts the view of decision-makers to the industrial structure as it exists. A wider and more forward-looking regeneration concept will help all parties concerned to understand that closure may be a necessary part of an attempt to establish an industrial structure with better prospects for sustained work.

On the microeconomic level, it is important to direct rehabilitation to production and management in existing industrial enterprises where problems usually occur in the following areas: marketing, finance, product diversification, poor management, inadequate supply of key industrial raw materials, or inappropriate technology. There is therefore a need for introducing effective and dynamic marketing; concentrating human, physical and financial resources on a few manageable projects or markets; analysing market trends more closely; and paying greater attention to technological development. It is toward this end that a systematic programme of industrial rehabilitation should be launched.

It is equally important to assist developing countries in determining which sectors demonstrate the greatest need for such measures. In doing so, the emphasis should always be on the more efficient utilization of existing industrial capacity rather than on new investment; the latter should not be considered until every aspect of the former has been thoroughly examined. The establishment of regional networks between enterprises for mutual self-help would be another important aspect of rehabilitation.

However, before a serious effort can be made to carry out detailed rehabilitation of industry, it is necessary to diagnose in depth the precise reasons and scope for the problems, the constraints now faced by industry, and the increasing challenges in a particular sub-sector and a particular country. For this reason it is important to avoid treating industrial rehabilitation as a mere micro/technical issue.

It is essential to fully assess the nature and magnitude of underlying constraints for two reasons: first, to be able to assess the general viability of many rehabilitation efforts; and second, to identify the precise type of measures, investment or market studies, policy and institutional issues, and technical matters which need to be examined in greater detail as part of the subsequent effort of detailed rehabilitation work at the sub-sector and plant levels. In other words, only with the broad classification of current problems and their causes and with an initial estimation of the appropriateness (in economic terms) of rehabilitation can targeted technical assistance projects be designed and launched to selected activities of the industrial sector in various African countries. Rehabilitation would thus avoid re-establishing previous conditions for production, but would establish a new basis for viable production and growth. It is in this connection that the issue of regional and sub-regional cooperation appears vital. In many instances rehabilitation of industries presupposes enlargement of the narrow domestic market, joint raw material supplies by several neighbouring countries, or other types of common activities. Appropriately-designed rehabilitation programmes therefore need to be based on an assessment of possible cooperative modalities among some African countries in selected sub-sectors.

Applying the top-down approach

Each country is first reviewed in its international context. Macroeconomic or country-level analysis includes key characteristics of the country's administration and economy, including general fiscal and monetary policies. At the sectoral level, manufacturing is reviewed in terms of overall character-istics, major problems and constraints, trade, and assessment of policies and institutions relating to the sector. The relationship of manufacturing to agriculture is given special consideration, since for most countries agro-related industries are the most important. In addition, agro-related industries can be the basis for establishing an industrial tradition based on locally available raw materials.

At the sub-sector level, overall characteristics, major problems and constraints, linkages, and policies as they relate to the sub-sector are analysed. The sub-sector is also examined at the branch level. Finally, at the plant level, a detailed analysis is made of the rehabilitation needs of particular firms, with specific recommendations for rehabilitation efforts. This 'top-down' approach is diagrammed in Figure 5.1.

A feature of the 'top-down' approach is to carry out rehabilitation analysis as a team effort – integrating the policy, economic, technological, managerial, financial and marketing dimensions. In order to gain first-hand knowledge of the plants' rehabilitation needs and the economic environment in which they operate, a UNIDO field mission includes industrial and macro-economists, industrial engineers, policy impact specialists, and experts in finance, marketing, and management. In addition, the team is supported by national experts in each of the same areas of specialization. The importance of the team approach cannot

111

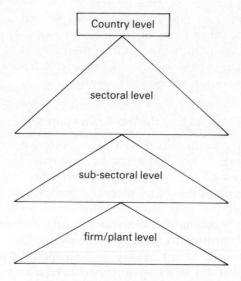

Figure 5.1 The 'top-down' approach

be overemphasized. It is crucial that it be made up of highly-motivated and competent professionals with solid and relevant development experience. It is the team that performs the diagnostic surveys and interviews government officials, industry representatives, and representatives from various donor agencies based in the country; it also formulates recommendations not only for specific rehabilitation projects but for improvements in the overall economic policy environment. The members must be able to work effectively with entrepreneurs, plant managers, and government officials responsible for the development of the industrial sector. The composition of the team facilitates the production of final reports covering all the issues – from macroeconomic to plant specific – including recommendations and follow-up measures.

FINDINGS OF THE REHABILITATION STUDIES

The type of industry to be rehabilitated depends on a government's development priorities and assessments for long-term viability. The governments of Angola, Liberia and Zambia have all attached top priority to the provision of basic needs. The agro-based industry was therefore the most logical sub-sector to study for rehabilitation. Additionally, the backward and forward linkages in the food processing sector are quite extensive. The projects would therefore contribute both to the integrated and balanced development of the industrial sector and to the socio-economic development of the country as a whole. The choice of agro-based industries is also harmonious with regional projects currently being developed for several industrial sectors in sub-Saharan Africa. The final selection of plants to be studied is based for the most part on the following general criteria:

1 The plants should be centrally located due to time and transport constraints.
2 Both the public and private sectors should be represented to reflect the current role of public enterprise and the growing role of private enterprises.
3 The plants should have good future economic potential and thus be viable rehabilitation projects.
4 In view of the shortage of domestic credit, the need to finance rehabilitation externally must be taken into account – candidate plants must therefore display sufficient promise to be potentially attractive to foreign sources of funds.
5 In order to enhance the impact of eventual rehabilitation efforts, the selected plants should exhibit a maximum number of interlinkages.

For the three countries studied, a detailed analysis was made of the rehabilitation needs of four firms. This analysis of plants included one firm from the following three branches: meat processing, animal feed production and vegetable oil processing (palm oil in Liberia). Given its importance to the food products branch, the packaging materials industry was studied in Angola and Zambia. The remaining branches analysed were wood processing in Liberia and flour milling in Angola. In addition, the conversion of a former Angolan sugar estate into an agro-industrial complex was studied at the special request of the

113

government. The plant-level surveys cover the following subjects: plant history; management and organization; financial structure; buildings, installations and production processes; inputs; product range; plant performance, cost and price structure; markets and competition; and constraints. The ownership of the plants studied is as follows: Angola – 3 private and 1 public; Liberia – 1 private, 1 public, and 1 mixed with a 67 per cent government interest; Zambia – 3 public and 1 private.

Angola

By the mid-1980s, Angola's industrial output had dropped to less than one-half of the output of the early 1970s. This was caused by long years of civil war and South African intervention, as well as by a serious shortage of skilled and professional workers at all levels of the economy and the administration. These continue to be the major obstacles to industrial development in the country.

While Angola's manufacturing enterprises were generally established to process domestic resources, they have remained dependent on imported intermediate goods, machinery and spare parts. The war's disruption cut off most industries from their raw material base, and the serious drain of financial resources limited the importation of machinery and spare parts. Additionally, the food processing branch suffered particularly from a shortage of lower and intermediate-level technicians and management, as well as from earlier agricultural pricing policies which also contributed to the shortage of inputs.

In an effort to revive its faltering economy, the Angolan government introduced a package of economic reform measures, Saneamento Economico e Financeiro (SEF), in January 1988. These economic reform measures include the privatization of much of the retail and wholesale sector; increased financial autonomy and responsibility for state enterprises; regional decentralization; the introduction of a foreign exchange retention scheme as an incentive for non-oil export industries; liberalization of the traditional rigid price-control system; improvements in monetary policy; and reform of the investment law. Whereas the Angolan Government had been committed to a centrally-planned economy in the past, the authorities now look to the new decentralization initiatives to help revive the manufacturing sector.

With regard to the domestic environment in which manufacturing operates, the mission concluded that:

1 Short-term economic stabilization measures as suggested by the SEF should be harmonized with overall development objectives in order to create the right long-term environment for industrial regeneration.
2 Recovery and development of the agricultural sector is a prerequisite for industrial development.
3 A large-scale programme of public works is needed to improve the physical infrastructure.
4 General education and technical training deserve high priority in order to increase the availability of qualified personnel.

Liberia

Throughout the 1980s, the Liberian economy has suffered severely from mismanagement and a decline in raw material earnings. The growing differential between the official and parallel market rates for the two legal currencies – the US dollar and Liberian dollar – has exacerbated problems.

The government responded to the economic crisis by launching the Economic Recovery Programme in 1986 and by agreeing to allow a team of US experts (the OPEX team) to participate in the management of the public sector in 1987 and 1988. While the OPEX team succeeded in improving government revenue collection and the functioning of certain aspects of the industrial infrastructure, it did not solve the government's financial problems.

The main objectives of the Economic Recovery Programme are to improve management in the public sector and to implement measures leading to renewed growth. This can be achieved *inter alia*, by improving the productivity of Liberian farmers and by strengthening industrial production based on the country's wide range of natural resources.

Liberia's manufacturing sector is small. Its share in GDP decreased from 10 per cent in 1979 to approximately 7 per cent in 1986. The most important branches are food products and beverages, accounting for over 50 per cent of gross output in 1985. There is considerable potential for wood processing, and recent government measures are designed to stimulate this activity. It was evident to the mission that the government is

115

displaying increasing determination in its efforts to tackle its economic problems.

Some of the general observations and recommendations are similar to those formulated for Angola and Zambia. These include the need for improvements in physical infrastructure and training, less administrative interference in public enterprises, greater reliance on domestic raw materials, and the introduction of allocation systems for foreign exchange to purchase essential parts and inputs. Specific recommendations include the formulation of a coherent policy framework, not only for the manufacturing sector but also for the economy in general, and strict adherence to the new Investment Code so as to increase the confidence of potential investors in the Liberian economy.

Zambia

Zambia's dependence on copper mining is the key characteristic of the economy, and a major cause of the country's present economic difficulties. Low copper prices have forced the country to borrow heavily, and the combination of the continuing low prices and an increasing debt service burden has led to a serious foreign exchange shortage. This, in turn, has resulted in stagnation in the highly import-dependent manufacturing sector. The 1987 Interim National Development Plan represents an attempt to diversify away from copper and to find new ways of saving and generating foreign exchange, by emphasizing domestic resource-based industries that produce both basic consumer goods and non-traditional exports.

Most of Zambia's larger industries are government owned, and political interference has been common. The present reform measures are viewed as serious attempts to liberalize and stabilize the economy, and to provide a sound basis for rehabilitation programmes.

To a certain extent, the general problems of Zambia are similar to those of Angola. The suggestions for improvement in the industrial environment, such as reducing government interference in economic affairs, have certain parallels to those formulated for Angola. In the case of Zambia, it was specially recommended to:

116

1   strengthen the government's capacity to formulate and implement appropriate measures and to monitor industrial development projects; and to
2   strengthen the advisory capacity with regard to rehabilitation and new investments of the Industrial Development Corporation (INDECO), an institution controlling the larger part of the country's industrial enterprises.

Plant-level findings

Several findings at the plant level were similar in all three countries. Problems include weak financial management, absence of proper quality control, and lack of proper maintenance procedures. Problems specific to Liberia are the pricing system, wastage, and top-heavy management in enterprises in which the government is involved.

In Angola, the major problems identified were absence of sales organizations, deficient middle-level management and management information systems, absence of systematic maintenance procedures and lack of spare parts, and raw materials shortages. These problems are largely an indication of the country's overall problems. The absence of sales organizations, for example, is partly the result of the fact that, at present, firms operate in a sellers' market. The absence of systematic maintenance is in part a result of the serious shortage of qualified technicians due to the war and the fact that the armed forces have priority in recruiting personnel.

Zambia's plants also suffer from weak middle management and a weak sales organization. The crucial issue of spare parts production could possibly be tackled by establishing a Southern Africa Development Coordination Conference (SADCC) Spare Parts Agency, which would both procure and distribute spare parts to manufacturers in member countries using computerized inventory management techniques.

FUTURE EFFORTS

The UNIDO rehabilitation missions to date, together with the industrial rehabilitation surveys, have provided clear evidence that our approach is a successful means of identifying key issues that affect the operation of plants and of formulating broad-based industrial rehabilitation policies. Our approach ensures that enterprise-level rehabilitation programmes are compatible and integrated into macrolevel industrial policy. The surveys provide clear recommendations for short- and long-term rehabilitation measures, including modifications to improve the institutional and economic environment at various levels, as well as clearly defined projects at the plant level.

UNIDO's rehabilitation studies will serve as the basis for a series of round table meetings on rehabilitation issues and projects. The first such meeting, held in Lusaka, Zambia from 8–10 March 1989, provided the opportunity for representatives of the Zambian Government, the four firms, UNIDO and other interested parties to review the findings and recommendations of the report in order to determine follow-up action in the form of technical cooperation and assistance (UNIDO 1989). Among the topics addressed were proposals regarding macroeconomic policies, financial and technical aspects of rehabilitation programmes, and necessary action in relation to industry-wide and international economic developments and issues. Participants included representatives from the World Bank, banking institutions, various embassies, and multilateral and bilateral organizations. Similar meetings covering the reports on Angola, Liberia, Tanzania and Morocco will be held at a later date.

The positive response to these studies and their follow-up on the part of African Governments, the international aid community and private business alike, points to the need to continue and expand the programme. Such expansion could take place in several ways. The most obvious way is to increase the number of countries studied. Another way would be to widen the scope to include industries other than those related to agriculture. Although agro-related industries will no doubt continue to play a key role in virtually all cases, industries such as non-metallic minerals, wood products, textiles, paper and printing, and metal products also have a potentially important role in many countries. With regard to agro-related industries, the analysis could be deepened to include a closer examination of the linkage between agriculture and industry and of the way in which developments in one sector influence those in the other. All of these approaches should help to strengthen rehabilitation and regeneration efforts.

In order for our programme to succeed, cooperation and

assistance on the part of the international community is essential. Most industrial rehabilitation projects require foreign technical and financial support, particularly in the acquisition of equipment and spare parts. Besides international financial assistance, African countries will require technical and managerial expertise to assist in selecting and procuring equipment and monitoring the plant rehabilitation. Following its initial surveys, an important element of UNIDO's rehabilitation programme is to mobilize and concentrate national and international resources and efforts to rehabilitate the plants. Intensified and focused international cooperation could generate a multiplier effect in industry and agriculture, thereby endorsing efforts to be undertaken by national entities.

Regional cooperation will also have an important role to play in regenerating African manufacturing. Given the small domestic markets and the difficulties in penetrating overseas markets, regional markets will be needed for growing industries. This implies measures such as harmonization of trade regulations, cooperation in improving the transport infrastructure, and organization of regional trade fairs. Regional coordination of rehabilitation and investment would also save resources in scarce supply. The shortage of qualified manpower, both at the enterprise level and in industrial development organizations, could in part be solved by pooling available planning resources and creating regional training institutes for higher-level manpower. Finally, cooperation among African countries would also strengthen their position *vis-à-vis* overseas suppliers and in overseas markets.

We believe the benefits of our 'top-down' approach to project rehabilitation will be experienced from the 'bottom–up' – from the plant, through the various levels, to the country level at the top:

1 First, the immediate beneficiaries of technical cooperation will be the specific enterprises selected. Through them, however, most small and medium-scale enterprises in the industry will gain through direct technical cooperation measures.
2 The agro-industrial sector will benefit from the analysis of branch problems and the methods suggested for tackling these problems. The diagnoses will serve as guidelines for other plants in the sector.

119

3 The entire industrial sector will benefit from the recommendations relating to the specific training and assistance required
   for the development of domestic rehabilitation capacities.
4 Finally, the government will benefit not only from the direct
   technical assistance to the enterprise, but also from the project
   recommendations for macro- and industrial-sector level policy
   changes designed to strengthen national industrial rehabilitation capacities.

The rehabilitation studies serve as a first step in the long
process toward regeneration of African manufacturing. Full
feasibility studies must be conducted as a follow-up to provide
effective guidelines for subsequent implementation. In the long
term, the ultimate and perhaps most important goal of UNIDO's
rehabilitation programme is to provide for a lasting capacity in
the country's overall economic framework to achieve its goals for
industry and economic recovery.

REFERENCES

UNIDO (1988a) 'Regenerating African manufacturing industry: country
briefs' (PPD.97), *Studies on the Rehabilitation of African Industry*, no. 2,
Vienna, November.
—— (1988b) 'The agro-based industries in Zambia and Angola: key
characteristics and rehabilitation issues' (PPD.102 and PPD.103),
Studies on the Rehabilitation of African Industry, no. 4 and no. 5, Vienna,
December.
—— (1988c) *Industry and Development: Global Report 1988–89* (ID/360),
Vienna.
—— (1989) Draft report on Round Table Meeting on Industrial
Rehabilitation, Lusaka, Zambia, 8–10 March 1989 (PPD.120) *Studies
on the Rehabilitation of African Industry*, no. 6, Vienna, June.

6

FINANCIAL ANALYSIS
Project or portfolio
Michael Yaffey

INTRODUCTION

The recent focus on rehabilitation as a mode of aided development has drawn attention to the need to define the benefit of project aid as (a) the effect of going ahead with an aided project minus (b) the effects of doing without it.

This double-barrelled analysis was never entirely absent from appraisal methodology; it is commonplace whenever extensions to an existing activity or enlargements of scale are under consideration, and it is quite normal when a prolongation of the life of a long-lived asset such as a tree crop is contemplated. Lease/purchase decisions are another example. These are all situations where the assessment of two plausible alternatives is imperative. Regrettably, however, the literature on the economic analysis of projects dwells on new starts, where the alternative to going ahead is to do nothing, and that is an option which is assumed to require no investigation.[1] Implicitly, the 'without the project' option has resource flows of zero, net present value (NPV) of zero, and no internal rate of return (IRR) (however these may be measured). Consequently the incremental benefit, derived by subtracting the 'without' case from the 'with', is identical to the 'with' case and can be ignored. It is useful, therefore, to have been reminded that the general case is one which requires the double-barrelled study ('incremental analysis'), or even a multiple-case study, while the all-or-nothing situation is the special case.[2]

121

DEFINITION OF THE 'WITHOUT' CASE BASED ON PRIOR DECISIONS

In order to get a correct calculation of the incremental net benefit, it is necessary to prepare both 'with' and 'without' cases to be optimal. It would produce an incorrect overestimate of the incremental net benefit, were a fully-prepared 'with' project case optimized as to choice of technique, location, scale, channels of distribution and so forth, while the 'without' alternative were poorly explored, arbitrary, and in general not the true second-best option.

However, just as the rehabilitation project needs to be appraised in the light of its possibly complex effects on the rest of the economy, so the 'without' alternative needs to be defined with regard to its possibly complex effects. Consider the case of a request for rehabilitation of an insolvent railway. Whether one is looking at financial or economic criteria, the best alternative to a series of rehabilitation projects may well be to close down the railway. Logically, that scenario ought to be examined. It will be necessary to consider whether in that case the traffic will diminish or switch to roads; and this will depend on what planning decisions have already been made for the provision of additional road transport, if any. Of course, if the decision to provide additional road transport has been delayed pending the decision on the railway rehabilitation, the two decisions are really one decision, and the road/railway alternatives should be appraised jointly. But if the decision was already taken as a separate decision, it must become part of the scenario for both the 'with' and 'without' studies. Quantification of the 'without' case, giving due recognition to whatever decisions have already been taken, is clearly a mammoth task. This is especially so for the economic, social and environmental appraisals, which bring non-railway costs and benefits into account. Even the financial appraisal will be concerned with assessing the general prosperity in the areas served by the railway in order to evaluate the revenues and associated uncertainties, both with and without rehabilitation.

In such a situation it may well be possible to develop the 'with' case out of the original pre-failure feasibility study, modified perhaps by annual budgets taken from a recent operating phase, whereas the 'without' case may be so complex and obscure as to be quite impossible to quantify with confidence.

122

A study of 'without' cases, conducted by the author on the rehabilitation appraisals undertaken by a major donor in the period 1982–6, found that in the absence of rehabilitation production was expected to behave as follows:

Total renewal rather than rehabilitation	2 instances
Renewal but output falling	3 instances
Output falling, same equipment	1 instance
Output static	8 instances
No output at all, same equipment	4 instances
No output, dispersal of assets	0 instances
Alternative equipment, rising output	1 instance
No 'without' case examined	2 instances

This indicates how the selection of the 'without' scenario can greatly affect the incremental analysis and how important it is that projects should be appraised even-handedly in this respect.

PROJECT AND PROGRAMME IN FINANCIAL ANALYSIS

If academic treatments of project appraisal tend to give a picture of economic analysis of projects taken in isolation, financial analysis certainly seems to look at one project at a time, or at best, one enterprise at a time.

It is sometimes assumed that the potential financier of a proposed rehabilitation is an investor with no important interests in the country concerned except the project in question. He may, however, have a stake in the failed activity which requires rehabilitation. In other words, there may be an existing debt. Because of history of failure, debt service is likely to be in arrears. Faced with two options – putting more money in, or refusing to do so – the financier compares his expected cash flows in the two scenarios and determines the net benefit of putting 'good money after bad'.

The determination is based on an arithmetical process which begins by subtracting the one set of financial statements from the other. The difference is the incremental income statement, incremental balance sheet forecast, and incremental cash flow. This last can be discounted to arrive at the NPV and the financial internal rate of return (FIRR) of accepting the proposal. The others can be used to assess the incremental return on incremental capital, using conventional ratio analysis techniques. Finally, gearing ratios, debt service cover ratios, and capital programme self-financing ratios can be calculated on the 'with figures' to check whether the total proposition is sound. These procedures may be called 'classic financial analysis'; as we shall see, however, there are problems in applying this approach to less-developed country (LDC) rehabilitation situations.

In both 'with' and 'without' scenarios it is necessary to appraise the borrower's ability to service the debt, and this involves looking at the commercial environment, so the financial analyst has to take some view of what assumptions to make as to the grand plan and the state of the economy. These assumptions may be optimistic or pessimistic; whichever, they should be the same for both scenarios, i.e. they should underpin the cash flow forecasts whether the financier does or does not accede to the request for new money in this specific project.

However hard it may be to choose the assumptions, the principles and purposes of the financier's analysis are clear providing he is only looking at one proposal at a time. If, however, his participation in one rehabilitation is going to influence the cash flow of another, and vice versa, additional data and additional computations are called for.

Faced with a single request for rehabilitation, on a take-it-or-leave-it basis, the financier may choose the better of the two options. Where two such projects are interrelated, the financier may accept either one, both, or neither; and the financial analyst has to consider four options, from which the most attractive can be chosen. With three projects there are eight options, and with four, sixteen. In general, for n projects, the number of options is two raised to the power of n. These numbers will rise further if there are unresolved alternative plans or specific contingency plans within any project.

In order to set out these options, the analyst has to collect expanded data on each project to show how it would behave in the various scenarios presented by yes/no decisions on the other projects. It will be obvious that in practice, four projects (sixteen options) will normally be beyond the bounds of practical possibility for this kind of analysis, and even three (eight options) may be too difficult.

The portfolio approach

This calls for a substitute methodology, a second-best technique of appraisal, in which the project interrelationships do not have to be quantified. In practice, such a technique is adopted frequently when it is assumed that every project is marginal in macroeconomic terms. In each project under consideration it may be assumed that product demand will grow and the economic climate will improve as a consequence of an extensive rehabilitation programme of sister projects – and perhaps also of policy reforms – but it is assumed that these results will obtain for each project currently under consideration regardless of whether any other specific proposal is accepted or not since they are all marginal.

This is more excusable than it might at first sight appear, since we are speaking here of financial, not economic, analysis. In economic analysis a decision not to go ahead with a major rehabilitation is likely to have non-marginal implications for other rehabilitation proposals which cannot be evaded. But in financial analysis, a decision not to invest in a rehabilitation proposal does not prevent the project from going ahead if another source of finance can be found. Many interrelationships are therefore *inherently not knowable* at the time of the individual financing decision.

In other words, if the same financier has an interest in a number of rehabilitations in the same country which can potentially reinforce each other, then the financial analyst who appraises a single project is in the same problematical position as the infantry officer who does not know the grand strategy and has to guess the ambient conditions. A local development bank may be in precisely this situation; this distinguishes the analysis appropriate to a local development finance institution (LDFI) from the analysis appropriate to a sporadic foreign investor.

In the extreme or limiting case (of course never found in reality) when one investor has a 100 per cent stake in all the projects of the country, the rehabilitation decision becomes a country-decision, and the reader will perceive that the financial analysis (when all the interrelationships are quantified and included in the calculations) becomes identical with the economic analysis (including the use of shadow prices). Unfortunately we cannot extrapolate to the situation where one investor has a lesser stake; it would be very convenient if we could compensate for the missing inter-project data by saying that if an LDFI has a 10 per cent stake in the country then its financial analysis should be that of individual projects subject to a 10 per cent adjustment in the direction of the economic analysis, but regrettably there is no evidence of any mathematical basis for such a procedure.

The LDFI with a large portfolio of projects many of which are requesting rehabilitation simultaneously, as is not uncommon, knows that the interrelationships must be strong, but it cannot quantify them. For each project, it is necessary to make a judgement as to how it will behave in an economic environment which itself is vaguely and judgementally defined.

The second-best technique, on which the LDFI is therefore forced to fall back in practice, seems to be simply the following:

1   Resolve those micro-problems which are due to failures of management or of inadequate capitalization; weed out those which cannot be solved, i.e. where the causes of the earlier failure at the micro level have not yet been fully diagnosed or cured.
2   Weed out or re-orientate those projects which are inherently inappropriate (perhaps originally 'politically motivated projects') – chiefly those with a built-in negative foreign-exchange flow.
3   Try to divide the clientele into market segments with separate risk factors and other operational indicators.
4   Seek to negotiate lines of credit for itself which are sufficiently soft to accommodate the rehabilitation problem. Specifically, grace periods should last not only through the implementation phase but well into profitable operation so as to pay off old debt before new debt bites.
5   Prioritize the demands of clients having regard to available lines of credit and the liquidity of the LDFI itself, and also the balance among sectors (or other categories of client) which the LDFI aims to have.

This portfolio approach involves many judgements of how each existing project will behave after rehabilitation in the economic climate which is to come. Such judgements may rely on data of past performance from an earlier 'golden age', but more commonly will rely on the similarity of the project to other

126

projects known to have been successful in other countries, plus confidence in the management, plus collateral security, plus a high FIRR (or quick pay-back). This is in some respects a return to traditional (1950s) banking; it places a high premium on the experience of the banker – including international experience – and places no great trust in forecasts of financial schedules. It harks back, also, to the quick decision-taking of post-war occupied Europe when ex-industrialists pressed the military authorities for permission to reopen their factories (or those of their defeated opponents). This approach may not be sophisticated but it has merit since it reposes confidence in available types of information in accordance with their qualities.

The LDFI's analytical framework at the portfolio level will be further clouded if it has been lending to finance activities with no proper corporate structure (village committees), or which have no proper Balance Sheet (government departments), or are not directly revenue-earning (social infrastructure). As Kitchen (1987) remarks, financial restructuring appears to be irrelevant in such cases, but the difference is merely one of degree, since some plan needs to be agreed upon to remove the financial shortfalls which cause failures in these areas too.

At the country level, the framework of analysis for decision support seems even more unsatisfactory than it is at the portfolio level. It would appear that we do not have any framework for the analysis of sovereign states as single investment opportunities. Consider the rhetorical question of the grounds on which such-and-such a country should be rehabilitated: that question can perhaps be answered on philosophical grounds, but not, it seems, on economic or financial grounds. Ask the question, and you may elicit the reply: we have no choice, we require rehabilitation. Ask further, and you may elicit unconvincing references to natural fertility, human potential, and the tempting attraction of participating in the expanding world economy. It may be that at this country level there are covert benefits, political benefits, which would sustain examination if disclosed, but certainly there is no financial or economic analysis at the country level to justify (nor to count against) a rehabilitation programme.

Quantifying the cash injection that is needed

An activity which is failing goes through a period of financial distress during which repeated applications for additional finance (equity or debt) may be made, and several potential banks or other backers may be approached in a piecemeal fashion for various sums. It is by no means regular practice to respond to each of these by calling for total reappraisal or even for the preparation of a revised comprehensive financial plan. It sometimes happens that several requests are granted before the alarm bells are sounded sufficiently loudly for the financiers to insist on seeing the whole picture. This is in accordance with the portfolio approach outlined above, but not in accordance with the project-level approach of the sporadic outside investor. In general, any supplemental request, where the same foreign backer is asked to put in more money to implement the same activity, will initiate a reappraisal. Anticipating this, borrowers will tend to delay such requests until the piecemeal opportunities have been exhausted. Therefore, the reappraisal tends to come after, rather than before, the period of financial distress.

At this stage, several problems have arisen calling for additional cash:

1 Cash and other current assets have been depleted, and need to be rebuilt to the working balances appropriate to a rehabilitated activity in full spate.
2 Current liabilities (creditors) may have risen above normal levels, and long-term debt service may be in arrears. These need to be paid off.
3 Normal replacement of fixed assets has probably been postponed, and a major programme of replacements may well be needed.
4 Normal maintenance may have been neglected or postponed, and an accelerated maintenance programme will be required to refurbish and repair existing assets.
5 An accelerated training programme may be needed to train or retrain staff.

Addition of these requirements indicates the cash injection needed. There will remain the questions, who should provide it?, and whether as equity or as debt?, bearing in mind that it should be a relatively attractive proposition.

Table 6.1 An example of financial analysis

	Equity (£'000)	Debt (£'000)	Total (£'000)
Balance sheet as last published	10	40	50
Subsequent estimated losses	–20	–	–20
	–10	40	30
Expected next year: operating losses	–10	–	–10
extraordinary losses (maintenance backlog and reorganization costs)	–15	–	–15
	–35	40	5
Additional capital needed: rebuild working capital		40	
premature replacements		28	
			68
Total finance required, split in desired ratio 40:60	29	44	73
Cash injections wanted	64	4	68

The thrust of the financial analysis is well shown in Table 6.1 by a numerical example (reproduced from Tribe and Yaffey 1988).

The thinking runs as follows. Funds totalling £45,000, needed to recognize losses up to now and during the period before self-sustainment becomes possible, must – by their nature – be a charge to the profit and loss account, that is, a charge against equity not against the LDFI. The value of equity stood at £10,000 in the last seen accounts and so will fall to –£35,000. Since the debt stands unforgiven at £40,000 the balance sheet total (net asset value) must be £5,000. A further £68,000 is needed to rebuild assets to required levels; the total will then be £73,000. Not wishing to extend the gearing (leverage) ratio beyond its normative prudent level, the LDFI is willing to finance not more than 60 per cent of this, which is £44,000. But this is only a slight increase on its existing stake; it calls upon the client to put in the other £64,000, if he can.

Unfortunately this is not likely to be attractive to the equity holder. The £64,000 may be unavailable; certainly it cannot come out of previous profits. Regarded as an incremental investment necessary to safeguard the existing investment (£10,000) it is hardly likely to be attractive. The sponsor may well look at his last set of accounts, which told him (albeit out-of-date) that he could walk away from the situation with £10,000 in cash and reflect that that would be preferable.

This analysis sets the scene for negotiation between the parties, at the level of the single project.

From the financier's point of view, the cash flows which are hypothesized in any particular proposition have to be compared with the cash flows (if any) expected to come out of the project if he declines to participate in rehabilitation. As we have noted, the latter scenario does not necessarily imply that the project will not receive rehabilitation, and if there are uncertainties here, the analyst might well use expected values (in the probabilistic sense) rather than central estimates. This will, of course, make the 'without' option less attractive; if he holds himself aloof from further participation the expected value of the future debt service is likely to approach zero (unless the debt is official and is officially rescheduled under Paris Club arrangements). These features of the 'without further investment' case must, of course, tend to enhance the apparent incremental benefit of providing fresh cash.

It may be noted in passing that the cash flows referred to here are all financial transactions between the entity conducting the project and the financier. They consist of lending, debt service, share subscriptions, and dividends. They differ from the resource flows used in economic analysis in a number of ways:

1 Resource flows use the penalty principle rather than the transactions principle. For instance, an enterprise which if rehabilitated will retain an existing asset rather than release it to the rest of the economy is penalized (debited with the opportunity cost of that asset as revalued) although no transaction occurs.

2 Resource flows compare the scenarios of rehabilitation versus

130

non-rehabilitation, whereas financial cash flows study the participation of a financier in rehabilitation versus non-participation.

3 Resource flows may be expressed in shadow prices rather than contractual prices.

4 Financial cash flows tend to be the subject of contractual agreement in current prices and so are rarely expressed in constant prices, except sometimes in the case of future dividends, which are not contractual.

The debt–equity ('gearing') problem

Operating problems during the previous period have probably eroded the equity base (losses are debited to equity); when the accounts are brought up to date the remaining equity may be negative, or may be too low to meet the gearing requirements of the lenders. This indicates how much of the additional cash should be provided by (existing or new) equity-holders, but frequently these cannot provide it, and therein lies the problem which is the crux of the negotiations on which the financial analysis bears.

This is an area in which economic models, which have become prevalent in the USA, are particularly unhelpful in the LDC context. I refer to the capital asset pricing model (CAPM) and the arbitrage pricing theory (APT). These have been summarized in Brealey and Myers (1984), Franks, Broyles and Carleton (1985), Kitchen (1986), and elsewhere. They appear to depend on the following features:

1 Both equity and debt are assumed to be expressed in negotiable instruments traded in a near-perfect market.

2 Operators in the market have by trading reached a consensus as to the expected return on each kind of financial asset, which expresses the market's view of its riskiness.

3 Projects in which one can invest can be regarded as similar to financial assets in having a distinct risk, assessed by market consensus.

4 The riskiness of a single asset can be expressed as a percentage of the riskiness of equity and/or debt as a whole.

5 The rational investor will hold a portfolio made up of a spread of assets representative of the total available in the market, plus a further amount of risk-free investments in accordance with

the investor's own aversion to risk (and borrowing pattern) where applicable.

6 This theory does not assist the investor in assessing the riskiness of an individual asset, but it is assumed that all other investors will have done so, and therefore the risk is already well reflected in the market price at which the investor can acquire it.

Quite apart from any criticisms one might make of the application of this group of models in the USA, where they are less than fully proven, the LDC circumstances are clearly different. The instruments are in general not negotiable, the market is far from perfect, and a distinct dualism, or treblism exists in the structure of the market. We have, on the one hand, foreign investors whose concepts of acceptable gearing ratios may be based on specific experience of lending to LDCs, whose own sources of funds may be partly soft, and who therefore are unlikely to be greatly influenced by the consensus of their domestic financial markets. On the other hand, we have indigenous market operators, who may be divided into private investors and the LDFI/government sector, hence the treblism. The private investors whose equity base is eroded can only survive by borrowing, pushing the gearing ratio to the limits tolerated by lenders; under these circumstances, working with other people's money, their risk aversion is likely to be irrelevant. To be more precise, since their own net assets are small or more likely negative, their preferences as to debt or equity holdings are hardly likely to be free choices in the continuum supposed by CAPM and APT.

The LDFIs, whose ability to invest in new assets of any kind is limited to the on-lending of lines of credit under the conditions imposed by the ultimate lenders, are compelled to set aside their preferences and lend as permitted, with a strong apparent inclination therefore towards medium-term private sector lending. Their own risk aversion is rendered nugatory by the combination of, on the one hand, a strong desire for rapid and risk-free pay-back at the project level, and on the other hand, a mandatory remit or directive at the country (portfolio) level to rehabilitate extensively almost at any cost. The solvency and profitability of the LDFI depend on the sum of the margins it derives from all its sub-loans, so project-level analysis is vital; yet no project will succeed unless there is a comprehensive programme involving the rehabilitation of a large number of projects simultaneously, so the portfolio approach is also vital. Hence the dilemma and the ambivalence in each case.

The ambiguous nature of debt–equity swaps

The debt–equity swap, which is the main feature of financial rescue in a major rehabilitation, and is inevitably a nodal point in negotiations with existing equity holders, therefore presents itself to the debt-holding LDFI in a double light. At the project level such a proposition may seem unattractive, while at the portfolio level it may seem desirable or even inescapable.[3]

The scenario being assumed here is that of a country which has undertaken major policy changes in agreement with the IMF; several devaluations have occurred; borrowers have suffered dislocations and losses leading to erosion of equity, to the point of going negative, in enterprise balance sheets; borrowings for the import of capital goods have emerged in those same balance sheets as vastly inflated debts in local currency terms; inflation is still continuing, and there may be further devaluations; liberalization and credit squeezes are depressing sales prospects except for those few enterprises which are export oriented. Debt service payments to LDFIs have therefore dried up or will soon do so, and there is no realistic prospect of ever clearing the inflated debts, generally speaking, unless there are massive overseas subsidies in one form or another. The majority of projects in the LDFI's portfolio (sub-loans, since LDFI equity has itself also been eroded and can no longer finance lending operations) are in arrears with debt service. As part of the total national programme, government representatives on the board of the LDFI have imposed a policy whereby overseas funds are sought for the purposes of rehabilitating this majority, in the hope that the entire portfolio will be brought back to some kind of normality. A sponsor makes a request within that programme, and the amount of additional cash which is needed is estimated by adding the requirements as enumerated above.

If this new money is injected as additional debt, unless the project can be reoriented as an export project (which is not usually possible), there is no serious hope of debt service. The existing debt is already beyond hope of servicing. The LDFI would prefer the sponsor to inject new equity, since the equity in the enterprise has already been eroded and the gearing ratio has become derisory, even without new borrowing. However, the sponsor cannot or will not do so. Other business activities conducted by the same sponsor have been subjected to the same difficulties.

This harsh but common reality sometimes appears to go unrecognized. It should be borne in mind that, for a favourable decision, an appraisal report should be satisfactory both in the incremental analysis and in the 'with' case. It is the cash flow from the 'with' case that will have to service the capital (new and old). Sometimes a very favourable incremental analysis generates a strong demand for rehabilitation, which appears to overlook the unsatisfactory 'with' situation. It is this error which gives rise to the suggestion which is sometimes proposed that a 'revolving fund' be created which will finance one rehabilitation after another.

The inescapable conclusion is that if the project cash flow after rehabilitation will not permit debt servicing, no more will it permit equity servicing as a substitute. If the LDFI injects equity or converts existing debt to equity, it will not receive a satisfactory dividend stream that would enable it to service its own debt.

The only conceivable exception or qualification to this statement is that which arises when the project cash flow will be affected by the strength of the incentive available to the sponsor. If debt burden is lightened to the point where a distributable surplus can be earned, notwithstanding that the bulk of these dividends will accrue to the LDFI, the sponsor may be more induced to devote time and energy to the good management of the enterprise than if the case is hopeless. Depending on the personal time preference and risk aversion of the sponsor, such a surplus could be made available either immediately in the form of a limited managerial salary (perhaps with bonuses), or rather later in the shape of a minuscule share of the general dividend or capital gain, or in postponed form in the shape of a much larger shareholding, following the reconversion of the LDFI's equity back into debt.

In any event, the LDFI faces a slow and insecure payoff on its new money, and what it is buying by this is time and energy devoted to the good management of the enterprise. The latter is what the national programme and the portfolio policy require.

The sponsors are not putting in capital, but management. They can hardly call themselves sponsors at all. There are, of course, instances where the sponsor is a good, committed manager, whose efforts have been frustrated for reasons beyond his or her control. But in many cases the LDFI can achieve better management by evicting the sponsor from the scene and bringing in, or promoting, specialist managers. However, this may require receivership and/or bankruptcy proceedings, which even on a small scale can be damaging to the institution bringing them, and on a portfolio scale can be damaging to the government. The LDFI may be debarred from taking a strong line with the previous owners. In that case, the new money and the debt–equity swap represent a political decision to subsidize the beneficiaries at the expense of the LDFI – not for the first time, of course. If such is the situation, the gain which the project will derive from the time and energy of the owner-manager is not likely to be so large as to justify the subsidy element regarded as an incentive. This is the scenario in which, at the project level, a debt–equity swap with or without new money may be unattractive, while at the portfolio level it may be inescapable.

A foreign development finance institution (DFI) which has invested in a sick project is not likely to be under quite the same pressure, and has a relatively free choice between putting in new funds, putting in a receiver (or it may have other sanctions open to it under specific agreements with the sponsors), or selling off its stake at a discount, possibly to some other (incoming) investor who is prepared to accept payment in local currency as a way of meeting local costs. Brazil, Chile and other western hemisphere countries have opened up channels for such transfers. However, inward investment is the subject of negotiated concessions in any event, and it is not clear whether the benefit accruing to existing owners requires an equal extension of state subsidy to the incomers, or whether there is a net gain to the economy taken from the outgoing DFI. According to Blackwell and Nocera (1988), claims that all parties gain from debt–equity swaps are certainly suspect.

The LDFI presses for more up-to-date accounts, for more sponsor equity, for service of the existing debt, for more diligence by management coupled with more monitoring and rights of intervention by the LDFI, though it may recognize a severe limitation on its own skilled manpower when it comes to intervention in such forms as part-time directorships and manager-receiverships. It wants to rehabilitate its entire portfolio but is willing to make exceptions from its project-level criteria only if these are not too numerous. It wants to avoid public wrangling but considers it has been misled by the client in the past and is wary of further misrepresentation in this supplementary request. Its arrears of interest have been accounted for, not as bad debt written off, but in the form of a level of profits less than the profits would otherwise have been; its arrears of principal have not as yet affected its income statement at all, and the directors have not as yet been asked to approve a write-off.

The client naturally presses the LDFI to provide a financial package with which the enterprise will be viable. This means that the total debt service, on old and new debt, must be within the limits of the available cash flow after allowing for some appreciable flow to the sponsor. The alternative is to close down the enterprise, with the bank taking losses; it is in the client's interest to maximize these hypothetical losses and the fuss and publicity which that route would involve. The client may also have an interest in the continuation of the activity in order to derive collateral benefits of a semi-hidden nature, such as temporary cash borrowing facilities, free vehicle maintenance, access to fuel and other goods at discount prices, some free labour for personal services, secure parking for vehicles, perhaps some access to foreign travel, and the like. Potential loss of these rights (or wrongs) can be a powerful, albeit unspoken, bargaining counter. Furthermore, in cases where the client has two or more businesses which share in a common pool of funds, bank assistance to one represents assistance to the group; all cash is fungible. If the bank will provide one of the enterprises with a truck, another will be relieved of that necessity and can purchase some stock, for example. The LDFI may actually welcome this informal pooling of resources even though it makes individual project analyses somewhat fictitious, and the ratios indicating gearing and liquidity of the individual company or project are thereby blurred. In extreme cases the LDFI may base its lending decisions primarily on its assessment of the owner and the immediate management team rather than on any financial statements – again a reversion to an earlier form of banking, possibly medieval.

When negotiation results in a debt–equity swap, this represents neither a satisfactory solution, nor a successful avoidance of loss for the LDFI. Whether it represents the avoidance of a greater loss in the long term can be revealed by the incremental project analysis, but in some projects it may represent putting good money after bad to incur an even greater loss (in financial analysis terms), in compliance with a general political-economic directive at the portfolio level.

Likewise it is not inconceivable that the foreign providers of the lines of credit supporting such sub-loans are acting in compliance with a political–economic directive rather than in genuine expectation of maximizing their incremental net benefits in terms of either financial or economic analyses. That directive, however, does not normally extend to the necessary overt softening of conditionality so that existing debts can be forgiven or alternatively new debts provided on such terms that no repayment of them is actually to be anticipated. Some rehabilitation credits may be in such a form as to permit sub-borrowers to escape repayment, but not without embarrassment to the LDFI which mediates the lending.

CONCLUSION

The conclusion is that classic financial analysis is difficult to apply in LDC rehabilitations. The occasional foreign investor with one or two projects requiring rehabilitation may adopt the classic approach, but a specific enquiry as to the project riskiness will be necessary, unaided by the market assessment of risk which is assumed to be available under the CAPM and APT models.

The LDFI investor has the following further handicaps:

1 Conditional interconnection between proposals waiting in the queue, which are known to be substantial but cannot be quantified because they are too numerous and too hypothetical to warrant investigation, given the perpetual difficulty of data collection at any time.
2 Untraceable movement of funds among sister enterprises.
3 Conflict between appraisal recommendations at the level of the

individual project, and rehabilitation policy at the portfolio level.

4   Associated with the above, an ambivalent attitude to risk, and therefore to the debt–equity preference.

5   Difficulty of reconciling the terms and conditions of overseas lines of credit with the very large unrequited transfer which is known to be needed to re-finance past losses.

In these circumstances the LDFI is compelled to revert to an earlier form of banking practice, more judgemental, more reliant on the personal assessment of borrowers and on collateral security, and mistrustful of financial projections generally. The LDFI will tend to try to resolve its dilemma by seeking an inducement to close the gap between what seems safe to lend at the project level and what is required to be lent at the portfolio level. To the extent this cannot be accommodated by overseas loans on soft terms, an ambivalent or vacillating policy may persist.

NOTES

1   For recent examples with this characteristic, see Squire and van der Tak (1975) or Bridger (1986). It is not hard to find others.

2   The application of incremental analysis to rehabilitation situations is explored in Tribe and Yaffey (1988).

3   This ambivalent attitude by the LDFI is another problem with the CAPM–APT model which requires an unambiguous measure of the riskiness of debt and of equity.

REFERENCES

Blackwell, M. and Nocera, S. (1988) 'The impact of debt to equity conversion', *Finance and Development*, June.

Brealey, R. and Myers, S. (1984) *Principles of Corporate Finance*, 2nd edn, London: McGraw-Hill.

Bridger, G. (1986) 'Rapid project appraisal', *Project Appraisal*, vol. 1, no. 4, December.

Franks, T.R., Broyles, J.E., and Carleton, W.T. (1985) *Corporate Finance: Concepts and Applications*, Boston: Kent.

Gasper, D. (1985) 'Bargaining in project appraisal and evaluation', Project Planning Centre Discussion Paper no. 116 (old series), University of Bradford.

Kitchen, R.L. (1986) *Finance for the Developing Countries*, Chichester: Wiley.

—— (1987) 'Projects rehabilitation and capital restructuring: principles and practice', *Project Appraisal*, vol. 2, no. 3, September.

Squire, L. and van der Tak, H.G. (1975) *Economic Analysis of Projects*, Baltimore: Johns Hopkins University Press for World Bank.

Tribe, M.A. and Yaffey, M.J.H. (1988) 'The planning and appraisal of rehabilitation projects', 2 vols, Development and Project Planning Centre, University of Bradford (training materials in private circulation).

7

THE ECONOMIC APPRAISAL OF REHABILITATION PROJECTS

Michael Tribe

INTRODUCTION

This chapter focuses particularly on the economic issues associated with the appraisal of rehabilitation projects in less developed countries.[1] The first section will discuss some definitional issues which could cause some confusion if they are not made explicit. The second section reviews some of the fundamental economic concepts as they relate to the appraisal of rehabilitation projects. The third section focuses particularly on the question of incremental analysis, and the fourth outlines other special features relating to the economic analysis of rehabilitation projects in less developed countries. The final section summarizes some of the conclusions.

DEFINITIONS

It is apparent that the terms 'project rehabilitation' and 'rehabilitation project' have intriguing differences in meaning beyond those which are simply syntactical. Practitioners in the world of project design and implementation often tend to regard a 'project' as having (usually implicitly) a clear beginning, middle and end, with the final act being the formal commissioning, the start of the operation phase and the preparation of the 'project completion report' (Hillebrandt and Meikle 1989; Meikle 1989; McCulloch 1986). This comparatively restricted definition of a project tends to be particularly associated with international aid agencies. If this restricted definition is used in the context of 'project rehabilitation' then it may be taken to refer strictly to the regeneration of projects which have 'stalled' before reaching the commissioning or operation phases of the full project cycle (Baum and Tolbert 1985; Baum 1978).

If, however, we use a wider definition of 'project' which includes the operation stage, then the two terms 'project rehabilitation' and 'rehabilitation project' involve less contradictory definitions. 'Projects' may not necessarily be so clearly time-bound – the regeneration of projects which have 'stalled' during the implementation phase is simply one of a continuum of types of project rehabilitation. The definition of 'project' in this context is more akin to the concept that a development bank might use, so that the 'operation' phase is of direct interest to the financial institutions (even beyond the period when loans are repaid). This is not to suggest that aid agencies have no interest in activities for which they have provided the investment finance, simply that in the past their reporting systems have tended to finish at, or very soon after, the commissioning stage. Development banks tend to retain direct contact with clients in a way which is not directly analogous to aid institutions.

Rehabilitation projects, in this wider definitional sense, involve putting an economic activity back into its previous good condition in at least some sense (Tribe and Yaffey 1988: 1).[2] However, even with projects that have not reached the commissioning stage, during the period between the original 'project identification' and the perception of the need for rehabilitation, the world has changed (perhaps rendering the original project design obsolescent) and markets may have changed. It would therefore be quite wrong to see rehabilitation simply in the context of restoring the project to the state that was originally intended. It is necessary to reconsider the entire project design and to undertake an appraisal which considers the alternative uses of the resources tied up in the 'failed' project, and the implications of the 'failure'.

The 'failure' will ultimately be evident at an economic level (i.e. failing to deliver the goods or services which were anticipated) and will also have financial and technical dimensions. It is necessary to have explicit criteria for failure, and to have a view of why such failure occurred. The reconsideration of the project design in the process of preparing a rehabilitation exercise requires an assessment of the causes of failure, and the 'designing-in' of conditions which have a good chance of ensuring the success of the rehabilitation (Tribe and Yaffey 1988: 9–10, 33–4). Such redesign may have to allow for the fact that far from taking over 'goodwill' from the failed activity the rehabilitation may have to overcome 'badwill', perhaps in the form of suspicion on the part of suppliers and customers alike. If the blame for failure can be attributed to management or organizational factors, then the redesign has to address itself to these questions.

The type of rehabilitation which will be required will depend critically on the reasons for project failure. Civil war, earthquake, economic crisis, and management failure create completely different dimensions for prospective rehabilitation. Not least, it should be obvious that it is not a sufficient reason for rehabilitation simply that 'something' existed before, or that implementation has started and so should be completed. The issue is whether there is economic justification for the rehabilitation (which commits additional resources to those already in place in order to provide a stream of goods and services in the future) and, by association, whether an alternative course of action (including non-rehabilitation) might be economically more rational.

Let us take as a fictitious but plausible case an extreme example of a likely course of events. Suppose that an industrial project is established on the basis of superficial financial analysis prior to a structural adjustment programme (SAP), and without proper economic appraisal. The SAP involves substantial devaluation of the currency and changes to internal relative prices following price decontrol. As a result of the reduction in economic distortions the project falls into a decline due to reduction in demand and in financial profitability, and, after a period, is put forward for prospective rehabilitation. Using financial analysis there is now no way in which the project can be made financially viable – it was never economically viable. Rehabilitation does not proceed, and closure follows with dispersal of the fixed assets and workforce.

This sketchy illustration shows how proper economic analysis might have prevented the initial commitment of resources to the project. The original go-ahead was given on the basis of an extremely short-sighted financial investment decision. When rehabilitation is carefully considered it is refused quite properly, but the refusal situation might never have arisen if a better investment decision had been made in the first place. Discussion of the economic analysis of project rehabilitation therefore has to incorporate the alternative, *inter alia*, of closure and/or abandonment as a potentially better option on national economic criteria.

ECONOMIC FOUNDATIONS FOR THE APPRAISAL OF REHABILITATION PROJECTS

Many texts do not clearly recognize that the fundamental basis of the economic appraisal of projects is 'incremental analysis'.[3] In this context 'incremental' means comparison of the alternative 'with project' and 'without project' situations.

The economic basis for much of project appraisal is that of the 'opportunity cost' valuation of resources prospectively to be used in, or created by, projects. Thus, an unemployed resource (such as the assets tied up in a failed project) which has no alternative use, has a zero opportunity cost, and therefore a zero price. If this unemployed resource has an alternative use then it has a positive opportunity cost, and therefore a positive price.[4]

Both Baum and Tolbert (1985) and Gittinger (1982) refer clearly to the concept of 'sunk costs' in the context of rehabilitation projects:

> In most countries, a large part of the investment program is made up of ongoing projects. Since it is the incremental returns (ignoring all sunk costs) that are relevant to the decision whether or not to invest, as a starting point it is sound practice to protect allocations to all ongoing projects that are indivisible and whose implementation is well advanced. . . . Similar considerations apply to maintenance, rehabilitation, and output balancing projects . . . all of which may entail relatively small investments that yield high economic returns.
>
> (Baum and Tolbert 1985: 433)

> Sunk costs are those costs incurred in the past upon which a proposed new investment will be based. Such costs cannot be avoided, however poorly advised they may have been. When we analyze a proposed investment, we consider only

future returns to future costs; expenditures in the past, or sunk costs, do not appear in our accounts.

In practice, if a considerable amount has already been spent on a project, the future returns to the future costs of completing the project would probably be quite attractive even if it is clear in retrospect that the project should never have been begun. The ridiculous extreme is when only one dollar is needed to complete a project, even if a rather poor one, and when no benefit can be realized until the project is completed. The 'return' to the last dollar may well be extremely high, and it would be clearly worthwhile to spend it. But the argument that because much has already been spent on a project it therefore must be continued is not a valid criterion for decision. There are cases in which it would be preferable simply to stop a project midway or to draw it to an early conclusion so that future resources might be freed for higher-yielding alternatives.

For evaluating past investment decisions, it is often desirable to do an economic and financial analysis of a completed project. Here, of course, the analyst would compare the return from all expenditures over the past life of the project with all returns. But this kind of analysis is useful only for determining the yield of past projects in the hope that judgments about future projects might be better informed. It does not help us decide what to do in the present. Money spent in the past is already gone; we do not have as one of our alternatives not to implement a completed project.

(Gittinger, 1982: 55)

The concept of 'sunk costs' arises because in economic terms 'bygones are bygones' – when resources have been used to create fixed assets those assets do not, other things being equal, have to be created again and they can therefore be regarded as 'free'. Baum and Tolbert, and Gittinger, make it perfectly clear that the 'sunk cost' principle is combined with treating rehabilitation as 'incremental'. Thus, in Gittinger's figurative terms, only one dollar may be sufficient to convert a 'stalled' uncommissioned project into an ongoing concern: equally, one dollar may be sufficient to convert a failed activity into an operating concern. Baum and Tolbert make it equally clear that careful manipulation of the economic and financial analysis may allow projects to advance to implementation despite the fact that they are intrinsically unacceptable within the normal appraisal criteria, and then subsequently a 'rehabilitation' or 'completion' project may be added on the grounds of 'sunk costs' and 'incremental analysis':

> It is not uncommon to come across situations in which the sunk-cost argument has been elevated to a fine art form: an agency, while pleading for funds for incomplete projects on the basis of sunk costs, may be simultaneously starting other submarginal projects, presumably to produce candidates for future financing under the sunk-cost doctrine! To avoid such abuses, it is important that the analysis also focus on the total project, including sunk costs, to determine whether, with hindsight, the original decision to proceed with the project was well founded and, if not, what should be done to avoid the recurrence of similar mistakes. The issue of sunk costs also highlights the need for sound sector work to guide the selection of individual projects . . .
>
> (Baum and Tolbert 1985: 436)

It will always be possible to falsify or manipulate the data associated with financial and economic analysis in such a way that unviable projects appear to be viable. The degree of alertness and honesty of the people who check and double-check the calculations is, of course, variable. Equally, the degree of confidence which can be placed on the accuracy of even the most painstaking economic and financial analysis is variable given the extent of uncertainties about the data which is used (see, for example, Pack 1988: 363; Papps 1987: 331). However, if we are at all serious about attempting to consistently improve the quality of investment decisions it is appropriate that more careful attention be given to the criteria used for the acceptance of rehabilitation projects than has been the case in the past.

The approach to the economic analysis of rehabilitation projects which has emerged from the work of Tribe and Yaffey (1988) has three elements to it:

1 Because of the lack of clarity concerning the utilization of the 'sunk cost' approach it should be abandoned and replaced by an 'opportunity cost' criterion for the valuation of the assets

of the activities which are prospectively to be rehabilitated. Thus, assets which are already in place should be valued according to their alternative use. This may be referred to as a 'penalty' approach to valuation, and does not relate directly to the alternative 'transactions' approach which owes more to financial analysis.

2   The basic method of calculating the economic project worth would then relate to 'incremental analysis' and would consist of the 'with' project worth minus the 'without' project worth. In the context of the above remarks on the problems of falsification and uncertainty the margin of error in the estimation of the 'without' project worth in particular makes the likelihood of an over-estimation of the incremental project worth very high.[5]

3   In order to allow for the difficulties associated with point 2, and to allow for the points made in the quotations from Baum and Tolbert and from Gittinger, in addition to passing the test of acceptability under the incremental project criterion, the rehabilitation project should also have an acceptable 'with' project worth.

This additional condition is adopted in an attempt to ensure that only basically sound projects are rehabilitated.

It should be evident that the economic analysis discussed here should be undertaken on the basis of the usual criteria of such exercises, including the consistent use of shadow prices, conversion factors and a realistic discount rate.

THE USE OF INCREMENTAL ANALYSIS

The 'mechanics' of using incremental analysis has been described fully in Tribe and Yaffey (1988: 40–57) as well as in Tribe (1989b) and Yaffey (1989).

First and basically, the 'with' project worth should be calculated using the full operating costs and revenues, together with the value of the existing assets taken over from the 'failed' project (based on an opportunity cost criterion) and the additional investment put in for the rehabilitation. Second, the 'without' project worth should be calculated using the full operating costs and revenues (if the project will struggle on in the absence of rehabilitation) together with the value of existing assets. Third,

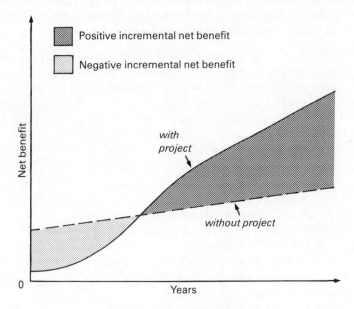

Figure 7.1 Incremental project worth
Source: Gittinger (1982:48)

it should then be apparent that the 'incremental' project worth will simply be the 'with' project worth minus the 'without' project worth. Gittinger has a diagram which makes the essential principles clear, and this is reproduced as Figure 7.1.

Because the value of the existing assets is written into both 'with' and 'without' resource flows, they are cancelled out, so that the 'incremental' project worth based on this 'opportunity cost' criterion is consistent with the 'sunk cost' approach. However, the method of calculating rehabilitation project worth which is recommended here has two advantages over the 'sunk cost' approach:

1 The explicit calculation of the 'incremental' project worth by subtracting the 'without' case from the 'with' case reduces the chances of erroneously, or intentionally, mis-specifying the true nature of the incremental case.
2 It is necessary to calculate the 'with' case as well as the 'incremental' case if the suggested decision rules (outlined in

the previous section) are to be followed. If the opportunity cost of the existing assets is not costed into the 'with' rehabilitation case, then the project worth will be overstated.

It should also be apparent that in the estimation of 'with' and 'without' project worths, both cases should be 'optimized'. There will be a number of possible rehabilitation scenarios involving different project designs and different extents of rehabilitation, and the 'with' case which is actually specified should therefore be the preferred one. Equally, in the 'without' case, there will be a number of possibilities including 'struggling on' and 'closure'.

Quite clearly any 'struggling on' project worth which is lower than the value of 'closure' would be inferior as an option, so that 'closure' would be the optimum 'without' project worth. There are special problems associated with the estimation of the value of closure, particularly related to the valuation of assets which may, or may not, be dispersed subsequently, and the extent to which the labour force is entitled to compensation (which has a real economic cost) (Cole 1987). However, it should be possible to resolve these issues satisfactorily.

A further question relates to the valuation of existing fixed assets. Strictly speaking, in economic terms, this should be the net present value of the best use of the assets. However, this net present value (or project worth) cannot be calculated without first having a value to write in for the existing assets. Therefore, this strict interpretation involves an inevitable circularity of argument. In theoretical, or strictly 'academic', terms this question could be resolved simply by reverting to an incremental analysis based on a 'short-cut' approach excluding the 'with' and 'without' cases and going directly to the 'incremental'. However, there are several operational reasons for preferring the longer version, including 'with', 'without' and 'incremental' project worths and the decision rules suggested above. This means that valuation of existing assets should usually be based on a professional valuer's report, modified if necessary by shadow pricing criteria. This operational approach short-circuits the circularity of the theoretical argument.

OTHER SPECIAL FEATURES OF THE ECONOMIC APPRAISAL OF REHABILITATION PROJECTS

It has been made clear earlier in this chapter that the discussion takes it as a *sine qua non* that shadow pricing and other elements of the economic analysis of projects are fully integrated into the approach to the appraisal of rehabilitation projects which has been outlined. Emphasis has been placed on special features such as the interpretation of opportunity costs when there are existing assets in place, and the use of incremental analysis in an effective operational manner.

However, there are special features of 'recovery programmes' in less developed countries which require particular attention in the context of the economic analysis of rehabilitation projects. Three such features can be identified:

1   The comparatively small size of many less developed countries means that the implementation of a few major rehabilitation projects can change the economic environment sufficiently to alter the opportunity costs (shadow prices) of a wide range of resources. For example, recovery programmes tend to require significant amounts of foreign exchange which tends to be provided for particular projects or programmes which, in turn, may considerably boost export earnings, thus contributing additional 'free' foreign exchange. This type of development is likely to affect the opportunity cost of foreign exchange.

2   The implementation of 'recovery' or 'structural adjustment' programmes tends to incorporate a wide range of measures, including attention to the official exchange rate, price control systems, interest rates etc., and in the process the 'economic control system' is often transformed. The effect of such a transformation is often to bring market prices and shadow prices closer together, i.e. to reduce 'distortions' (World Bank 1983: Chapter 6). However, it is also likely that the effects of such 'adjustments' alter shadow prices in a 'second round' set of effects. Since rehabilitation projects are often part of such programmes this makes the prediction of relative shadow prices (or even of relative market prices) difficult.

149

3 Where recovery programmes follow prolonged economic crises, civil unrest or international conflict, the 'foundations' of the economy may be very difficult to determine, so that the 'economic scenario' may be equally difficult to define. The economic analysis of all projects, and rehabilitation projects in particular, may consequently become a matter of conjecture.

The theoretical basis of shadow pricing, particularly as it applies to the use of 'border prices' as adopted by most economic institutions, is marginal analysis. In principle, the marginal input, if not available from domestic sources, has to be imported, the marginal output, if not sold on the domestic market, has to be exported. The heart of the economic analysis of projects therefore lies in some form of marginal cost pricing (Papps 1987). Of course, untraded inputs, discount rates and the appropriate foreign exchange rate cannot be handled by appealing to 'border prices'. The fact is that structural adjustment programmes and the like are not simply making marginal adjustments to the economy – they aim to make structural changes to the economy, meaning that there is an anomaly associated with marginal analysis of projects in a period of deliberate structural economic change. Such economic analysis may give results which are an inaccurate pointer to future events (and to project economic performance in particular).

These circumstances add a further layer of uncertainty to those to which we are accustomed in the undertaking of the economic analysis of projects, and which are particularly likely to apply to rehabilitation projects within 'recovery' or 'structural adjustment' programmes.

A further set of problems relates to the questions of intrasectoral priorities and of intersectoral allocation of resources in an economic planning or coordination context.

For individual projects, particularly in the public sector or where public sector decision-making is involved (as, for example, for larger private sector investments where tax concessions or other preferential treatments have been applied for) clear criteria are required as a basis for accept/reject decisions. It is inappropriate that such criteria, or decision rules, should be varied significantly for different sectors or sub-sectors. In the case of rehabilitation projects Tribe and Yaffey (1988: 47–53) and Tribe (1989a) have demonstrated that, depending upon the precise method of handling the resource flow data, the project worth can vary substantially. This implies that some projects might be accepted when they do not really satisfy the acceptance criteria, and others might be rejected when they are in fact acceptable. It is important that an agreed method of calculating rehabilitation project worth be defined and then used consistently (perhaps through being defined in the terms of reference for the preparation of individual project reports).

Some sectors or sub-sectors of the economy may have structural characteristics which make the universal adoption of a single set of decision rules on an economy-wide basis impossible. Yaffey has explored this issue in his cross-sectoral survey of rehabilitation projects (Tribe and Yaffey 1988: Chapter 2). For example, health, education and water projects do not easily lend themselves to the same kind of cost–benefit analysis as industrial or agricultural projects. In some sectors the use of the cost-effectiveness method of project appraisal is obviously not directly comparable with the cost–benefit analysis used in other sectors. Therefore, an investment programme (which includes investment in both public and private sectors) would need to specify a sectoral allocation of resources which is determined on some criterion other than relative project worth. Then, within the programme for each particular sector the selected accept/reject criteria can be used for individual projects.

The significance of this sectoral allocation of resources relates to the question of priorities for rehabilitation within recovery programmes. If there has been a prolonged economic crisis, a war, or some other catastrophic set of events, it is clearly impossible that the entire economy could be rehabilitated at the same time. It is therefore necessary for priorities to be established which may not necessarily relate directly to the level of project worth. For example, it will often be the case that the rehabilitation of infrastructure projects is a high priority because of the beneficial 'external' or 'knock-on' effects that they have on a wide range of other projects, and that the establishment of projects which have a good prospect of high net foreign exchange earnings will also have a high priority. Establishment of such priorities cannot simply relate to a rank ordering of projects according to project worth.[6]

A number of these questions are raised or developed in Tribe (forthcoming), in which the role of rehabilitation in Ghana's recent Economic Recovery Programme is discussed. It is quite clear that within the Public Investment Programme 1986–1988 the question of the criteria for acceptance or rejection of individual projects was an issue which had to be settled clearly (Republic of Ghana 1987: iv). A cut-off economic internal rate of return of 15 per cent was adopted for most sectors together with cost- effectiveness criteria for the health sector, implying that the 73 projects (out of 201) characterized as 'rehabilitation' in nature satisfied the established criteria (accounting for about 55 per cent of the proposed public sector investment). On the question of priorities the Public Investment Programme established a set of 21 'Supercore' projects of which 8 were rehabilitation, accounting for 66 per cent of 'Supercore' investment. It is notable that the 'Supercore' included a higher proportion of rehabilitation investment compared with the programme as a whole, and that for some sectors a very high proportion of projected investment was to be rehabilitation in nature (100 per cent for three sectors, and 97 per cent for a fourth). It also included a high proportion of infrastructure projects (transport and communication: roads and highways in particular). Further, it is also notable that the Progress Report on the Economic Recovery Programme placed strong emphasis on the role of rehabilitation projects (Republic of Ghana 1985). This is not very surprising given the extent of the economic decline over the previous ten to fifteen years, and the state of the economy in 1982/3 at the start of the Recovery Programme (Tribe forthcoming; Huq 1989: 1–32).

SUMMARY AND CONCLUSIONS

In discussing the issue of project rehabilitation it is advisable to take a broad view of 'projects' so that evaluation of past events is carried through into the design, appraisal, implementation and operation of the rehabilitation in the context of the project cycle. It is also necessary to take a broad view of the options for the future, so that closure, abandonment or benign neglect are alternatives to rehabilitation which may be economically justifiable in many circumstances. Project 'failure' has to be defined, and can arise through a range of causes at various stages of the project cycle. A clear identification of these causes, and of means to avoid similar problems in the future, is a necessary part of the rehabilitation project report.

The fundamental basis of the economic appraisal of rehabilitation projects is 'incremental analysis', but in this context a distinction has to be made between 'theoretically' ideal appraisal methods, and those which are 'operationally' appropriate for the project analyst or practitioner.

In this context it has been suggested that the concept of 'sunk costs' be abandoned for 'operational' purposes, with the substitution of the consistent use of the concept of 'opportunity cost', particularly with regard to the valuation of existing fixed assets.

A consistent set of operational decision rules is required as part of the 'Terms of Reference' for rehabilitation project reports. Tribe and Yaffey (1988) have suggested that the 'incremental project worth', calculated by subtracting the 'without project worth' from the 'with project worth', should be acceptable and that in addition the 'with project worth' should also satisfy the usual rules of economic acceptability (i.e. positive net present value, benefit–cost ratio greater than unity, and/or economic internal rate of return greater than the test rate of discount).

In the context of major economic recovery or structural adjustment programmes it has to be recognized that normal marginal economic analysis may break down as the project operating environment changes with the implementation of such programmes. This is significant since such programmes have often included a substantial number of major (and minor) project rehabilitations.

Intersectoral, and to some degree intrasectoral, resource allocation criteria – especially the establishment of priorities as between 'acceptable' projects – cannot depend only on the results of project worth calculations. The establishment of criteria for such priorities remains as a major issue which still has to be explored thoroughly.

A brief outline of recent Ghanaian experience brought the discussion to a conclusion, illustrating the clear relevance and significance of the issue of project rehabilitation for African economic conditions at this time.

NOTES

1 A literature search of the *Journal of Economic Literature* index and of the Development and Project Planning Centre's own library in early 1987 produced only one relevant reference – Sauermann (1979). The report on the rehabilitation of the Ugandan economy (Commonwealth Fund for Technical Cooperation, Seers and Belshaw (eds), 1979) also relates to the national and sector levels of the economy rather than to the level of the project.
2 The pair of bound volumes produced by Tribe and Yaffey (1988) were supported by a financial contribution from the British Council.
3 This issue is discussed exhaustively in Tribe and Yaffey (1988: 40–57) and in the texts by Baum and Tolbert (1985) and Gittinger (1982). The papers by Tribe (1989a) and Yaffey (1989) also explore many of the issues raised by the use of incremental analysis in the economic and financial appraisal of rehabilitation projects.
4 A limiting case is that of the resource which has an alternative use, but where the cost of *transferring* it to that use is very high (e.g. for transportation and installation) and is greater than the intrinsic value in that use. In this case the 'net opportunity cost' would appear to be negative, but in reality the alternative is to leave the resource where it is, thus avoiding the costs of transfer, and the opportunity cost of the resource would then be zero. Another limiting case would be where there are substantial de-commissioning costs for, e.g. a nuclear power station, which can alternatively be used for a period with comparative safety for the production of electricity – the economic cost of not using the resource may sometimes be higher than that of using it. A third limiting case might apply to the exhaustion of non- renewable resources such as coal, oil, tin, clay, etc., where the costs of closure often include those of putting the 'site' back to a tolerable environmental condition.
5 This issue is explored more fully in Tribe (1989a).
6 Faber raises a number of these issues in Chapter 8 in this volume.

REFERENCES

Baum, W.C. (1978) 'The World Bank project cycle' *Finance and Development*, vol. 15, no. 4, December.

Baum, W.C. and Tolbert, S.M. (1985) *Investing in Development: Lessons of World Bank Experience*, New York: Oxford University Press for the World Bank.

Cole, S. (1987) 'The economic costs of plant closure', *Project Appraisal*, vol. 2, no. 1, March.

Ghana, Republic of (1985) *Progress of the Economic Recovery Programme 1984–1986 and Policy Framework 1986–1988*, Accra.

—— (1987) *Public Investment Programme 1986–1988*, vol. 1 – Main Report, Accra.

Gittinger, J.P. (1982) *The Economic Analysis of Agricultural Projects*, 2nd edn, London and Baltimore: Johns Hopkins University Press for the Economic Development Institute.

Hillebrandt, P.M. and Meikle, J.L. (1989) 'Construction project rehabilitation: policies for improved resource use and performance' in M.A. Tribe (ed.), *Proceedings of the Conference on Project Rehabilitation in Developing Countries*, Development and Project Planning Centre, University of Bradford.

Huq, M.M. (1989) *The Economy of Ghana: The First 25 Years Since Independence*, London: Macmillan.

McCulloch, M. (1986) 'Project frameworks – a logical development for more effective aid', in *British Overseas Aid in 1985*, London: HMSO/Overseas Development Administration .

Meikle, F.S. (1989) 'Tools for the analysis of project performance with findings from an example of their use in reviewing a number of Egyptian projects', in M.A. Tribe (ed.), *Proceedings of the Conference on Project Rehabilitation in Developing Countries*, Development and Project Planning Centre, University of Bradford.

Pack, H. (1988) 'Industrialization and trade', in H. Chenery and T.N. Srinivasan (eds) *Handbook of Development Economics*, vol. 1, Amsterdam: Elsevier.

Papps, I. (1987) 'Techniques of project appraisal', in N. Gemmell (ed.) *Surveys in Development Economics*, Oxford: Basil Blackwell.

Sauermann, H. (1979) 'On the economic and financial rehabilitation of West Germany 1945–1949' *Zeitschrift für die Gesamte Staatswissenschaft*, vol. 135, no. 3, September.

Seers, D. and Belshaw, D.G.R. (eds) (1979) *The Rehabilitation of the Economy of Uganda*, 2 vols, Commonwealth Fund for Technical Cooperation, London: Commonwealth Secretariat.

Tribe, M.A. (1989a) 'The planning and economic analysis of rehabilitation projects', in M.A. Tribe (ed.), *Proceedings of the Conference on Project Rehabilitation in Developing Countries*, Development and Project Planning Centre, University of Bradford.

—— (forthcoming) 'Project rehabilitation in Ghana's Economic Recovery Programme', mimeo, DPPC Discussion Papers (new series), no. 14.

Tribe, M.A. and Yaffey, M.J.H. (1988) 'The planning and appraisal of rehabilitation projects', 2 vols, Development and Project Planning Centre, University of Bradford (training materials in private circulation).

World Bank (1983) *World Development Report*, London and New York: Oxford University Press for the World Bank .

Yaffey, M.J.H. (1989) 'Financial analysis: project or portfolio', Chapter 6 in this volume.

Part IV

PROJECT REHABILITATION: POLICY AND EXPERIENCE

Part IV

PROJECT
REHABILITATION:
POLICY AND
EXPERIENCE

8

PROJECT REHABILITATION
Getting the issues right
Mike Faber

INTRODUCTION

The first three sections of this chapter deal with general issues –
(i) the macro and sector policy contexts in which rehabilitation
projects are likely to be undertaken, (ii) a primitive typology of
needs and opportunities, and elements of dereliction, both causes
and effects, which will need to be remedied if rehabilitation is to
be successful, and (iii) the question as to whether the private
foreign investor can be reattracted, particularly in circumstances
where he may feel he was badly treated last time. The fourth
section deals with a case study of an actual rehabilitation project,
providing a description of the rehabilitation of the Ashanti
Goldfields mine in Ghana. In the final section some guidelines
are suggested based upon the earlier argument and the case study.

MACRO AND SECTOR CONTEXTS

The quality of a project is not independent of the policies being
pursued that will affect the performance of that project. For while
good policies cannot make a bad project good, bad policies have
made many a good project bad.

This statement is true for all projects, but it is particularly
relevant for rehabilitation projects. The reasons why rehabilitation may be necessary are many, including deteriorating
external environment. But unquestionably such reasons also
include unrealistic or impractical policy choices in the past and/or
failures to modify earlier policies when new (and usually less
favourable) circumstances had rendered this necessary.

It is a feature of nearly all rehabilitation projects that they take place in countries which have suffered a period of economic decline and that they require some foreign funding – whether that be from bilateral aid agencies, the World Bank, regional development banks, or from agencies like the IFC (International Finance Corporation), the CDC (Commonwealth Development Corporation) or even (possibly by way of a debt: equity swap) through direct foreign investment. Such agencies will normally only be prepared to proceed if the government of the country where the project is to be located has already accepted an IMF and/or World Bank stabilization and adjustment programme.

The projects themselves are thus likely to be cast in the context of a programme of policy reforms: indeed the covenants and conditionalities attached to the project may be viewed as part of that programme, or at least will need to be consistent with it. In the design of any rehabilitation project, it is therefore necessary to be aware of what items of conduct are likely to be covered in such programmes. Each programme is of course unique, but the ingredients – if not the precise mix – are normally the same. From the work of Killick (1984) and Mosley (1987) a table has been synthesized which lists the most common ingredients of those programmes.

In Table 8.1, the asterisks in the column on the left display the importance which the IMF has usually attached to various reforms, either as preconditions of their stand-bys or as conditions to be subject to performance criteria. The number of asterisks is a measure of their importance, in terms of a mix of both frequency and intensity. The data are from Killick (1984), interpreted by the author. The numbers in the columns on the right are taken from Mosley (1987) and indicate the percentage of structural adjustment programmes negotiated between 1980 and 1986 in which these particular conditions occur. The cut-off point has been set at 49 per cent, but the original Mosley article includes other conditions that occur less frequently than that.

A PRIMITIVE TYPOLOGY

Which of those measures and policy reforms will be most relevant for a particular project will depend upon where that project is located and what specific reasons have rendered it in need of rehabilitation.

Table 8.1 IMF upper tranche stand-by arrangements and policy reforms required for World Bank structural adjustment loans

IMF Pre-condition	Performance criteria		World Bank 1980–6 % in SALs
***	***	Exchange rate adjustment credit ceilings	
	***	–Total domestic credit	
	***	–Credit to govt /public sector	
	*	–Credit to private sector	
***	***	Interest rate policy	
**		Pricing policies	
		–agricultural prices	73
		–energy prices	49
**		Tax measures	70
		Reduction of payment arrears	
***		–to IMF	
	**	–to others	
	*	Minimum forex reserve target	
	· *	Restrictions on new external debt	
	*	Reduce specified public expenditures	
	*	Liberalization of trade and payments	
		–remove import quotas	57
		–improve export incentives and support	76
	*	–liberalize payment mechanisms	
		Resource mobilization	
		–reform budget and reduce deficits	70
		–improve financial performance of PEs	73
		–strengthen management of external borrowings	49
		Use of resources	
		–change industry incentives	68
		–revise public investment priorities	59
		Institutional reforms	
		–strengthen capacity to implement public investment programme	86
		–increase efficiency of public enterprises	57
		–improve support for agriculture (marketing etc.)	57
		–improve prospects and support for industry	49

Source: Adapted from Killick (1984) and Mosley (1987).

Table 8.2 A primitive typology of needs and opportunities

Public sector

(a) Standard departmental
   –education
   –health
   –general administration (customs, tax)
   –public security

(b) Economic infrastructure
   (provision out of general public taxation or rates)
   –roads
   –water supply
   –sewerage
   –flood control etc.

(c) Parastatals (Mark One)
   (production for monopoly sale, with or without subsidy)
   –postal services
   –telephone services
   –railways
   –harbours
   –electricity

(d) Parastatals (Mark Two)
   (production for export or competitive sale domestically)
   –airlines
   –mining corporations
   –parastatal factories
   –state farms
   –state marketing boards
   –state shops, etc.
   –financial services

Private sector
   –agriculture
   –mining
   –manufacturing
   –commerce, finance, etc.

Rehabilitation of creditworthiness

All sciences start with the tedious business of collection of samples, classification and tabulation. In Table 8.2 a primitive typology is offered which distinguishes by sector and by mode of financing the activities which provide the prime candidates for rehabilitation projects. The list is extensive. It seeks to move from the provision of standard government services, through traditional infrastructure projects, to different types of para-statals. Private sector rehabilitation and the rehabilitation of credit-worthiness are added simply as reminders that these need to go hand-in-hand with rehabilitation in the public sector, and that it cannot be assumed that these will happen of their own accord.

Of course there is nothing sacred about these particular classifications. One classifies according to the use one has in mind. Some of the items in (b) could be put into (c), some of those in (c) could be put into (d), and some of those in (d) could be privatized, which is what certain of the aid agencies would like to see accomplished.

Most aid agencies, particularly the bilaterals, will probably feel most comfortable in respect of rehabilitation projects in categories (a), (b) and (c) – since these are the areas where the original aid-assisted projects were most likely to be located. The present author's main interest is in projects in areas (d) and in the private sector. These can be amongst the most difficult of all rehabilitation projects, since they involve restoration of production at an internationally competitive price. But they are also amongst the most vital since such projects are likely to be direct producers of foreign exchange, and therefore a means of loosening the import strangulation that besets the rest of the economy.

The financing of rehabilitation projects is likely to differ from the financing of the original projects. Although some foreign exchange and some expenditure of a capital nature will nearly always be required, expenses – a considerable proportion of many rehabilitation projects – are likely to be in local currency and/or to be of a recurrent cost nature. The financing of these costs is in some ways similar to the financing of general balance of payments support by way of a programme loan. Alternatively, agencies may find this a convenient use of blocked or counterpart funds. For the rehabilitation of projects in the private sector of firms or industries that are operating well below capacity, access to more foreign exchange for imported materials is often necessary if output and exports are to expand substantially.[1]

The following is a list of sixteen causes and effects of dereliction compiled from the author's own experience:

1 Decrepit capital stock.
2 Very little access to foreign exchange.

3 Shortage of spares and replacements.
4 Inadequate stocks of materials and finished goods.
5 Poor maintenance, but often combined with great ingenuity in effecting repairs.
6 Frequent break-downs.
7 Insufficient revenues due to: charges or prices too low, and uncollected; inadequate subsidy; erosion of capital allowances by inflation.
8 Inadequate local credit.
9 Over-staffing (thus low productivity labour force).
10 Untrained technicians (and inability to retain trained ones).
11 Overstretched and underqualified management (often spending time on the wrong work).
12 Salary and wage levels too low.
13 Obsolete technology (resulting in non-competitive or unexportable product).
14 Late deliveries of product (resulting in loss of orders).
15 Frequent failures of supporting infrastructure, (power, rail, ports, phones, slow and unreliable service from public administration). Each can therefore convincingly blame the failure of others for its own poor performance.
16 Poor morale and incentives; sense of hopelessness.

All are likely to need attention if a project is to be successfully rehabilitated.

CAN THE FOREIGN INVESTOR BE RE-ATTRACTED?

Recently the author was asked to comment upon an 'investment incentives scheme' being put in place by a government hoping to attract direct foreign investment. The scheme included: a ten-year tax holiday; the right to carry losses forward, beyond the ten years, for income tax purposes; an initial allowance; generous capital allowances; expensing of some capital expenditures, e.g., in mining[1]: an export allowance, which effectively reduces the tax rate on profits earned on products sold abroad; exemption of a range of customs duties; a One-Stop Agency to help the foreign investor obtain all necessary consents and permissions.

One's reaction was that this list of concessions and incentives was, if anything, too generous. But I also felt obliged to point out eight other matters which the incentives code did not mention, all of which would in fact be on the potential investor's mind (although he might not mention them) just as much as any of the points mentioned in the code. These were:

1 The track record of the government in dealing with earlier foreign investments.
2 The maintenance of a realistic exchange rate.
3 The ability of the government to control domestic inflation (or, if not, its willingness to index certain allowances and costs for tax purposes).
4 The country's reputation for workforce discipline.
5 Conditions, including the control of crime and marginal tax rates and the issuance of work permits, that would make it possible to attract and retain skilled personnel.
6 The reliability (and cost) of power and other publicly-provided services.
7 The attitude, efficiency, honesty and promptness of the bureaucracy and the extent of bureaucratic requirements.
8 The likely impact of foreign debt servicing obligations in the competition for foreign exchange, where this had to be provided by the central bank.

Of these eight 'other matters', the first is probably the most important. And here an unpalatable fact has to be faced. Just as a good track record will bring down the supply price of capital and minimize the number of assurances and covenants the investor will insist upon, so a poor track record increases the supply price of capital and increases too the number of assurances, guarantees, conditionalities and covenants that the provider of foreign capital will insist upon. Repentance is fine, but it does not immediately change the record. And it is the record primarily which determines the requirements.

The very difficulty of re-establishing a track record leads to one other conclusion. Direct foreign investment is sometimes paraded as a likely lead-force in achievement of economic recovery and as a means of replacing financial flows from the commercial banks. Experience suggests that the dimensions of the flows required are unlikely to be comparable, and that direct private investment from abroad is much more likely to follow recovery than to lead it.

THE CASE STUDY: ASHANTI GOLDFIELDS

The Ashanti mine in Obuasi, Ghana is the largest underground gold mine in the world, outside the Republic of South Africa and the Soviet Union. With 11,000 people on the payroll, it is Ghana's biggest single employer (other than government and the Cocoa Marketing Board), and characteristically contributes about one-fifth to the country's export earnings.

The rich gold ores of Obuasi had been worked by traditional methods as far back as the seventeenth century, but the history of the modern mine really starts with the acquisition of a lease on behalf of what was to become the Ashanti Goldfields Corporation (AGC) in 1895 and its subsequent confirmation by the colonial governor of the Gold Coast in 1897.

AGC owned and operated the mine as an independent enterprise until 1968 when the company was taken over by Lonrho. The following year the government of Ghana was granted 20 per cent of the shares of the company and the right to purchase a further 20 per cent[2] in return for the abolition of the 5 per cent royalty and a new 50-year lease – the previous lease being due to expire in 1987. The government also acquired the right to appoint four members to the company's twelve-member board.

In 1972, the National Redemption Council seized power and declared a policy of majority state ownership (55 per cent) for all major mining projects. Negotiations with Lonrho followed but failed to reach agreement as a result of which, at the end of the year, the Ghana government issued a decree which effectively gave it 55 per cent of a new Ashanti company having the exclusive right to mine the Obuasi deposit with the other 45 per cent plus the management responsibilities being left with Lonrho. A 6 per cent royalty was imposed as well.

In 1974 agreement was reached with Lonrho on management arrangements, but no agreement was to be reached on the issue of compensation – its amount, method and timing of payment – for another ten years. By 1982 then, consistent with the deterioration in the entire Ghanaian economy, the company was operating at a post-tax loss. But a recovery in the dollar price of gold and the 1983 devaluation of the cedi improved the company's position. In 1984, Lonrho accepted the sum of £2.8m[3] that had been offered a dozen years earlier. By that time the

166

US$160m rehabilitation project was in prospect, and one might speculate that Lonrho may have been influenced by the knowledge that the IFC would not proceed with its financing until the dispute over compensation had been settled.

During the years of general decline in Ghana, production at Ashanti fell by 56 per cent from 533,025 ounces in 1971/2 to 232,156 ounces in 1981/2. This fall in fact paralleled the declines that had been recorded for Ghana's other primary commodity exports. Over the same period cocoa exports fell by 45 per cent,[4] tropical timber exports by 81 per cent, bauxite exports by 69 per cent, and manganese exports by 88 per cent. Thus there is evidence that some of the reasons for Ashanti's declining production were systemic, in the sense of being part of what was happening to Ghana's whole economic system and part of a generalized reaction to a whole set of macroeconomic policies,[5] rather than special to the industry itself.

However one must be careful here. Although the causes may have been in that sense systemic – overvalued exchange rate, rapid inflation, import strangulation, a ramshackle taxation structure, emigration of skilled workers, inadequate cash flow – such causes invariably have different impacts on different types of industry.[6]

Dealing with rapid inflation is itself costly, but for modern industry there is an additional cost arising from the fact that the tax relief available from capital allowances will rapidly be eroded by price rises. Theoretically these prices might be offset by investing in a sinking fund, but in practice the interest rate in Ghana was kept well below the rate of inflation. In consequence a large part of replacement expenditure, as well as expenditures on exploration and development (the activities which, in mining, are required to locate and delineate the new ore bodies necessary to sustain production), had to be financed out of post-tax profits.

AGC, as a major foreign exchange earner with an overseas shareholder, was to some extent protected from the worst consequences of the economy's decline. Although gold production had fallen by 56 per cent during the 1970s, actual tonnage milled had fallen by very much less, and the fall in production was to a considerable extent a consequence of the rise in the gold price from an average realized price of US$90.29 per ounce in the year to 30 September 1973, to an average realized price of US$576.52

per ounce in the year to 30 September 1980. As the price rose, the cut-off grade was lowered in accordance with conventional 'sound mining practice', leading to a smaller gold output per ton milled. (Economists may like to note this as an example of a short-term backward sloping supply curve.) However as equipment got older, and the areas being mined further away from the main shafts, the tonnage milled would have fallen further but for the investment made possible by the IFC loan, which has not only refurbished old equipment but allowed for an expansion of tonnage milled.

By 1983 the structure of fiscal charges which confronted Ashanti was as follows:

1   a royalty of 6 per cent;
2   an export levy of 20 per cent;
3   a minerals duty at a rate variable between 5 per cent and 25 per cent which normally worked out for Ashanti at 10 per cent;
4   a corporate income tax at 45 per cent.

Of these charges all but the last were levied on gross revenues, with the first of them being independent of the enterprise's profitability. However, as a backhanded form of compensation for the overvalued exchange rate, the company was granted a variable Gold Export Bonus calculated on gross revenue. In 1982, when the gold price dropped, this bonus was increased from 10 per cent to 20 per cent.

Fifty-five per cent of any distributional income thereafter would be paid out to the government as majority shareholder, although the price for this shareholding had still not been agreed, or paid.

This set of charges did not constitute a fiscal regime likely to encourage investment in expansion, even if Ashanti – properly structured and properly treated – could have been a highly profitable company. What in fact was happening was that a government desperate for revenue, and especially for foreign exchange, was using it as something of a milch cow.[7] No wonder morale was low; no wonder so many Ghanaians with skills that could be employed abroad, decided to leave.

But there is this to be said for a battered and run down industry. If you take the industry as it is and if you regard rehabilitation expenditures as new investment, then the return from the expenditure required to revert to a much improved proportion of previous production levels can be extraordinarily high.

Even after the previous summer's devaluation of the cedi by 1,000 per cent, a first analysis of the figures presented in 1983 produced four stark conclusions:

1   With no tax change and no expansion, AGC would be unviable within two years.
2   If AGC were to attempt to borrow to expand but remain subject to the current Ghana tax regime, the project would not be feasible because debt service payments would not be adequately covered and the shareholders would have to inject new money to keep it going with doubtful prospects of dividends.
3   With an appropriate new tax regime, the project and AGC could be rendered highly profitable with government still retaining, in one form or another, over three-quarters of the present value of the discounted cash flow.
4   However, under any sensible new fiscal regime, there would be a brief period (probably between 18 months and two years) when the government's receipts from AGC would fall below what they had been getting from the old arrange- ments. After that, the new regime, in association with the new project, would yield the government a very great deal more money.

In physical terms the rehabilitation and modernization programme at Ashanti involved two basic projects.

1   A five-and-a-half-year programme of shaft sinking – two major ore access shafts and one ore-hoisting shaft. One of these in the southern section of the ore body has already been opened and reduces the underground walking of the miners and the distance which the ore has to be hauled by a mile.
2   A three-year re-equipment and modernization programme which will include improvement in the treatment of refractory ores (parts of the ore body where separation of the gold from the host body of material is particularly difficult) and a new plant for the treatment of tailings – in other words, for mining the dumps for residual gold left behind when the price was lower and separation techniques less sophisticated than they are today.

169

As a result of these, both the quantity of ore processed and the recovery rate will be improved. By the end of the project gold production should be up by between 55 and 60 per cent, from a low of some 250,000 ounces a year in 1983/4 to an estimated 398,000 ounces in 1990. The total cost of these works including accumulated interest is expected to be some US$160m.

The financing has been arranged as follows. Half of the funding will be provided from AGC's own cash flow, and a substantial amount ($30.5m) will be provided by export credits. For the balance, IFC – who put the package together – is making a US$45m loan to AGC, US$22.5m for its own account and US$22.5m for the account of participating commercial banks, including Standard Chartered and Union Bank of Switzerland (UBS) as lead banks and also Manufacturers Hanover Trust, Banque National de Paris and Handelsbank NW of Zurich. In addition IFC is making a stand-by loan of US$10m, of which US$5m is for its own account and with US$2.5m each for the accounts of Standard Chartered and UBS.

Most of these loans will carry a fully commercial interest rate, fixed at 14 per cent. The main commercial bank loans will be fully repaid after eight-and-a-half years, IFC's main loan will be completely repaid after twelve-and-a-half years, and the stand-by loans – if they are required – will be repaid after thirteen-and-a-half years.

The middle price for gold assumed in the original project appraisals was US$350 per ounce; recent prices have averaged around US$420. As part of the deal, Ashanti was guaranteed that it could retain 45 per cent of the foreign exchange from its own export sales. Because of the higher-than-projected gold price, the government has urged that this level of retention could be reduced, but – backed by the IFC – Ashanti has resisted this on the grounds that some of the loans are denominated in currencies other than the dollar, and the repayment obligations of these have in fact become more onerous. There is an additional profits tax (APT) in the new fiscal regime which would be triggered when the internal rate of return on the new investment (looked upon as a new project) exceeds 17.5 per cent. The expectation is that this will become payable in 1989, indicating that the rate of return will have been exceeded, and failing any unforeseen disasters, should only climb higher after that.

170

From the losses of 1983/4, AGC recovered to a profit of US$30m in 1987. The projects themselves are 'on track' physically and financially, and are likely to be completed within 2 per cent of the original cost estimate.

The government's new taxation policy for the mining sector was an important part of the programme of structural reforms at that time. The changes made to the fiscal regime were few, but major in their impact:

1 The royalty remained unchanged at 6 per cent.
2 The export levy was reduced to a maximum of 6 per cent, variable downwards under specified circumstances.
3 The minerals duty was replaced by an additional profits tax (APT) at a rate of 25 per cent which would only be triggered when the internal rate of return on the project reached 17.5 per cent.
4 The corporate income tax remained unchanged at 45 per cent.

5 The capital allowances were greatly improved.
6 An investment allowance of 5 per cent was claimable.

This package did the trick, in that it was acceptable to the shareholders and the government and satisfied the lenders, although there were some discussions as to what might have to be done if either the funding ratios or the debt cover ratios (by which the IFC sets much store) did not display satisfactory values.

Two further issues which emerged are worth mentioning because they are likely to recur in similar rehabilitation projects.

The first concerns the valuation of the existing assets in a run-down project. This is likely to be of importance if the investor assisting the rehabilitation is taking an equity stake; it is also of importance if a fiscal charge based on rates of return calculations (such as the APT) is introduced, because a value has to be assigned to the contribution to future output of the existing assets.

The second point concerns that period when the revenues that the government has been taking out of the project have to be reduced – before they can later grow again. Where this occurs, it is helpful if the rehabilitation can proceed simultaneously with a structural adjustment loan, or some other form of sector or programme loan which might help compensate government for this temporary fall in revenue.

171

SOME GUIDELINES TOWARDS THE POSSIBILITIES FOR PROJECT REHABILITATION

Experience to date and the case study cited suggest a number of propositions that can be put forward as a guide towards the identification and design of rehabilitation projects.

1 In circumstances of economic decline, it usually makes better sense to invest in the rehabilitation of existing projects than in the construction of new ones.

2 Given the right policy framework, such rehabilitation projects are capable of showing high rates of return.

3 The right policy framework embraces appropriate macroeconomic policies (exchange rate, control of inflation, containment of government deficit, etc.) as well as appropriate sector policies (pricing policies, controls, lease and licensing regimes, labour policies, etc.).

4 Such a policy framework may require extensive changes to earlier policies – even when these have met with fair success.

5 Most rehabilitation projects are likely to occur in countries already undertaking externally negotiated programmes of policy reform; indeed the covenants attached to the project may themselves form part of that programme.

6 Some rehabilitation projects are likely to involve considerable expenditures in local currency and those of a recurrent nature. If recipient governments are involved in an IMF programme with tight credit ceilings, they may be unable to meet these expenditures themselves.

7 Blocked and counterpart funds may be useful sources for financing the local cost ingredients of rehabilitation projects.

8 Differences exist between rehabilitation of infrastructure and rehabilitation of entities producing for the market, but the rehabilitation of one type is both dependent upon and useless without the rehabilitation of the other.

9 Often it is not the management of the project itself which had caused failure, but the economic and policy environment in which it operated.

10 But rehabilitation projects can also run into unforeseen problems i.e., policy conditions are not met; supporting services are not refurbished; cost overruns occur; value cannot

be agreed for run-down assets; the previous organization may be reluctant to yield managerial control.

11 Good track records reduce the supply price of capital; bad ones increase the required rate of return as well as leading to demands for additional assurances, guarantees and covenants.

12 Even when longer-term capital and foreign exchange for imports has been obtained, short-term local credit can be a problem; a strong partner eases its availability.

13 The abolition of restrictive rules and regulations may be the cheapest and most cost-effective way of achieving the rehabilitation of many projects.

14 Rehabilitation projects can act as 'bright spots'. Each successful one makes the next easier to establish. When a sufficient number of them exist, the whole economy will be on the way to recovery.

But it would seem right to end on a cautionary note. Much may be possible in individual project rehabilitation, but full recovery in many LDC economies may still have to await better prices for commodity exports, fair access to growing OECD markets, lower interest rates and an extinction of a major portion of the country's external debt – in other words a reversal of those trends and influences that have contributed so much to making the rehabilitation of so many projects necessary in the first place.

NOTES

1 One possibility would be to set up a foreign exchange facility off-shore for short-to-medium term finance and to invite private sector firms to tender competitively for access to it by way of the interest rate they would be prepared to offer, with repayments being made in foreign exchange. To avoid abuse the facility itself would have to be the agency which monitored and paid for the required material imports; and to secure repayment it would also have to operate an escrow account into which the proceeds from the consequent export sales would initially be paid.

2 Later, Ghanaians were to be upset by the fact that those shares would have to be paid for in cash, whereas Lonrho had been able to acquire the whole of AGC with an issue of its own shares and debentures.

3 Lonrho had acquired AGC for 15m in 1968, and had asked for 6.1m for the transfer of the 35 per cent of AGC which would have taken the government's holding from 20 per cent to 55 per cent. In the

autumn of 1988 stockbrokers valued Lonrho's interest in AGC at around 100m.

4 *Ghana: The Cocoa Sector*, IBRD Working Paper, Western Africa Programs, Dept 1, Div. B, Adjustment Report no. 4702–GH, 3 October 1983, p. 14.

5 The right policy framework embraces appropriate macro policies (exchange rate, control of inflation, containment of government deficit, etc.) as well as appropriate sector policies (taxation regime, pricing policies, executive probity and efficiency, leasing and licensing regimes, labour policies, etc.).

6 Theoretically, for a company that exports and is obliged to use the official rate of exchange, an overvalued exchange rate results in artificially cheap costs for some inputs (to the extent that these can be imported at the official rate of exchange), but also an artificially low price for that part of its output which is exported. Since the whole of Ashanti's output is exported while only some 40 per cent of its inputs (by value) need to be imported, the loss of revenue obviously far exceeded any savings on cost. Moreover, an overvalued domestic currency itself causes a shortage of foreign exchange, so that production delays and cutbacks may be caused by the difficulty of getting adequate or prompt foreign exchange allocations.

7 'Put bluntly, the treasury cannot go on feeding off the capital of the existing mine while at the same time seeking capital to finance the mine's expansion' was how an internal report put the matter to Ghana's current Minister of Finance.

REFERENCES

Government of Ghana (1983) 'A principled approach to designing a tax regime for mining in Ghana', Accra.

Killick, T. (ed.) (1984) *The IMF and Stabilisation: Developing Country Experiences*, London: Heinemann Educational Books, with the Overseas Development Institute.

Mosley, P. (1987) 'Conditionality as bargaining process: structural adjustment lending, 1980–86', *Princeton Essays in International Finance*, no. 168, October.

9

REHABILITATION OF MANUFACTURING IN SUB-SAHARAN AFRICA
Some macroeconomic issues
John Weiss

INTRODUCTION

At a general level, this discussion raises the question of the link between macroeconomic adjustment programmes and micro-level measures to rehabilitate industrial investments. The focus is on economies of sub-Saharan Africa because not only is the need for rehabilitation in these economies a major priority, but also because their production structure is such that many of the industrial goods currently produced in these economies are clearly uncompetitive in international terms. Current thinking on economic policy reform suggests there is no contradiction between macro adjustments and industrial project rehabilitation. However this can be questioned by dropping the assumption that all manufacturing output is traded, since it is generally traded activities that will benefit from the price signals of current reform packages.

In sub-Saharan Africa manufacturing production has barely risen during the 1980s and in several economies has fallen significantly (see Table 9.1). As is well known, countries in the region inherited a weak industrial base at independence, geared in a typical 'colonial' pattern towards agro-processing activities for export and simple consumer items for the home market. In comparison with higher-income developing economies there has been relatively little development of inter-industry linkages through the production of basic industrial intermediates, with a low share of heavy industry – intermediates and capital goods – in the industrial structure.

Whilst in most countries of the region there is some local

Table 9.1 Recent manufacturing performance in
sub-Saharan Africa: selected economies

	Annual growth of manufacturing (%) (1980–6)	Share of manufacturing in GDP (%) 1965	1986
Ethiopia	3.7	7	10
Zaire	−0.7	16	n/a
Uganda	−0.3	8	5
Tanzania	−4.6	8	6
Somalia	−3.4	3	6
Central African Republic	−0.6	4	4
Kenya	4.1	11	12
Zambia	0.6	6	20
Sierra Leone	2.0	6	4
Sudan	0.0	4	7
Ghana	−1.9	10	12
Senegal	4.1	14	17
Liberia	−5.0	3	5
Zimbabwe	1.3	20	30
Nigeria	1.0	7	8
Sub-Saharan Africa[a]	0.3	9	10
Low-income economies[b]	4.8	10	11

Source: World Bank (1988), Tables 2 and 3.
Notes: [a] Total for the region
[b] Excluding India and China

production in virtually all International Standard Industrial
Classification (ISIC) three-digit branches, this is generally of a
considerably lower quality, and often of considerably higher price
to that of foreign alternatives. Production has only survived
through either import protection, or by serving a separate
segment of the market to that met by imports, with relatively little
manufactured goods exported from the region.

INDUSTRIAL REHABILITATION

Rehabilitation in these countries can take several forms. Critical
in the short term is general import support for the balance of
payments. Here multilateral and bilateral donor aid is given not

for individual projects, but for the purchase of parts, components and raw materials that can stimulate an increase in production. Capacity working is typically very low often due to a scarcity of foreign exchange for the purchase of critical productive inputs. This general import support can be controlled in various ways by recipient governments: some may wish to determine the precise allocation of individual import products between enterprises, whilst others allow varying degrees of enterprise flexibility (for example by open general licences that allow registered producers to import what they feel they need without a specific licence for a particular product).

As a longer-term measure individual enterprises may be selected for rehabilitation. This will involve investment in new plant and equipment often with a significant training component to allow staff to deal with the complexities of the new plant. This type of aid is often undertaken by individual donors who take on rehabilitation of specific enterprises.

Also, as a more general form of support, donors, particularly multilaterals, can set up general lines of credit through the domestic banking system. These will offer local finance to enterprises wishing to undertake rehabilitation, a method often used as a means of reaching small and medium size enterprises who would not normally be identified for specific enterprise rehabilitation by donors.

In addition in most countries in the region new investment expenditure qualifies for generous tax concessions, chiefly in the form of holidays from taxes on profits and dividend distribution for periods often from five to ten years. This is frequently part of a general attempt to revive private sector investment.

Rehabilitation under these various headings is basically a series of supply-side measures aimed at providing productive inputs, new capital assets, and financing facilities to enterprises judged to be in need of rehabilitation. However what must not be lost sight of is the general market environment in which these enterprises operate. In many activities market rehabilitation may be just as important as technical issues relating to the revival of production. However the market environment will be governed by macroeconomic policy, particularly in relation to foreign trade controls, government expenditure and the exchange rate. The type of macroeconomic reform introduced in these economies in

177

recent years is briefly discussed below in order to identify those parts of manufacturing that may have particular difficulties in achieving an adequate market expansion.

MACROECONOMIC REFORMS

The general picture of the region in the 1980s has been of economies characterized by substantial external and internal imbalances, often with severe scarcities of commodities.[1] Parallel markets had developed in response to scarcities and government controls, with often very major differences between official and parallel market prices. The essential features of the adjustment programmes introduced in many countries of the region have much in common with earlier efforts at stabilization and adjustment, particularly in Latin America.[2]

The key elements are a combination of reduction in aggregate expenditure – led by a reduction in the government budget deficit – plus shifts in relative prices through various measures including exchange rate adjustments, tariff reform, trade liberalization, and removal of price controls. The overall effect, initially, of a package of this type is almost always recessionary, and in many instances also inflationary as large nominal devaluations raise import prices.[3] However precise measures of inflation will depend on how the relevant price index is compiled. In several countries post-reform prices have risen very dramatically relative to previously controlled official prices, but probably significantly less so in comparison with earlier parallel market prices. The short-run recessionary impact of the reforms arises through the real cuts in government expenditure, combined with any immediate contractionary effects of devaluation – for example a redistribution from wages to profits with a fall in real wages, or higher foreign debt service burdens in local currency.

The objective, however, is to move the economy along a new growth path – illustrated as a U-shaped curve – with an initial contraction, followed by a recovery, as resources move internally in response to the new price signals of the reform programme. The seriousness of the initial downturn is acknowledged to vary, as will the speed of the recovery; however, where a reform programme is accompanied by foreign exchange inflows – particularly for general balance of payments support – these may

Table 9.2 Composition of manufacturing value-added: selected African economies, early 1980s (%)

	Food products[b] (31)	Textiles wearing apparel leather (32)	Machinery and equipment production (38)	Others	Manufacturing value added per capita (US$)	Index of similarity[c]
Ethiopia	42.1	32.5	2.6	22.8	12	43
Kenya	37.9	12.0	18.8	31.3	34	66
Tanzania	24.8	28.7	11.5	35.0	9	63
Zaire	23.9	26.5	17.2	32.4	7	63
Zimbabwe	14.5	19.1	19.1	47.3	145	76
Zambia	11.1	24.1	20.2	44.6	67	72
NICs[a]	9.4	12.6	37.7	40.3	529	80

Source: UNIDO (1985), various tables.
Notes: [a] Average for S. Korea, Brazil, Argentina, Mexico, and Singapore.
  [b] Figures in brackets refer to ISIC classification.
  [c] Index comparing structure of individual country with that of developed economies (100 = total similarity). See original source for details of the index.

partially counteract the negative short-run effects of the reforms on internal demand.

STRUCTURE OF MANUFACTURING IN LOW-INCOME ECONOMIES

As noted, the structure of manufacturing production in Africa is dominated by 'traditional' activities such as food processing, and textiles and clothing. This is illustrated in Table 9.2 which compares manufacturing composition in selected economies with that in both developed economies and a sample of newly industrializing economies (NICs). However, another critical difference, not brought out in the table, lies in the fact that in the region there is a tendency for a significant proportion of manufacturing output to be uncompetitive internationally and thus to be non-traded; non-traded goods are defined here as those whose use or production affects the domestic economy – through output or price changes – rather than affecting the trade balance.

There is a tendency in textbook discussions to treat all manufacturing as internationally traded, so that goods either compete with imports or can be sold abroad as exports.[4] However, this can be misleading in low income economies where domestic manufactures are often high cost or low quality by international standards. All manufacturing output may be potentially trade-able, in that broadly similar goods are sold on the world market, but for many of these economies local manufacturers, in many production lines, may be either serving a different market seg-ment to that met by imports, or protected from import competition by quota or tariff barriers.

The quantitative significance of the distribution of manufacturing output between traded and non-traded goods will clearly vary between economies, and between forms of local enterprise. Large-scale formal sector enterprises based on for-eign technology – the classic form of import substitution activity – will generally be competing with imports, even if local costs are considerably higher, unless import controls are tight. However, small-scale formal sector producers, and those in the informal sector, may be producing goods of a quality and specification so low as to make exporting impractical, but which can be produced

180

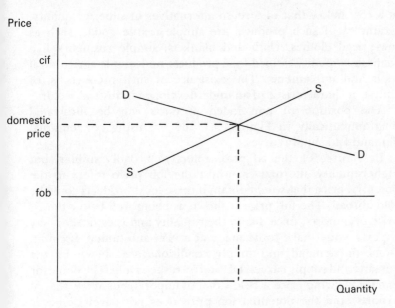

Figure 9.1 Non-traded manufactures: quality differences

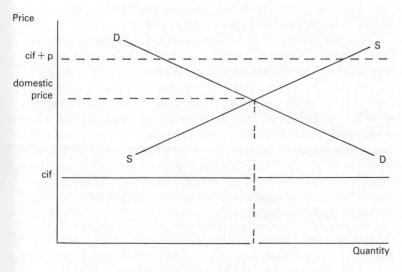

Figure 9.2 Non-traded manufactures: quota protection

at a cost below that of foreign alternatives of superior quality. Examples of such products are simple textile goods, such as low-priced clothes, cloth and blankets, simple cosmetics like soaps, low-quality canned food products, and simple agricultural tools and implements. The existence of such products is, of course, a characteristic of an underdeveloped industrial sector.

The position of non-traded products can be illustrated diagrammatically in Figures 9.1 and 9.2 using conventional demand and supply curves.

In Figure 9.1 the cif price refers to broadly similar, but higher-quality alternatives, whilst the fob price refers to the potential price that would obtain if these local products could be sold abroad. The fob price is shown as being well below the cif price of imports, since due to their quality and specification any exports would have to be made at a very substantial discount. Domestic demand and supply conditions are shown by the demand and supply curves, DD and SS respectively. The domestic market-clearing price is below that of imports, but above that of exports, and the potential fob price does not cover domestic production costs. Due to their quality and price differences such goods serve a different segment of the market to imports, and can only be exported at a price that does not cover costs. Therefore their domestic production has no direct effect on the trade balance – through either import substitution or exports.

Figure 9.2 illustrates the situation where domestic producers operate at costs above the cif price of imports, but where import competition is prevented by either prohibitive tariffs or quota restrictions. The curves DD and SS again represent domestic demand and supply conditions respectively. Now the cif price is raised by a premium p – due to either quotas or tariffs – so that the domestic market-clearing price is below the cost of imports entering the domestic market. Domestic production again has no direct effect on the trade balance; imports do not enter the domestic market, so local production does not substitute for imports, and exports are not possible given high domestic costs relative to world levels.

TRADED AND NON-TRADED ACTIVITIES AND ECONOMIC REFORM

The significance of the distinction between traded and non-traded sectors of manufacturing is that one would expect only the traded sector to benefit from the relative price changes associated with the type of economic reform programmes introduced in the region in recent years. Of central importance is exchange rate policy generally aimed at devaluing the real exchange rate to improve incentives for production of traded goods.[5] Table 9.3 summarizes movements in the real rate in eight countries in the region.

In all but one country the real rate in 1987 is much below that of the early 1980s.

The central importance of the exchange rate in the reform programme advocated for the region is illustrated in influential World Bank reports on policy reform in Africa: World Bank (1981) – the so-called Berg report – and World Bank (1984). On a priori grounds one would expect a devaluation of the exchange rate to benefit all activities producing internationally traded goods. A nominal devaluation raises all prices denominated initially in foreign currency, relative to those denominated in local currency. Provided domestic wages and other local costs do not rise by as much as the nominal devaluation this will create a relative price change in favour of traded activities, and thus a real

Table 9.3 Real exchange rate indices (1982 = 100) in selected African economies[a]

	1983	1984	1985	1986	1987
Gambia	99.0	91.3	100.4	78.2	80.0
Ghana	183.4	25.7	18.6	12.3	8.7
Nigeria	118.4	160.5	145.5	89.2	27.8
Sierra Leone	128.3	146.7	137.9	123.4	52.0
Somalia	95.6	147.9	103.7	67.8	n/a
Uganda	78.2	37.5	61.2	69.3	179.6
Zaire	81.5	45.5	40.9	44.1	36.9
Zambia	91.7	78.7	71.8	35.8	28.8

Source: Roberts (1989), Table 2.
Note: [a]Real exchange rate is period average exchange rates for US dollar deflated by ratio of indices of local consumer prices to industrial countries export prices. A fall indicates a depreciation. n/a = not available.

183

devaluation. The normal prediction of a simple two commodity trade model, with wage and price flexibility ensuring full employment, is that a real devaluation shifts the composition of output towards traded goods.[6] However, it is necessary to distinguish different possible outcomes for different categories of manufacturing, rather than treat the sector as a whole as producing traded goods. Manufacturing exporters are the only group of producers who will gain unambiguously from a devaluation. On the demand side, where they are not price takers on the world market they can use the devaluation to set prices below those of their competitors. Where world prices are given to exporters devaluation raises local currency returns, and thus, other things being equal, encourages resources to shift into export production. Any downturn in domestic demand generated by adjustment policies will free exportables sold domestically for the export market, and thus a decline in domestic income will have a beneficial rather than negative effect on export prospects.

For import-competing or import-substitute products the outcome is less obviously positive. Domestic producers gain on the demand side, since with rising import prices in local currency they can under-price imports. Alternatively if prices of domestic import substitutes rise over time in line with the rise in import prices – so that the law of one price operates – whilst there will be no positive demand effect, local import-substitute producers will receive a boost on the supply side, since their prices will have risen relative to those of non-traded activities, attracting a shift of resources in their favour. However import-substitute production, as it is aimed at the domestic market, is clearly affected negatively and directly by any downturn in domestic demand associated with adjustment policies.

Finally non-traded manufacturers are likely to be affected negatively by devaluation and the associated income adjustments. There will be a positive relative price effect on demand, where traded goods prices rise relative to non-traded goods. However, unless cross-elasticities of demand are high this will be unlikely to outweigh the short-run effect of a fall in income on domestic demand. Furthermore, as net users of foreign exchange non-traded activities will find their costs rise as a result of the increase in import prices. This will be particularly significant in low-

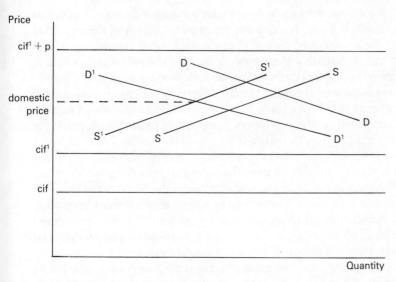

Figure 9.3 Non-traded manufactures: quota protection post-devaluation

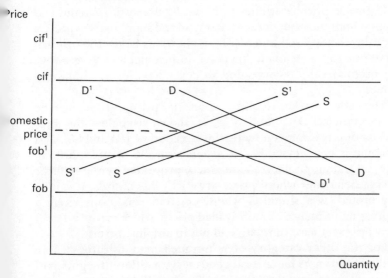

Figure 9.4 Non-traded manufactures: quality differences post-devaluation 1

income economies where import-intensity of manufacturing production is high.

Non-traded manufacturers who produce non-traded goods as a result of quota restrictions on imports may find their market position weakened if trade liberalization – in terms of a reduction in quota controls – is a major element of the policy reform package. Where quotas are weakened significantly or replaced totally by protection through tariffs, this type of good may switch category to become traded with the possibility of a loss of market share for domestic producers if previously frustrated demand for imports can now be satisfied.

Domestic manufacturers who remain subject to quota protection post-devaluation may find that they are unable to raise their output prices in line with the rise in the local cost of imports. Domestic market-clearing prices will be above import levels due to the scarcity premiums created by quotas. With devaluation the most likely outcome is that scarcity premiums will be eroded, and that domestic prices will be determined by domestic demand and supply conditions. For example, Figure 9.2 can be modified as in Figure 9.3, so that cif[1] is the import price at the new exchange rate, and the margin p has been reduced by devaluation.

Domestic price continues to be set by domestic demand and supply conditions, but now new demand and supply curves prevail after devaluation (D^1 and S^1). D^1 is shown as below the original curve due to an assumed downturn in income, and S^1 as above the original supply curve due to cost increases for imported inputs.

The new market-clearing domestic price, given by the intersection of D^1D^1 and S^1S^1, is shown as below the pre-devaluation price, given by the intersection of DD and SS. This outcome is not inevitable – it depends on the relative shifts in demand and supply curves – and can be prevented by oligopolistic pricing behaviour where prices are sticky downwards. It can be interpreted as a situation where demand conditions exert a depressing influence on non-traded prices, which create a fall in their prices, at least in relative, if not in absolute terms.

For the other category of non-traded manufactures, where quality differences mean local goods serve a different segment of the market to imports, the situation is slightly different, as illustrated in Figure 9.4. Here as in Figure 9.1 there is a big gap

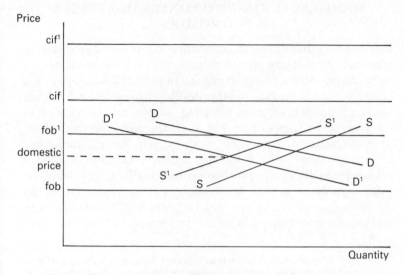

Figure 9.5 Non-traded manufactures: quality differences post-
devaluation 2

between alternative cif and fob prices, because of the large
discounts that would have to be offered to break into export
markets. If the new market-clearing domestic price is still
between the cif and fob prices nothing has changed post-
devaluation; this is illustrated in Figure 9.4, where cif[1] and fob[1]
are the world prices at the new exchange rate and D[1] and S[1] are
the new demand and supply curves.

In Figure 9.5, however, the devaluation has been sufficiently
large to bring the new export price fob[1] above domestic costs of
production, as shown by the new supply curve S[1]S[1], and the
domestic price is below the fob price, so that exporting is now
viable. Here these goods have crossed over into the traded
category, and new exports have been stimulated by a sufficiently
large real exchange rate change and domestic production
conditions which are not so import-intensive for rising costs to
offset the exchange rate shift. This latter scenario is, of course,
one of the most favourable outcomes of reform programmes,
with the generation of new non-traditional exports in response
to the exchange rate change.

MANUFACTURING RESPONSES IN AFRICAN ECONOMIES

It is obvious that different economies will respond in different ways and at different speeds to particular reform packages. In sub-Saharan Africa, where in general industrial development has been carried less far than in other developing regions, a relatively small proportion of manufacturing output can be classed as internationally competitive. This is evidenced by the small share of manufactured exports in total exports for all but a few economies (see Table 9.4). This means that there is only a relatively small export branch of manufacturing to gain from the price signals of a real devaluation. Furthermore, given the acknowledged difficulty of expanding non-traditional exports in low income economies it is surely not very realistic to anticipate

Table 9.4 Manufactured exports in selected African economies, 1986

	Manufactured Exports US$ (million)[a]	*Share in total Exports (%)*
Ethiopia	3	1
Malawi	39	16
Zaire	88	6
Tanzania	58	17
Somalia	1	1
Central African Republic	47	33
Kenya	192	16
Zambia	21	3
Sierra Leone	72	57
Sudan	32	6
Senegal	185	29
Liberia	6	1
Nigeria	99	2
Ivory Coast	289	9
Ghana	22	2
Zimbabwe	365	36
Average low income economies[b]		32
Middle income economies		52

Source: World Bank (1988), Tables 8 and 12.
Notes: [a] at current prices.
[b] excluding India and China.

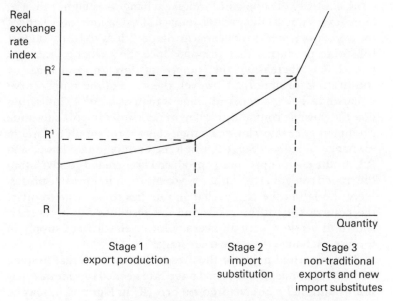

Figure 9.6 Supply of foreign exchange from manufacturing

that a significant proportion of manufacturing output will shift from the non-traded to traded category as illustrated in Figure 9.5. It is well known that simply changing the exchange rate is, on its own, rarely enough to establish a major export drive – with issues of quality control, infrastructure, marketing links and so forth, to be resolved.[7] One would expect, therefore, that in the medium term at least the bulk of manufacturing will be sold on the domestic market – either as non-traded goods or as import-competing import substitutes.

These arguments can be illustrated diagrammatically as in Figure 9.6, which shows a supply curve for foreign exchange from manufacturing rising in response to a rise (that is depreciation) in the real exchange rate index. Figure 9.6 gives a series of stylized stages to indicate different responses within manu- facturing to the price signals from devaluation.[8] At Stage 1 existing export-oriented manufacturers respond positively to devaluation. The magnitude of their additional foreign exchange earnings will be greater the higher is underutilized production capacity. At this stage the supply response to a given change in the exchange rate

– the elasticity of supply of foreign exchange – is higher than at later stages due to the greater impact of exchange rate changes on export-oriented producers. At Stage 2 it is existing import substitute producers that respond once the exchange rate has passed R1, increasing the supply of foreign exchange by substituting for imports. However, the slope of the supply curve is shown as being steeper at Stage 2 than at Stage 1, indicating that the possible counteracting forces restricting import-substitute producers generate a lower average elasticity of supply of foreign exchange. Finally at Stage 3, when the exchange rate has passed R2, producers that previously produced non-traded goods shift to the traded category with either new exports or import substitutes. Here the fall in the real exchange rate has to be large to offset the poor quality of the goods and the response of producers is shown to be slow, with an average lower elasticity of supply of foreign exchange than at earlier stages.

The important point for the present discussion is that in some African economies the real exchange rate needed to generate new non-traditional manufactured exports (R_2 in Figure 9.6) may be below the long-run sustainable level – as determined by demands for foreign exchange, capital flows, and socially acceptable real wage levels. Therefore actual rates may remain above that necessary to trigger significant new exports.

The central hypothesis of this paper is that in African economies it will often be the case that a significant proportion of manufacturing production will be non-traded for the two main reasons of quota protection and quality differences. If this hypothesis is correct it implies that as non-traded products, such manufactures will receive little boost from the price signals generated by exchange rate depreciation. Non-traded activities will look to the domestic market for their demand stimulus and will have their prices set by internal demand and supply conditions. This is where the potentially contractionary effects of adjustment programmes may undermine the domestic markets for particular products, and thus counteract the supply-side rehabilitation efforts noted.

DOMESTIC MARKET EXPANSION

In most African economies there is still considerable scope for import substitution, although clearly this should be relatively

Table 9.5 Imports as a percentage of apparent consumption: selected
products in selected African economies (early 1980s)

Vegetable oils and fats (ISIC 3115)	
Kenya	91.6
Tanzania	67.0
Zambia	45.1
Ghana	70.6
Animal feeds (ISIC 3122–01)	
Sierra Leone	29.7
Uganda	16.3
Congo	32.7
Cigarettes (ISIC 3140–07)	
Ethiopia	21.1
Sudan	45.6
Cotton fabrics (ISIC 3211–28)	
Chad	31.1
Senegal	78.6
Zambia	9.8
Ghana	7.3
Ivory Coast	34.6
Footwear (ISIC 3240)	
Angola	90.9
Kenya	11.9
Malawi	23.7
Mozambique	47.6
Somalia	21.3
Zambia	15.5
Kraft paper (ISIC 3411–25)	
Ethiopia	13.4
Mozambique	64.0
Sudan	62.9
Nitrogen Fertilizer (ISIC 3512–01)	
Mozambique	56.4
Tanzania	90.0
Zambia	80.1
Ivory Coast	79.4
Soap (ISIC 3523–01)	
Ethiopia	51.7
Sierra Leone	42.7
Zambia	44.2
Ghana	42.1
Cement (ISIC 3692–04)	
Ethiopia	17.6
Malawi	20.5
Uganda	71.5
Tanzania	9.3
Ghana	53.8
Ivory Coast	50.3

Source: UNIDO (1985), Table 7.

efficient, so that local costs exceed world prices by a margin that can be justified by infant industry or externality arguments. Using data from the United Nations data base, Table 9.5 gives the share of imports of selected products in national consumption in selected countries.[9] The figures refer only to products where local production is established and omit products where there is as yet no local capacity. Across a range of manufactures, therefore, where there is currently some local production capacity a significant part of the market currently supplied by imports remains to be captured.[10]

How far markets for manufactures will grow in the short to medium term will depend in large part on developments in agriculture. As the main export sector, agricultural producers should gain directly from a devaluation. Further, a shift in the domestic terms of trade in favour of agriculture, as advocated for example in World Bank (1981), is a major plank of current policy reform in the region. Rising agricultural incomes through higher exports and domestic prices can provide a major source of demand for non-traded manufactures – for example simple consumer items like clothing and processed foods, or simple agricultural tools and implements.

The success of a strategy of basing industrial development on income growth in agriculture will depend on several factors. First, and perhaps critical, is the supply response within agriculture to higher producer prices. If due to various supply bottlenecks, or simply because of normal crop gestation periods, higher output is not forthcoming, the rise in producer prices may not have a major impact on total agricultural incomes. Second, there is the impact of higher agricultural prices (and therefore food prices) on the incomes of urban dwellers. Rising food prices will lower urban real incomes and thus reduce demand for manufactures. How far this counter effect of a shrinking urban market is significant will depend on the relative size of rural and urban markets for manufactures. Third, there is the question of the import content of demand from the rural sector. Clearly the higher this is the weaker will be the demand effect on domestic manufacturing from a rise in agricultural incomes. One would expect these considerations to vary between economies, but in general there is the expectation that in the region, on balance, rising agricultural prices and incomes should stimulate non-traded manufacturing. However, the speed of the process and the extent to which it counteracts other recessionary pressures in the economy will clearly vary.

IMPLICATIONS FOR REHABILITATION

If the view of manufacturing put forward here is correct it implies a need to rehabilitate the market and not simply the supply conditions of industrial projects. The concept of market rehabilitation can have different dimensions. At the project level it implies the need for enterprises to move from ideas and practices drawn from an economy of scarcity and parallel markets, where virtually anything produced can be sold, to those relevant to a more competitive environment in terms of the availability of goods. Domestic producers will have to learn to design, market and package goods to meet consumer requirements even if the main focus is on the domestic rather than the export market.

Going beyond individual enterprises to the industrial branch, as an aggregation of enterprises, market rehabilitation implies that demand growth will be adequate to cover the full capacity sales of enterprises in the branch. Trade policy has a critical role in relation to existing import-competing producers, and those that will become import-competing once trade liberalization has removed quota barriers to imports. Here it is important to stress that liberalization, in terms of removal of quantitative restrictions and rationalization and reduction of import tariffs, should not be carried so far as to remove the basic protective margins enterprises need for survival. Protection policy for market rehabilitation must avoid the well-known errors of past import-substitution that established permanently high-cost producers with no incentive to lower costs or improve quality. Market rehabilitation in this context requires designing protective measures – based largely on tariffs – that grant rehabilitated enterprise adequate protection in the short- run, but which build into the tariff system a form of shifting protection that declines over time as a means of stimulating greater enterprise efficiency. Further, the initial level of protection should be based on an assessment of domestic costs in comparison with the price of imported alternatives, so that obviously high-cost activities, with no infant industry potential nor beneficial externalities, should not qualify for protection.

193

Finally, for both import-substitute and non-traded manu-facturing, aggregate demand growth in the economy will be a vital element in market rehabilitation. If internal demand expansion is slow and export prospects for manufacturing are poor there is the danger that foreign grants and credits will go unutilized, if local firms do not have the confidence to borrow for sale to a depressed internal market. A fully-worked out scheme for adjustment that notes the importance of internal demand and rejects the reasoning of orthodox measures still remains to be developed[11]. However, the situation of manufacturing in many economies in the region can be cited as evidence of the need to develop such an alternative perspective.

NOTES

1 World Bank (1981) (1984) and (1989) give the World Bank view on reform in the 1980s. For a critical discussion of the World Bank position see the essays in Ravenhill (1986). For a more recent survey of the position in sub-Saharan Africa see Ravenhill (1988).

2 See Choksi and Papageorgiou (1985) for a discussion of the lessons of this experience.

3 Krugman and Taylor (1978) stress the potentially deflationary short-run impact of a devaluation.

4 For example, Morley (1988), p. 145.

5 Please and Amoako (1986), two economists closely associated with the Berg report, state that: 'Exchange rate policy, in the Bank's view, has to be a central part of any realistic policy framework to achieve African growth and structural objectives' (p. 142).

6 For example, Dornbusch (1980: Chapter 6); see also Corden (1989) for a discussion of the adjustment costs of macroeconomic reform.

7 Weiss (1989) discusses export promotion policies in Jamaica, and points to the limited impact of exchange rate policy.

8 The discussion is stylized in that it assumes only export expansion from existing producers at Stage 1 – the easy stage of export promotion – and only expansion by existing import substitute producers at Stage 2. Finally at Stage 3 only previously non-traded producers are assumed to respond. Clearly, in practice, additional foreign exchange would come from a combination of sources at each stage.

9 In discussing the prospects for further import substitution Ravenhill (1986) cites a Figure of 35–45 per cent of the consumer goods market

in Africa as being supplied from imports. Such aggregate figures are difficult to verify.
10 Some of the papers in Fransman (1982) illustrate problems of import-substitution in the region.
11 Taylor (1988), Chapter 5, begins to sketch out a structuralist alternative.

REFERENCES

Choksi, A. and Papageorgiou, D. (eds) (1985) *Economic Liberalisation in Developing Countries*, Oxford: Basil Blackwell.
Corden, W.M. (1989). 'Macroeconomic adjustment in developing countries', *World Bank Research Observer*, vol. 4, no. 1.
Dornbusch, R. (1980) *Open Economy Macroeconomics*, New York: Basic Books.
Fransman, M. (ed.) (1982) *Industry and Accumulation in Africa*, London: Macmillan.
Krugman, P. and Taylor, L. (1978) 'Contractionary effects of devaluation', *Journal of International Economics*, vol. 8, November.
Morley, R. (1988) *The Macroeconomics of Open Economies*, Aldershot: Edward Elgar.
Please, S. and Amoako, K.Y. (1986) 'OAU, ECA and the World Bank: do they really disagree?', in J. Ravenhill (ed.) *Africa in Economic Crisis*, London: Macmillan.
Ravenhill, J. (1986) 'Africa's continuing crises: the elusiveness of development', in J Ravenhill (ed.) *Africa in Economic Crisis*, London: Macmillan.
—— (1988) 'Adjustment with growth: a fragile consensus', *Journal of Modern African Studies*, vol. 26, no. 2.
Roberts, J. (1989) 'Liberalising foreign exchange rates in Sub-Saharan Africa', *Development Policy Review*, vol. 7, January.
Taylor, L. (1988) *Varieties of Stabilisation Experience*, Oxford: Clarendon Press.
UNIDO (1985) *Handbook of Industrial Statistics 1984*, New York: UN.
Weiss, J. (1989) *Industrial Policy in Jamaica in the 1980s*, Development and Project Planning Centre, Occasional Paper no. 13, University of Bradford.
World Bank (1981) *Accelerated Development in Sub-Saharan Africa: An Agenda for Action*, Washington, D.C.: World Bank.
—— (1984) *Towards Sustained Development in Sub-Saharan Africa*, Washington, D.C.: World Bank.
—— (1988) *World Development Report*, Washington D.C. and London: Oxford University Press for the World Bank.
—— (1989) *Africa's Adjustment and Growth in the 1980s*, Washington: World Bank and UNDP.

10

THE POLITICAL ECONOMY OF PUBLIC ENTERPRISE
Rehabilitation in developing countries
Paul Cook and Martin Minogue

INTRODUCTION

Public policy in LDCs has given a high prominence to the rehabilitation of ailing public enterprises in recent years. This stems in part from pressures of the rising cost to the economy, in the form of subsidies to support loss-making enterprises. Overall deficits of public enterprises in LDCs averaged almost 4 per cent of GDP in the mid-1970s as compared to an average of 1.7 per cent in the industrialized countries (Short 1984). Further, around 25 per cent of these deficits were met by direct foreign borrowing so that during the period 1976–8 public enterprises accounted for more than half of the outstanding external debt (World Bank 1988). The pressure to improve the performance of the public enterprise sector is reinforced through the conditions of World Bank structural adjustment and IMF stabilization lending. In a survey of 94 Fund-supported adjustment programmes in LDCs during the period 1980–4, it was found that 68 of the programmes included policy recommendations relating to non-financial state enterprises, aimed mainly at improving financial performance (Mosley 1988).

Pressure for reforms to public sector enterprises comes at a time when not only is there a concern for their poor performance but also a perceived change in approach towards development policy and process (Cook and Kirkpatrick 1988). With the election to power of strong conservative governments in a number of key industrialized countries and the disillusionment with state planning and large-scale government intervention, there has been a general shift in the dominant paradigm towards a neo-classical, market-oriented view of development. In terms of policies the neo-classical approach has called for a reduction in the size of the public sector, the removal of government regulations and controls, and the creation of competition and greater reliance on the market mechanism for allocating resources. In turn this has had a marked effect on the specific policy proposals made for the public enterprise sector.

This contribution uses preliminary research on the prospects and problems of public enterprise reform, including privatization, in three countries (India, Pakistan and Thailand) to construct an appropriate explanatory framework for policy reform in less-developed countries. The first section examines the theoretical reasoning behind the current proposals for reforming public sector enterprises. The second section notes the slow progress that has been made with implementation. The third section shows that economic arguments for reform have been predominant but finds that economic analysis, although necessary, is not sufficient either to explain why the practical implementation of reforms – especially those to change ownership – has made limited progress, or to provide an appropriate set of recommendations for future action. The fourth section develops a political economy framework that integrates economic and non-economic factors to explain the progress (or lack of it) of policy reforms to public sector enterprises. The final section summarizes the advantages of adopting a broad model for analysing policy reforms.

REFORM STRATEGIES

The reform strategies that have been advocated for public enterprises have taken a number of forms. First, there have been pressures to change to partial or complete private ownership, which is designed to lessen political intervention in the operations of public enterprises. If this has not been contemplated then arguments have been put forward to institute internal reforms to simulate private sector operation while retaining the enterprise in public ownership (Berg 1982, Ayub and Hegstad 1987, World Bank 1983). The latter has often been through establishing holding companies to manage a group of public enterprises. It has often been the case that the degree of public ownership has varied considerably under this institutional arrangement. Overall it has been anticipated that these changes will reduce the overly complex networks of dysfunctional and bureaucratic controls faced by public enterprises by simplifying the objectives they pursue. Second, and related to this, has been the pressure to reform or rehabilitate public enterprises on the basis of property rights arguments (agent–principal). Here it is suggested that a change in the structure of property rights, from complete government ownership to one where management have a more direct stake in an enterprise's future, will improve efficiency of operation (Furubotn and Pejovich 1972). A third element concerns the argument that public sector monopolies need to be broken up to improve productive efficiency. This has involved two principal strands. First is the suggestion that there is a need to foster competition through many firms being able to compete in the same market. Second, stemming from the contestable markets literature, is the argument that actual competition in the sense of many firms competing is not necessary as long as the threat of potential competition exists. This would occur if the artificial controls that inhibit entry were removed making markets more contestable (Baumol and Willig 1986). Finally, a change in the structure of ownership either to full or partial private ownership has been seen as desirable, since it will impose the discipline of capital markets on the enterprise to maximize profits and avoid take-over or bankruptcy.

These arguments for economic efficiency have placed many of the other reasons for reforming public enterprises in the background. These concern the use of public enterprises as instruments for the pursuit of distributional goals, in terms of employment, and as counterweights to the concentration of private market power and the threat of foreign ownership.

Experience with reform of public enterprises

The actual experience with privatization, in the form of complete divestiture, has been modest (Nellis 1986, Cook and Kirkpatrick 1988, Killick and Commander 1988). Even within the wider definition of privatization used by many LDC governments that includes ownership change through joint venture and the introduction of private sector management in a public enterprise, change has remained slow.

The slow pace and lack of implementation has been attributed to a variety of predominantly economic factors. These include: the constraints to changing ownership given by the problem of determining the appropriate valuation for the sale of public assets; the difficulty of disposing of public enterprises owing to insufficiently developed capital markets; the associated difficulty of finding large individual buyers; and the uncertainty as to the economic benefits to be derived from reform, where these concern attempts to increase economic gains from enhanced levels of competition.

Importance of non-economic factors

Our own more recent research in India, Pakistan and Thailand gives additional support to this conclusion by documenting the relatively low level of implementation of reforms, with particularly halting progress towards divestiture (Cook 1988, Cook and Kirkpatrick 1988, ODI 1986). Further, our findings suggest that the economic constraints that have commonly been identified represent only a partial explanation for these trends. It is apparent that the selection of rehabilitation programmes and the effectiveness of implementation, whether involving owner-ship change or not, is closely related to the political and institutional development in each country.

Our concern here is to produce a more balanced explanation than is usually offered of the reasons for this 'implementation gap'. Given the well-canvassed problems of performance in public sector enterprises, and the overt donor pressure for the introduction of privatization programmes, why has the response been so limited and ineffective? The bulk of the privatization literature (see Cook and Kirkpatrick (1988) for a comprehensive survey) has concentrated on detailed assessment of the economic costs and benefits of restructuring policies, while paying only lip-service to problems of implementation and political resistance.

In our own research, discussion of the constraints which surround institutional and policy change in this field consistently produced a response addressed to non-economic factors. These included:

1 A belief that the response of bureaucracies involved in formulating and implementing rehabilitative policies might

cover a range of reactions from reluctant support to downright opposition and recalcitrance. For example, in Pakistan this can be seen within the bureaucratic decision-making process. Privatization of Pak-Saudi Fertilizer and Dandot Cement, with considerable assets, was held up because of a disagreement within the Ministry of Finance over who would finance the underwriting costs of the transfer to private ownership if the issues were not fully subscribed. Similarly, disagreement within the government over the degree and type of concessions that should be given to potential owners of divested businesses, has slowed implementation. Reluctance to change the operating principles of public enterprises can also be detected from the concern shown by the bureaucracy over the erosion of influence that may occur when private investors join the boards of wholly or partially privatized enterprises.

Moreover, resistance to privatization in Pakistan is not confined to the bureaucracy. Holding corporations, that were established as part of an earlier reform programme for public enterprises, may themselves suffer as a result of privatization and, therefore, offer resistance. Although this is unlikely to happen with those gaining from privatization, some, like the State Cement Corporation, would clearly lose if the smaller profitable enterprises under its control were sold to private interests.

In India, a recent report has alluded to the prevalence of public enterprises as conduits of 'black' money. The report links leakages of public expenditure for public enterprises to 'an important source of unaccounted funds for political finance of elections and inter-election political manipulations' (NIPEP 1985). Factors of this kind may well underlie political opposition to privatization, especially from those who have been beneficiaries of such leakages (Pendse 1988).

2   a recognition that the response of labour, especially where public sector unions are strongly organized, well entrenched and politically well connected, is likely to be one of intense resistance. This is likely to be most prevalent where the opposition stems from the fear of a loss in employment security, weakened collective bargaining powers, poor employment conditions and generally diminished rights to organize once privatization takes place. In the context of some

countries, Thailand for instance, this depends heavily on the type of privatization envisaged (ILO 1987). Some strategies that do not involve a direct change in ownership, because the government maintains a controlling interest, would not substantially change workers' rights, since labour relations would still be governed by the rules and laws associated with the public sector as opposed to the private sector. In the former, unions are likely to be stronger, as evidenced by their size and stability of membership (Cook 1988). In cases where outright privatization is envisaged, workers' rights and their bargaining positions are likely to suffer owing to the lower degree of employment security and the tougher policy of employers towards both employees and their unions.

3 to a greater or lesser degree, a continuing attachment to the view that public sector enterprises serve other than commercial purposes, including an implicit or disguised welfare function. In the case of India this can be seen in the employment obligation which extends into the private sector as well as the public sector. The strength of this obligation can be illustrated by reference to the privatization of scooters (the only recent example) which could only take place after the government granted the new owners concessions over labour retrenchment. The importance of employment protection can also be seen in Pakistan, in the decision not to sell textile plants in Baluchistan even though they are economically unviable. In this case, they have actually been closed down but not legally liquidated; nevertheless the government continues to pay the labour force.

4 a persistent view that the state must retain a clear responsibility for economic management and an associated competence in management and administration. It is notable that all three countries, India especially, have a commitment to centralized economic planning. Under these circumstances it would be difficult to inject private sector management disciplines, which characterize commercial enterprises facing competition, into the public sector. In the case of Thailand, for instance, this would entail a potentially infeasible challenge to the entrenched practice of short-term placements of inexperienced managers, often drawn from military ranks, in senior positions in public enterprises.

5 in the cases of India and Pakistan, but less so in Thailand, a concern with political accountability. In India, a clear link is perceived between legislative accountability and the political responsiveness of public sector organizations. The incorporation of social and economic welfare objectives in the Indian constitution, and the strong value attached to the achievement of social welfare objectives through centralized economic planning, reinforce an evident reluctance by the central bureaucracy and political leadership to consider retrenchment of the public sector.

In Pakistan, a conditioning feature is the high level of political uncertainty in the post-Zia period. The return to democratic civilian government and a political leadership which has electorally committed itself to a programme of state-led welfarism may create a political climate hostile to a dilution of centralism, and will certainly produce a conflict of view with donor agencies.

ANALYSIS OF ECONOMIC AND POLITICAL INTERACTIONS

It is evident from these and other studies (Ascher 1984, Brett 1988a, Craig 1988, Nelson 1984) that economic management and economic performance are unquestionably political matters. Consideration of the issues of policy and management involved in the rehabilitation of public sector enterprises, especially where the innovative thrust takes the form of liberalization and privatization programmes, requires an explanatory framework capable of integrating the economic and political factors which are explicit in all substantial areas of state economic policy in less developed countries. Not only do economists 'tend to analyse policies in ways that ignore essential political reactions', they also tend naïvely 'to assume that a policy's stipulations will be straightforwardly translated into reality' (Ascher 1982). Ascher recognizes that an 'economic accommodation' model at least allows for a dilution of policy intentions by the reactions of economic actors, but rightly challenges the ability of this model to grasp the complex range of reactions to economic policies which emerge through the political process.

It is necessary to construct a less narrow framework for

economic and political interactions to do full justice to the complexity of these interrelationships. Such a framework will incorporate the economic postulates of rehabilitation policy but will then proceed to consider the impact and significance of non-economic factors, particularly those identified with 'politics'. Politics must, however, be dealt with much less crudely or sceptically than is customary in economic analysis. To reach a full understanding of the weight to be attached to politics, it is essential to examine several components: the public policy process, the political system which determines the decisions which emerge from that process, and the administrative system which is responsible for the implementation and evaluation of such decisions. What *should* happen (formal plans, rational solutions, external donor preferences) is invariably subordinated to, and conditioned by, these ineluctable internal political and administrative processes which determine what, in practice, actually *does* (or does not) happen.

In the first place, then, it is necessary to examine the public policy process in less developed countries in order to delineate the whole range of administrative and organizational constraints which will limit the implementation of privatization and related policies (for a full examination of the problems of policy implementation in LDCs see Grindle 1984). As Brett points out 'State structures in the Third World are widely regarded as rigid, inefficient, overstaffed, and corrupt . . . [and] . . . the orthodox form of public service organisation is seriously deficient in many ways' (Brett 1988b).

Restructuring reforms are, of course, intended in part to address precisely this problem: but how can we expect a rigorous and efficient implementation of such reform policies when the principal instrument of implementation must, and can only be, the defective bureaucracy itself? Only where the bureaucratic machinery is driven hard by a political leadership strongly committed to specific reform is the state bureaucracy likely to deliver those reforms effectively (as, for example, in Korea, see Park 1986).

But this combination of efficient bureaucracy and firm political commitment is uncharacteristic in less developed countries. Rothstein (1976), discussing politics and policy-making in the

Third World, has drawn attention to the

> difficulty of breaking out of a set of powerful constraints upon
> the political process: . . . constraints such as elite corruption
> and conflict, segmented and mistrustful groups, the centrality
> of the political struggle in the absence of alternative
> structures of power. . . . These are powerful constraints, and
> they clearly limit the results that can reasonably be expected
> from the policy making systems of developing countries.
>
> (Rothstein 1976: 695–6)

He goes on to point out that 'weak governments have enormous
difficulty in controlling or altering policies once made.
Procrastination, altering as little as possible, becomes a political
way of life' (Rothstein 1976: 695–6). Perversely, it may seem,
strong and authoritarian governments are no more likely to be
innovative than weak and ineffectual ones. In many less
developed countries, strong government means military government; and, as Shackleton points out 'the military (with some
exceptions) are no great supporters of the free market. They use
orders and regulations in their own field, and too often regard
similar controls over economic activity as appropriate. They are
themselves major beneficiaries of statism' (Shackleton 1987).

This leads inexorably into a question characteristically ignored
or sidestepped by development economists: how should we
handle the power relationships contained within the Third World
state? (see Nixson and Leeson 1988). This is especially significant
in a policy area which itself involves an ideological debate about
the proper limits of state power. The question of political power
raises further questions about political groupings and elites,
about conflict between groups and the tendency for any
substantive area of economic policy to become a political arena
in which group conflicts are played out. As Rothstein puts it:

> The political systems of many LDCs. . . . are split by sharp
> conflicts over very scarce resources between groups that mistrust
> each other and share only the desire to control the state for
> their own benefit. There is little consensus, there are insufficient
> resources to satisfy all groups, and the losers fear (with much
> justification) that they will be permanently denied access to
> the political arena and to their fair share of benefits.
>
> (Rothstein 1976)

This conceptualization compels some attention to what has been described as 'the suppressed question of the privatisation debate' (Killick and Commander 1988: 1472). Does privatization represent a shift in values about the most productive way of allocating resources? Is it likely to bring greater distributional efficiency? The practice of privatization appears, to Killick and Commander, to produce contradictions; on the one hand, 'the substitution of market-determined prices for the previously subsidised prices will create a group of unambiguous losers'; on the other hand, 'one of the motives behind the divestiture movement has been a desire to promote a 'crony capitalism', from which the relatives, friends and supporters of members of a ruling group are the chief beneficiaries' (Killick and Commander 1988: 1472–3). The focus here remains on the question, what are the distributional effects of privatization? Yet, as we have noted earlier, there has been relatively little practice of privatization in LDCs, surely not enough on which to base a confident discussion. We need to look through the other end of the telescope, and see that if benefits (whether economic or political) flow from existing public sector agencies to specific (and powerful) social and political groups, there will be resistance by these groups to policy changes which will alter or remove these benefits. Hood (1979) identified this as the problem of 'recalcitrance', that is, the resistance and antagonism of vested interests in the target population. If such groups, whether of labour or capital, are well-organized and politically well entrenched, the effective implementation of state policies is bound to run into difficulties. These difficulties will be all the greater, and the pace of innovation so much slower, if recalcitrant groups are located within the state and public enterprise bureaucracies themselves. Experience of privatization in developed economies has clearly demonstrated the organizational, political and financial costs involved in such resistance (Minogue and O'Grady 1985). Resistance is likely to be stronger (and either more costly, or more effective in preventing policy changes) in less developed economies, where public enterprise agencies often constitute patron–client networks which lead back directly into the political and bureaucratic elite groups responsible for policy reforms (Pendse 1988; Sandbrook 1988). In such cases, political commitment will be weak, and bureaucratic responses reluctant. It is clear that for effective policy change to take place, economic rationality must be supported by political will, which must be able to command organizational obedience. But if strong political values are attached to existing institutions, these values are likely to conflict with, and possibly override the economic values contained in policy innovations. The acceptance and implementation of economic reforms, is heavily dependent upon the political character of the public policy process.

CONCLUSIONS

It is not new to notice the significance of the interaction of economic, social and political factors: Myrdal (1968) long ago coined the term 'the soft state' to capture this interaction, and Hirschman (1970) almost as long ago constructed a valuable typology of the political constraints upon economic action. But their books would appear to have been left unopened by a later generation of development economists, who suffer from what might be called 'politics-blindness'. There are clear advantages in using a broad framework which integrates economic, political and administrative analysis of rehabilitation and policy reform. Such an analysis engages closely with the real policy implementation process in less developed countries. It provides a convincing explanation of policy failure, or ineffectiveness. It enables identification of the political and managerial constraints which may limit the possibilities of implementation, or determine which types of reforms are possible and which unpromising. From a prescriptive point of view, this political economy approach is a better guide than the conventional economistic approach which tends to assume away political and bureaucratic constraints. It offers, therefore, an effective method for considering what policy changes may be realistically prescribed, adopted and carried through. Moreover, this is a type of analysis which can be sensitively applied to differing political and policy systems. Finally, it offers a coherent and inclusive theoretical and research base on which to build a more effective practice, whereas analysis which examines economic factors and options alone will be incomplete, tendentious, and ultimately impractical. The application of a political economy approach to the current experience of privatization in LDCs would lead us to agree, with Brett, that the failure of the state to control its own servants should not simply be seen as an economic problem to be resolved by privatisation (i.e. by dismembering the state) but also as a political problem to be resolved by improving the political and administrative mechanisms which have failed.

(Brett 1988a)

It is the neglect of this insight which is the greatest weakness in the current analyses of public enterprise rehabilitation policy and practice.

REFERENCES

Ascher, K. (1984) *The Politics of Privatization: Contracting Out Public Services*, London: Macmillan Education.

Ascher, W. (1982) 'Political forecasting and development policy', *Vierteljahresberischt*, no. 90, December.

Ayub, M. and Hegstad, S. (1987) 'Management of public industrial enterprises' *World Bank Research Observer*, vol. 2, no 1, pp. 79–101.

Baumol, W. and Willig, R. (1986) 'Contestability: developments since the book', *Oxford Economic Papers*, vol. 38 supplement, pp. 9–36.

Berg, E. (1982) 'Changing the public–private mix: a survey of some recent experiences in LDCs', DM/83/10, IMF: Washington DC.

Brett, E.A. (1988a) 'States, markets and private power: problems and possibilities', in P. Cook and C. Kirkpatrick.

—— (1988b) 'Adjustment and the state: the problems of administrative reform', *IDS Bulletin*, vol. 19, no 4, pp. 1–11.

Cook, P. (1988) *Economic Liberalisation, Privatisation and State Enterprise Efficiency in Less Developed Countries*, Report to British Council/Overseas Development Association, September.

Cook, P. and Kirkpatrick C. (eds) (1988) *Privatisation in Less Developed Countries*, Brighton: Wheatsheaf.

Craig, J. (1988) 'Privatisation in Malaysia: present trends and future prospects', in P. Cook and C. Kirkpatrick (eds), *Privatisation in Less Developed Countries*, Brighton: Wheatsheaf.

Furubotn, E. and Pejovich, S. (1972) 'Property rights and economic theory: a survey of recent literature', *Journal of Economic Literature*, vol. X, no 4, pp. 1137–62.

Grindle, M.S. (1984) *Politics and Policy Implementation in the Third World*, Princeton, NJ: Princeton University Press.

Hirschman, A.O. (1970) *Exit, Voice and Loyalty: Responses to Decline in Firms, Organisations and States*, Cambridge, Mass.: Harvard University Press.

Hood, C. (1979) *The Limits of Administration*, London: John Wiley.

International Labour Organization (1987) 'Privatisation – its impact on labour relations in ASEAN', ASEAN Tripartite Symposium on Privatization, Chiang Mai, Thailand, February.

Killick, T. and Commander, S. (1988) 'State divestiture as a policy instrument in developing countries', *World Development*, vol.16, no 12, pp. 1465–80.

Minogue, M. and O'Grady, J. (1985) 'Contracting out local authority services in Britain', *Local Government Studies*, May–June, pp. 35–50.

Mosley, P. (1988) 'Privatisation, public-based lending and World Bank behaviour', in P. Cook and C. Kirkpatrick (eds) *Privatisation in Less Developed Countries*, Brighton: Wheatsheaf.

Myrdal, G. (1968) *Asian Drama*, London: Penguin Books.

Nellis, J. (1986) 'Public enterprises in sub-Saharan Africa', mimeo, Washington DC: World Bank.

Nelson, J. (1984) 'The political economy of stabilisation: commitment, capacity and public response', *World Development*, vol. 12, no 10, pp. 983–1006.

NIPEP (1985) *Aspects of the Black Economy in India*, Delhi: The National Institute of Public Finance and Policy.

Nixson, F. and Leeson, P.F. (1988) 'Development economics and the state', in P.F. Leeson and M.M. Minogue (eds) *Perspectives on Development: Cross-Disciplinary Themes in Development Studies*, Manchester: Manchester University Press.

Overseas Development Institute (1986) *Privatisation: The Developing Country Experience*, Overseas Development Institute Briefing Paper, London: ODI.

Park, Y. (1986) 'A system for evaluating the performance of government-invested enterprises in the Republic of Korea', *World Bank Discussion Papers*, no 3, November.

Pendse, D.R. (1988) *Privatisation: Myths and Realities*, Project for Economic Education, Bombay.

Rothstein, R. (1976) 'Politics and policymaking in the Third World: does a reform strategy make sense?', *World Development*, vol. 4, no 8, pp. 695–708.

Sandbrook, R. (1988) 'Patrimonialism and the failing of parastatals: Africa in comparative perspective', in P. Cook and C. Kirkpatrick (eds) *Privatisation in Less Developed Countires*, Brighton: Wheatsheaf.

Shackleton, J.R. (1987) 'The political economy of privatization in less developed countries', Unpublished paper to UK Development Studies Association Annual Conference, September

Short, R. (1984) 'The role of public enterprises: an international statistical comparison', in R. Floyd, C. Gray, and R. Short, *Public Enterprise in Mixed Economies*, Washington DC: IMF.

World Bank (1983) *World Development Report*, London and New York: Oxford University Press for the World Bank.

—— (1988) *World Development Report*, London and Washington, DC: Oxford University Press for the World Bank.

Part V

PROJECT REHABILITATION: MANAGEMENT AND INSTITUTIONAL ASPECTS

11

INSTITUTIONAL CHANGE AND PROJECT REHABILITATION
Hardware, software, and liveware
Tom Franks

INTRODUCTION

The term 'rehabilitation' is commonly used, in the context of the socially handicapped or deviant, to describe the process by which the deviant is brought to conform to society's norms and values. In development it has the same connotation: 'restoration to proper condition . . . effectiveness or normal life'; but there are a range of meanings within this general definition. On the one hand, it can mean a series of actions intended to restore a facility (human or physical) to the operating state for which it was originally designed. Very often, however, when development practitioners talk of rehabilitation, they are in fact referring to a process whereby the facility is changed so that its new operating state is different from that for which it was originally designed. We might call this 'renewal' or 'modernization', rather than 'rehabilitation'. 'Reform' is another word often used in a similar context, being particularly related to organizations or institutions. Reform in this case can have the same range of meanings, from changing the institution so that it functions as originally intended, to changing it so that it functions in new, and presumably improved, ways.

There are many examples of rehabilitation in modern development. On the one hand, structural adjustment programmes may be seen, at least by the donor countries and lending agencies, as designed to restore the economies of the recipient countries to a 'normal' condition. Institutional reform programmes are also common, not only in developing countries but in international agencies (Collins 1987) and in the industrialized countries as well. At the other end of the spectrum, rehabilitation

213

projects abound, covering a wide variety of sectors and countries. These range from the repair of infrastructural facilities (water supply systems in Uganda, school buildings in Sri Lanka) to the updating and improvement of industrial concerns and other productive assets (irrigation systems in Java, textile mills in Africa). Debt rescheduling and financial rescue packages may also be seen as rehabilitation efforts, either on an economy-wide scale or at the level of individual enterprises. Thus we can use the word rehabilitation to apply to a process of reform or renewal of the complete range of human, physical or financial assets for productive and non-productive functions.

REHABILITATION AND THE NEED FOR INSTITUTIONAL CHANGE

Rehabilitation, in its strict sense, implies that while there is change the overall effect of the change is to restore the situation to its original condition – in other words, change and no change. An understanding of this apparent contradiction is a key to understanding the essential differences between rehabilitation and other types of development. Whilst all development efforts imply planned change to improve conditions, rehabilitation is designed to restore the *status quo*. Thus, for a facility starting at state A, there may be a process of deterioration over time leading to state B (see Figure 11.1). At this point there may be a need for rehabilitation, implying change and restoration to state C, at which the level of performance is the same as state A. Alternatively, a policy of renewal or modernization may be followed, implying change and an improvement in performance leading to state D. New development, by contrast, starts from the position in which there are no existing facilities in the conceived form, implying improvement up to state E.

Rehabilitation is often a preferred option at the present time for a number of reasons. First, there may be a general desire, or indeed a necessity in the case of physical facilities such as water supply systems, to make existing assets work in the way they were originally designed. Second, the techniques of project analysis and appraisal may particularly favour opportunities for rehabilitation. The use of existing assets often means that the returns to the incremental investment required to raise

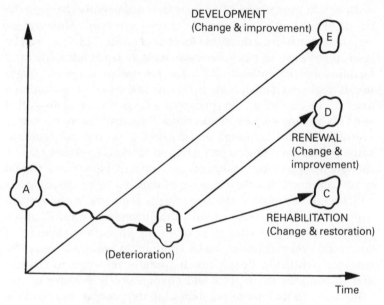

DEVELOPMENT
(Change & improvement)

RENEWAL
(Change &
improvement)

REHABILITATION
(Change & restoration)

(Deterioration)

Time

Figure 11.1 Rehabilitation and development

performance to the originally designed level are very high. Indeed there are many examples of rehabilitation projects which could in fact be seen as the final tranche of investment required to implement the project in the first place. Third, opportunities for new development may be limited, as available locations and resources become fully utilized.

In this consideration, however, it is necessary to distinguish between the use of physical assets and non-physical or institutional assets, the latter category comprising the organizations, procedures and people concerned with the operations of the existing system. If we call the physical assets the 'hardware' of the system, the organization and procedures make up its 'software'. There has been a tendency to include people within 'software' but it is helpful to think of people, with their complex attitudes, aspirations and behavioural patterns, as a separate and distinct category of assets – the human capital of the facility, which we might call its 'liveware'. These three categories, hardware, software and liveware make up the total assets or value of the facility.

Rehabilitation is very often a preferred alternative because the re-use of existing assets reduces the apparent level of investment required to achieve a desirable level of benefits. This may well be true in the case of physical assets such as land, infrastructural facilities and equipment which the rehabilitated system might use. It might even be thought to be true in the case of institutional assets. For instance, the presence of skilled or semi-skilled workers already employed may reduce the investment needed in recruitment and training, whilst existing procedural relationships such as land tenure patterns and marketing chains may be thought adequate for the rehabilitated system. However, it should not be assumed that the presence of existing institutional assets will necessarily reduce the investment required in the human capital of the facilities, or simplify the processes of rehabilitation. Whilst institutional change is often an important element of successful rehabilitation, achieving it in practice may be extremely difficult. People are frequently reluctant to change, and institutions themselves will change slowly because of this reluctance. In the case of rehabilitation the process may be made more difficult because the end result of the change may be a return to the original state, a process of change and no change which provides little motivation for those involved.

Another important factor in rehabilitation concerns the latent inability of organizations to change. Most organizations concerned with operating existing facilities are bureaucratic to a certain extent, in that there are established procedures and regulations for dealing with the situations that are commonly met during the normal operations of the facilities. Indeed, the bureaucratic properties of organizations in this situation are actually an asset. The end-users of the facilities expect a certain degree of regularity, stability and predictability from the organization, since otherwise they would not be able to plan or rely on that end-use. However, whilst stability is generally an asset during normal conditions, it does imply that such organizations are inherently reluctant to change. This may be particularly important for rehabilitation where the final result of the proposed change may be no different from the organization's avowed objectives at the present time. A further factor reinforcing this is that, commonly, bureaucracies are much more inclined to punish mistakes and deviations from established norms than to reward good performance or productive effort. Typically, therefore, project agents involved in a situation with potential for rehabilitation, will, at least in the first instance, be concerned to ensure that no changes take place. In that way, no blame or sanction can be applied to them. In new development, by contrast, there are no pre-existing procedures or conditions, and therefore no inherent constraint to accepting the changes which the investment is likely to bring.

Institutional arrangements existing prior to rehabilitation may well benefit some people connected with the project. Except in the case of complete failure and disuse of the facilities, some operations are being carried out which will be benefiting one or other group, perhaps a particular department within the organization, a certain group of traders, or a specified location of beneficiaries. Thus, while rehabilitation may seem to be of potential benefit overall, certain groups may stand to lose heavily from the proposed changes and are therefore being quite pragmatic if they oppose them. Here again, there is a contrast with new development which is designed to bring benefits to end-users and to reward project agents for their involvement in the investment through salary payments and incentives of various kinds. It is admitted that the reality often falls very short of the ideal and that investments often have unintended effects in disadvantaging those affected (including end-users, others in the environment, and project agents).

Nevertheless, such unintended negative effects are much more likely to occur in rehabilitation where patterns of service and delivery have already been established. Change nearly always involves conflict. In the case of rehabilitation, the conflicts may be particularly severe.

THE FRAMEWORK FOR INSTITUTIONAL CHANGE

In seeking to develop a framework for understanding institutional change, it is instructive to consider how management studies can help us. Much of such study has its origins in the industrialized countries and is often considered inappropriate in the context of developing countries. However, in the case of institutional change there is an unexpected relevance and we can find, at the very least, fruitful ways of beginning to think about the problems of implementing institutional change in support of rehabilitation. For instance, two seminal management studies of the twentieth century – the Hawthorne lighting studies of Elton Mayo and the longwall coal mining studies of Trist and Bamforth – were both concerned with assessing the effects of experiments designed to improve the productivity and working procedures of members of existing work organizations. Therefore, although the term 'rehabilitation' was not used directly, a process of reform and renewal of existing human capital was being described.

These and other studies are in fact helpful to our consideration of rehabilitation processes in a wider sense. They are part of the development of management thought from the Scientific Management School of the early twentieth century (which viewed both worker and organization in mechanistic terms) to the idea of a socio-technical system in which technical production modes are seen as underlain and interwoven with a social system relating the organizations and institutions involved. Both the Hawthorne studies and the longwall coal mining studies emphasize the inter-dependence of technical systems and organizational structure. Whilst neither of these relate to rehabilitation in its most narrowly-defined sense, in that both sets of measures were intended to improve productivity rather than to restore it to its originally designed state, yet both have important implications for many rehabilitation projects, which too often concentrate on changing the technical systems (the hardware), without at the same time assessing the necessary changes to the institutions that operate them (the software and liveware). The concept of a socio-technical system arose from the understanding that any production system requires both a technological structure and work organizations and procedures relating those who carry out the various tasks to one another.

Smith *et al.* (1982) have some useful general perspectives which can serve as a basis for a conceptual framework of institutional change. First, people are most willing to change if they are sympathetic to the changes and if they see the change to be in their best interests. The role of participation is very important to the acceptance of institutional change, since people generally like to have a say in change which affects them. In this respect, of course, rehabilitation is no different from other kinds of development: the importance of participation by the beneficiaries

218

and those involved is now constantly being stressed by development theorists and practitioners. Second, resistance is a normal and healthy reaction to proposed change. Institutions need to develop a degree of regularity and predictability in their operations or else they will not be able to perform their functions effectively. To do this they need, at least initially, to be able to resist forces tending to push them to change. Third, institutions must be viewed in the context of the whole, and not just selected parts. They are complex entities, and change in one part may well have far-reaching effects in other, quite separate parts.

With these perspectives as a basis, we can develop a framework for institutional change which has three major elements:

1 change of and for the individual;
2 change to organization structures and procedures;
3 change of organizational culture (ideology).

Such a framework closely follows analysis by Porter, Lawler and Hackman (1987) and Mitchell (1978).

Change of and for the individual

Change of and for the individual is an important element in a process of overall institutional change. It is not useful to design changes in the pattern of organizational systems and procedures if those who have to work the procedures are not themselves changing in a complementary way. It is rational that a human being's initial response to imposed change is one of resistance, since most people condition their lives to some degree to afford stability. Change threatens that stability and takes them into the unknown. Some writers have categorized an individual's resistance to change in two forms – systematic and behavioural. Systematic resistance arises from a lack of appropriate knowledge, skills and information. Behavioural resistance is emotional in nature and relates to reactions, perceptions and attitudes, such as perceived threats to status or suspicion of motives for change (Lawrence 1975).

Various methods of effecting individual change can be identified, some related to the psychological setting of the individuals themselves and some related to their work. The former category ranges from the direct use of information to various types of skills and sensitivity training. In the latter category job enrichment and job enlargement are examples of measures which try to change individuals by changing their work. Such measures, which have been much favoured in industry, are designed to increase the autonomy of individuals within the organization, thereby bringing about a change in their attitude and their responsibility towards the quality of their work.

Changes to organization structure and procedures

A second aspect of institutional change is to change the organization structure and procedures within which the individual operates. Such measures are often included during rehabilitation (for instance, new management structures, and operation and maintenance procedures for rehabilitated facilities). In considering such changes, Porter *et al.* (1987) distinguish between 'anatomical' features and 'operational' features. The former group comprises those which are evident in the organizational chart and include job titles and descriptions, formal roles, communication, and reporting relationships. 'Operational' features refer to institutional processes of job enrichment and enlargement described in relation to individual change. All such measures are intended to promote autonomy and the potential for self-realization by the individual, so as to assist organization change and increase organizational effectiveness. These, of course, may be accompanied and supported by changes in organizational authority systems, and appraisal and reward systems. All of these change the way the organization structure operates and may thus be used to promote organizational change in support of rehabilitation.

Changes to the organization culture

Some writers refer to organization structure and procedures as the 'visible' spectrum of an organization, implying parameters which can be clearly identified and defined and which are amenable, at least in theory, to considered adjustment in support of institutional change. Alongside the visible spectrum of an organization is an 'invisible' spectrum, whose constituent elements are, by contrast, neither readily definable nor amenable to adjustment by standard techniques. Such elements include the norms (unwritten rules of behaviour), beliefs and values, personal aspirations and goals, power networks, informal relationships, motivation, loyalties, and commitments. These are sometimes referred to as the organization's culture or ideology and are very important in determining the way the organization functions. Franks (1989) has described a recent survey of the cultures perceived to be operating in a number of development organizations. This survey highlights the significant differences that sometimes exist between the formal organizational procedures (for example, how decisions are made, how promotion is achieved) and the informal methods by which the organization actually works. Whilst the formal structure is often bureaucratic, the culture may be quite different in ways that may sometimes help and sometimes hinder the rehabilitation process and the effective functioning of the rehabilitated system.

INSTITUTIONAL PROCESSES SUPPORTING REHABILITATION

Motivation is an important process promoting institutional change in support of rehabilitation. However it is to be done, those concerned with rehabilitation must be motivated to take part in it and to support the objectives of the rehabilitation programme, otherwise those objectives will not be achieved. Participation is an important way of providing motivation, as with other development initiatives. People will support more readily those sets of actions to which they have been able to contribute at the planning stage, since they will internalize the programme objectives by early involvement. They may also, of course, contribute a significant amount in knowledge and understanding of the practical aspects surrounding the proposed programme, including the factors leading to the present situation and the likely or possible consequences of proposed changes. Managers of rehabilitation projects must therefore identify how best to involve existing or potential project agents and beneficiaries in the design of rehabilitation. Ideally these agents and beneficiaries should assist in identifying unacceptable operating conditions and in defining the objectives of rehabilitation, in order to support rather than subvert these objectives.

Information and communication systems are key elements in supporting successful rehabilitation. Even if they are not able to be actively involved in the planning process, project agents and beneficiaries must at least be fully aware of the proposed programme so that they understand its objectives and proposed procedures. As discussed, people naturally dislike change and will be reluctant to change unless they fully understand the proposal. This is likely to be particularly so in many rehabilitation programmes, where risk avoidance is an important and common behaviour, often for very good reasons.

Training has an important role to play in support of all planned change. In the case of rehabilitation there may be problems in training operators to improve performance in what is effectively the same job. How can the need for training be justified to an individual who is already performing the job for which the training is supposedly required. Alternatively, training may be required precisely because low levels of skill and ability contributed to the degradation of the facility in the first place. Once again, however, the incentive to undertake the training may be lacking in those needing it. Even where rehabilitation is not involved, training in developing country organizations is often less successful than desired because those who receive training use it as an active means of self-development and change jobs or seek promotion. The motivation for such actions is increased in rehabilitation, where the outward status of the individual may not change at all as a result of training. Rehabilitation runs the risk that the agents involved are required to change existing skills, habits and procedures without any necessary indication that they will be able to develop their own talents or that their situation at the end of the process will be different from that at the beginning.

A further element in institutional change is the use of external (or sometimes internal) change agents who stimulate or facilitate the change process. Smith and his co-workers (1982) divide change agents into three main categories, change generators, change implementors and change adopters. In the first two categories the agents can come from both within and outside the organization. In rehabilitation, external change generators (consultants) are commonly used to identify factors leading to deteriorating performance and to plan and initiate measures to rectify the situation. Very often, it is easier to perform these functions when coming from outside, since past experience and relationships within the organization will inhibit acceptance of changes originated by existing organization members. However, it is also necessary to recognize and support those within the organization who will readily adopt the proposed changes. Managers often need, therefore, to pay particular attention to the change adopters within the organization who can see the advantages of the planned changes and will adopt them as models for other organization members.

A set of 'anatomical' measures to change organizational structures concerns the establishment of project teams or matrix structures. These are discussed by Youker (1977). The underlying idea is that organizational change will be more readily achieved if there is a project or task orientation – projects and tasks implying an intended change within a specified time. Project teams are self-contained teams set up to achieve these objectives, whilst matrix structures attempt to graft a project or task orientation to an existing institutional structure which is established on functional lines. The use of project or matrix teams is one way by which an attempt can be made to modify a bureaucratic organizational culture. Both of these can be successful in promoting organizational change in support of rehabilitation.

Change in organizational culture has received particular attention in the management literature, through its emphasis on the influence of peer groups and the use of team or group processes. Organizational development techniques lay great stress on team building and on coping with conflict within organizational groups. They also stress the use of change agents as catalysts for change and the importance of feedback and review by participants of how the organization is functioning. Whilst much of this clearly has its origins in work done on business organizations in the industrialized countries, and finds a more receptive climate there, it is interesting to reflect on what modifications to the techniques may be necessary to make them appropriate in the situation of developing countries.

Support at the highest levels of the organization is necessary if institutional changes required for rehabilitation are to take place. 'Global experience indicates that planned (administrative) change, to be effectively implemented, requires unequivocal and sustained political support' (Collins 1987: 131). Senior managers and directors must internalize the objectives of rehabilitation as much as their operating staff if the whole process is to succeed.

REHABILITATION IN THE IRRIGATION SECTOR – THE INSTITUTIONAL ISSUE

Developments in the irrigation sector provide good examples of many of the points discussed so far. There is an increasing interest in rehabilitation in this sector as available water resources become fully utilized and new development becomes more expensive. Additionally, rehabilitation, in the form of modernization or renewal, has been practised for many years, as schemes are modified to allow for increased demands or new cropping systems. In the rice growing countries of the humid tropics, for instance, rehabilitation projects in the past decade were often designed to enable double or triple cropping of rice. As these countries reach self-sufficiency in rice, rehabilitation projects now often have as their objective diversification out of rice cropping, as well as general repairs and improvements to the water distribution system and procedures.

Hardware, software and liveware are all very important elements in the rehabilitation process. Irrigation development is capital intensive, with large engineering and construction inputs. (New developments often cost in the region of US$10,000/ha, whilst rehabilitation projects can be up to US$2,500/ha.) Attention to system hardware is therefore a major component of irrigation rehabilitation. At the same time software is very important to efficient and effective irrigation. Examples of such software include the operation and maintenance procedures for water delivery and allocation, and the water rights and land tenure systems that pertain on the scheme. Liveware is also an integral part of irrigated production, since it requires major skilled and unskilled labour inputs. Many types of production relations can be found on different irrigation systems but perhaps the most common situation involves a government agency responsible for the storage, conveyance and distribution of the water, whilst farmers or farmer organizations are responsible for the allocation of water to the fields and other agricultural practices.

An irrigation scheme is thus a good example of a

socio-technical system, in which a technical mode of production is underlain by a complex web of interlocking social and institutional systems. To be successful, rehabilitation of irrigation schemes requires attention not only to hardware improvements but also institutional change relating both to software and to liveware. For example, considerable attention is now focused on sustainability, which, in the case of irrigation, will often mean the ability of a scheme and its operating agency to continue operation without support and subventions from central government. Whether or not this can occur will depend, amongst other things, on software procedures (for instance can water charges be levied and collected in sufficient amounts to cover operating expenses?) and the skills, capabilities and attitudes of the farmers and managers involved. Rehabilitation, to make a lasting impact, will need to pay attention to all these factors.

Such points are made clearly in the conclusion to a working paper describing the rehabilitation of an irrigation scheme in Sri Lanka. The major premise underlying the present approach to the rehabilitation of the scheme is that the primary reason for poor system performance is the dilapidated condition of the system. Therefore, improving the physical system is the key to improved performance and all other efforts take second place to the major investment in physical improvements.

> There is no doubt that physical improvements are needed. However, our observations of the pilot field channel suggest that the basic premise of the project may not be entirely correct. From our observations, it would appear that the fundamental problems are *behavioural*, and not just physical. That is, changes in the behaviour of both the farmers and the officials (which together form an integrated social system), and the associated values and expectations, as well as physical upgrading are required if the performance of the Walawe Scheme is going to be improved.
>
> (Merrey and Jinapala 1988: 9)

Some examples of the problems encountered in irrigation rehabilitation are discussed by Burton and Franks (1989). Their discussion focuses on the government agencies responsible for supplying water. They note that these are often referred to as irrigation 'bureaucracies', because they notionally apply formal rules and procedures to water distribution and other operations. The farmers who use the agencies' services value the stability, predictability and accountability inherent in a bureaucratic structure. Even though the operational system may not be optimal, it is better for farmers to know clearly the way the system will behave, rather than for it to be uncertain and liable to unpredictable change.

The culture of an irrigation agency will determine to a large extent how that agency deals with farmers, how receptive it is to new ideas, how easily it will adopt new techniques or improved methods. As Moore (1981) puts it, 'aspects of the prevalent ideology of public service discourage realistic and useful administrative innovation'. This may occur particularly in the lower ranks of the agency where staff rely on a higher level of educational achievement and the personal prestige of attachment to government service to maintain their superior status over farmers. They cannot allow this to be jeopardized by allowing genuine participation to take place, in which they might appear as the equals or even the inferiors of the farmers. This is not always the case, of course, and many committed and know-ledgeable junior staff exist in irrigation agencies all over the world who are able to consult and discuss management requirements with farmers easily and on an equal footing. Most irrigation rehabilitation projects imply a more open and participatory management process; part of the important change required in the software of rehabilitation is to develop an organiz-ation culture which fosters such a process. This in turn requires an increased openness, technical knowledge and self-confidence on the part of the agency staff.

It is hardly surprising that irrigation agency staff are generally quite reluctant to change. In the case of rehabilitation projects, they are working within a known system with a known set of rules and procedures. As long as they continue to operate within those standards, no negative sanctions can be applied to them. If they become involved with the change implied by rehabilitation, not only are they stepping outside the norms, with all the risks that entails, but they are also likely to come into conflict with water users on the irrigated area who benefit from the existing procedures and correctly perceive that they stand to lose after the process of rehabilitation. Irrigation staff, particularly at the local level, may well be risk-avoiders in the same way that farmers often are. Rehabilitation, because it is a deviation from the norm, is a risk.

An interesting example of an irrigation bureaucracy at work was observed on the Rice Canal in Pakistan (Franks 1986). It was discovered that the same incorrect data on water abstractions and irrigated area were being reported year after year, the aim of the irrigation agency being to be able to communicate to the central organizations that 'there was no adverse change from previous years' practices, that abstractions had been maintained at normal levels, and that there has been no unusual losses, damage or crop failure'. It was also found that significant improvements to the condition of the irrigated area (which was suffering severe waterlogging), could have been obtained by some alteration to the dates of opening and closing the seasonal canal. Such measures, however, which are a form of rehabilitation, were likely to be strongly resisted by those at the head of the area who benefited from the late opening. As the irrigation agency's headquarters were also at the head, the engineer concerned would face extreme pressure from those benefiting from existing procedures and would suffer severe criticism if changes were made. The landowners at the head, who had developed over many years into a strong and influential pressure group, would be quite capable of sidestepping the engineer and going to his superiors or the local politicians, and could probably, in the final outcome, have him removed from his post. The incentive on the part of the engineer to become involved in the changes implied by a rehabilitation programme in conditions such as these is therefore minimal.

Another interesting example of similar bureaucratic rigidity is the case of senior irrigation officials responsible for the Gezira Scheme in Sudan. For many years farmers have been ignoring the established procedures for abstraction of water from minor canals. These canals were originally designed to be operated during daylight hours only, with water being stored in the minor during the night. Farmers found this unsatisfactory and gradually moved to a system of continuous 24-hour abstraction. Officials in the irrigation bureaucracy adamantly refused to accept that this was happening, despite evidence to the contrary (Francis and Hinton 1987). The Gezira Scheme is currently undergoing rehabilitation. It will be interesting to see if the irrigation officials can be persuaded to accept the logic of change in the established procedures.

However, in spite of these problems, there have been some notable successes in effecting change in irrigation bureaucracies. For instance, in 1975, proposals were prepared on behalf of the Indonesian government for new operation and maintenance procedures in one province. Two pilot schemes were established and the introduction and use of the new procedures monitored. In 1980 the procedures were officially adopted for use throughout the province and in 1982 a pilot training programme was initiated to train irrigation staff in the new procedures. The training programme has now been extended to all parts of the province. The introduction of the new procedures has taken time and considerable effort (not least in convincing senior staff trained in the previous procedures) but change has occurred, on the whole successfully. An important feature implicit in the new procedures is that they be updated gradually to a more sophisticated level as the need and the capabilities of both the staff and the farmers rise. This establishes that the process of change should be continuous if the irrigation systems are to remain flexible, adaptable and responsive to farmers' needs. Change can be implemented, though there are risks involved. It is the confidence of the staff within the agency that these risks are worth facing that leads towards an administration which is in touch with reality (Burton and Smout 1986).

One comprehensive attempt to change the whole organizational culture of an irrigation bureaucracy which has been well-documented is in the Philippines (Bagadion 1985). While much of this documentation concerns the development of the irrigators' organizations, there is a good deal on the changes required and effected in the implementing agency – the National Irrigation Administration. It is interesting to consider how many of the concepts of organizational development (OD) were used in this process even if they were not labelled as such directly. They included, for instance, the widespread use of pilot projects to develop successful methods and approaches, and a conscious effort to learn by feedback from previous experience. A further technique borrowed from the OD armoury was the use of change agents to introduce and catalyse successful approaches. Third was the use of particular groups to foster and support changes in organizational culture. In this case it took the form of a committee composed of irrigation agency officials, academics and representatives of the donor agencies which helped to:

identify agency procedures that interfered with successful work; to ensure that successful methods were written down for later use in training; to develop new agency capacities when field-level experience indicated that they were needed; to sponsor workshops to spread awareness of the new approaches within the agency . . .

(Bagadion 1985: 85)

Similar experiments have been going on in Sri Lanka concerning institutional innovation in the irrigation bureaucracy. The most interesting of these concerns the creation of the Irrigation Management Division (IMD) to provide a forum for the development of positive relationships between farmers and line agencies concerned with irrigation (Harding and Franks 1988). It is an attempt to change both the organizational structures and, to an extent, the invisible spectra of the agencies concerned with irrigation, to reduce their bureaucratic rigidity and make them more flexible and adaptive in responding to the demands of modern irrigated production. A particularly interesting aspect of the experiment is the decision, by the Sri Lankan authorities, to deliberately keep the organization of the IMD as small as possible, in order to avoid unnecessary expense and bureaucracy. A further sign of the move towards institutional change in the irrigation bureaucracy is the forthcoming management training programme within the Irrigation Department. This training should go some way towards providing individual change, to complement the various structural and cultural changes being introduced through the IMD. Together they should create a beneficial climate for the necessary software changes to support hardware changes in rehabilitation projects.

Whilst Burton and Franks (1989) concentrated attention on the problems of irrigation agencies, considerable work has been done with farmer organizations. In this regard there have been some notable successes such as the use of 'institutional organisers' to develop farmer organizations on the Gal Oya rehabilitation project in Sri Lanka, this particular example being well documented by Uphoff (1986). By contrast, the introduction of water users' associations in Indonesia has been less successful. These were introduced by presidential decree in 1984 but there are as yet few groups which are actually functioning as intended (the local term is that they are still 'sleeping'). There are no doubt many reasons why the groups are not yet functioning, but possibly a major cause is that the supposed beneficiaries – the farmers – can perceive no direct benefit to themselves in the arrangement. Failure to elicit active support resulted in failure, which was perhaps not at first readily apparent since the required committees were set up and meetings held. However, little of practical value materialized since the initiative was passively resisted by inactivity. Indeed few changes appear to have been made in the decision-making processes within the irrigation agency to cater for the water users' associations, which have been given no power to influence decisions outside the field units (which they already control). In this case attention had been given to changes to the visible spectrum of the organization (organization structures, committees, meetings) without the necessary complementary changes to the invisible spectrum (perceptions, attitudes, relationships) that make up the culture of the irrigation agency.

CONCLUSION

This discussion has highlighted three major elements of the rehabilitation process (see Figure 11.2). On the one hand, there is the important factor of improvements to the physical assets, or hardware. Such improvements must, however, be accompanied by institutional improvements to be fully effective. Within institutional improvements we can distinguish two strands, changes to and for the individuals concerned with the system (the 'liveware'), and changes to the organizations and procedures (the 'software'). Rehabilitation occurs within a time-frame, normally in a project or a programme, and transforms the existing system into the rehabilitated system. The rehabilitation process may be intended simply to restore the system to its originally designed operating state, or to modernize it to provide an improved level of services to its customers or beneficiaries.

To be successful a rehabilitation project must give sufficient weight to all three components in the process. Whilst this is also

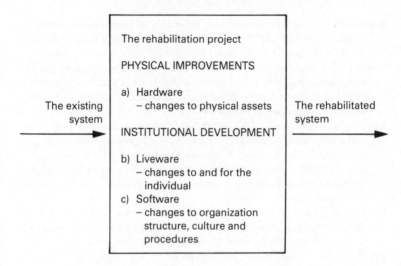

Figure 11.2 Rehabilitation processes

necessary in the case of new (greenfield) development, rehabilitation faces special difficulties in relation to institutional change. The re-use or improvement of existing physical assets is one of the reasons why rehabilitation is often an attractive proposition for owners, since it leads to high notional rates of return. Existing institutional assets (people, organizations and procedures), on the other hand, may pose constraints rather than opportunities because they are inherently difficult to change.

Overall, there may be little incentive for the institutions concerned with a rehabilitation project to change in the manner that is required. They already have established procedures to operate the facilities in one way and will naturally be somewhat reluctant to change these, particularly if the net result of the change is a restoration of the *status quo*. Additionally, some of those involved may correctly perceive that their interests are actually disadvantaged by the proposals and may therefore oppose them, overtly or covertly. The outcome may therefore be, at best, passive resistance, at worst, conflict and sabotage. Proposals for insti- tutional change and methods for affecting it therefore need special attention during rehabilitation.

231

REFERENCES

Bagadion, B.U. (1985) 'Developing irrigators' organizations: a learning process approach', in M.M. Cenea (ed.) *Putting People First: Sociological Variables in Rural Development*, Oxford: Oxford University Press.

Burton, M.A. and Franks, T.R. (1989) 'Successful rehabilitation: can old habits be changed?', paper given at Asian Regional Symposium on the Modernization and Rehabilitation of Irrigation and Drainage Schemes, Philippines, February.

Burton, M.A. and Smout, I.K. (1986) 'Training programmes for irrigation staff and farmers', ODI/IIMI Irrigation Management Network Papers 86/1d and 86/1e, London: Overseas Development Institute.

Collins, P. (1987) 'Implementing administrative reforms in international development organizations', *Public Administration and Development*, vol. 7, pp. 125–42.

Francis, H.R.H. and Hinton, J. (1987) *Minor Canal Management in the Gezira Irrigation Scheme, Sudan*, Interim Report, ODU Research Report, OD/93, Hydraulics Research Ltd, Wallingford, UK.

Franks, T.R. (1986) 'Water management on the Rice Canal System, Pakistan', *Irrigation and Drainage Systems*, vol. 1, pp. 5–18.

—— (1989) 'Bureaucracy, organization culture and development', *Public Administration and Development*, vol. 9, pp. 357–68.

Harding, T.M. and Franks, T.R. (1988) 'The matrix management of irrigation projects: integrated management of major irrigation schemes in Sri Lanka', *Agricultural Administration and Extension*, vol. 28, pp. 133–46.

Lawrence, P.R. (1975) 'How to deal with resistance to change', *Harvard Business Review on Management*, New York: Harper & Row.

Merrey, D.J. and Jinapala, K. (1988) 'On physical remodelling and institutional strengthening: an evaluation of the implications of the pilot field channel experience for the rehabilitation project at Uda Walawe, Sri Lanka', International Irrigation Management Institute. Working Paper no. 7.

Mitchell, T.F. (1978) *People in Organizations: Understanding Their Behaviour*, New York: McGraw-Hill.

Moore, M.P. (1981) 'The sociology of irrigation management in Sri Lanka', *Water Supply and Management*, vol. 5, part 1, pp. 117–33.

Porter, L.W., Lawler, E.E. and Hackman, J.R. (1987) *Behaviour in Organizations*, New York: McGraw-Hill.

Smith, M., Beck, J., Coper, C.L., Cox, C., Ottaway, D. and Talbot, R. (1982) *Introducing Organizational Behaviour*, London: Macmillan.

Uphoff, N. (1986) 'Activating community capacity for water management: experience from Gal Oya, Sri Lanka', in D.C. Korten (ed.) *Community*

Management: Asian Experiences and Perspectives, Connecticut: Kumarian Press.

Youker, R. (1977) 'Organization alternatives for project managers', *Harvard Management Review*, vol. 5, pp. 112–21.

12

PROJECT MANAGEMENT IN THE CONTEXT OF CHANGE

Farhad Analoui

INTRODUCTION

While the failure of a development project may have myriad causes, insufficient attention to managerial aspects is often a major factor. Rondinelli, for example, states that, 'Most attention has been paid to the financial, economic and technical feasibility and very little concern has been shown for the effectiveness of the management requirement of the development projects' (1980: 5). As long ago as 1974, Waterston argued that the presence of factors such as a lack of coordination, inadequate monitoring systems and inappropriate organization design played a decisive role in project failures. More recently writers such as Ashley *et al.* (1987) and Duffy and Thomas (1988) have claimed that the way project managers 'manage' must be considered the prime cause of project failures.

It does not come as any great surprise therefore to read that it has recently been recommended that, 'The supreme importance of good management for the success of a project must always be kept in mind' (ODA 1988: 72). The dominant tradition of project management, characterized by an overemphasis on predictability, control and general disregard for external factors, typically prescribes 'good management' as an all-embracing cure for project ills. Obviously what could be termed as 'good management' is somewhat disputable. It is a well-known fact that project managers have to cope with ambiguities, unpredictability and uncertainty. The 'traditional' approach to project management, it will be argued here, ignores the crucial role of management in terms of monitoring unpredictable and ever-changing external factors.

However, before we embark on this, the historical development of the prescriptive style of management with its unmistakable characteristics will be traced. Its implications for projects in general and those in need of rehabilitation in particular will be outlined. Then, in the light of this discussion, an alternative approach based on the descriptive philosophy for the management of development projects, in the context of change, will be offered.

THE PRESCRIPTIVE APPROACH TO PROJECT MANAGEMENT

The art of management in its modern-day form has not been achieved overnight. Its historical development can be traced back to the turn of the century when early attempts were made to conceptualize the industrial organization.

These early attempts emerged within the United States and came to be known as Scientific Management. This school advocated prescriptive management and organizations were primarily examined from the functionalist perspective. This soon grew to the point where it was, and has remained, the dominant sociological perspective.

> The functionalist paradigm provided the dominant framework for the conduct of academic sociology and the study of the organizations. It represents a perspective which is firmly rooted in sociology of regulation and approaches its subject matter from an objectivist point of view.
>
> (Burrell and Morgan, 1979: 25)

Not surprisingly, with the unavoidable advent of industrialization, continuous technological achievement and the growth in size and complexity of organizations, the need for regulation and order increasingly became the focus of attention.

The overwhelming preoccupation with 'objectivity' and 'regulation' meant that organizations and the relationships between their members were studied and analysed in attempts to establish a set of general principles and guidelines for their efficient operation. Observations and analyses made of such things as structural design, managerial and administrative knowledge and skills were thought to possess universal applicability

235

(Braverman 1974). The classical theory of management advocates that there is a best and most efficient way of managing organizations (Silverman 1970). This resulted from the combined efforts of a number of innovative theorists and writers on organization theory. They sprang from a variety of disciplinary backgrounds including psychology, sociology, scientific and administrative management, microeconomics and public administration. Prominent writers such as Taylor (1911), Mooney and Reiley (1931) and Weber (1947) were particularly interested in the ways in which the activities of people could be organized and managed in order to achieve maximum efficiency and productivity. The contributions made by writers such as Cyert and March (1963), Alfred (1965), Simon (1965), and Drucker (1970) are further examples of the prescriptive philosophy.

When considering the present state of organizations – including projects – and their management, either in Western societies or less developed countries, it is imperative to remember that the theories of Scientific Management and the notion that certain principles of organization are universally applicable have remained influential. For example, Fayol's (1916) thesis that eight basic functions (namely: deciding objectives, forecasting, planning, organizing, motivating, coordinating, controlling and communicating) represent the process of management in any organization, large or small, public or private, manufacturing or services, still forms the basis for many discussions concerning the management of development projects in the official textbooks provided by the funding agencies. This preoccupation with mechanistic objectivity can be traced back to the 'telling period' when the renowned theorist Weber (1947), a major pillar in the development of classical organization concepts and the founder of modern sociology, introduced bureaucratic organizations as being the 'ideal type' of organization (Pugh *et al.* 1976). The bureaucratic model has formed the basis of most organizations in the private and public sectors in today's developing countries. It is only recently that bureaucracy has been labelled as 'red tape' and acquired its negative connotations. For many years, bureaucracy was prescribed as being the most efficient organizational form and suitable for the management of complex organizations (Kast and Rosenzweig 1974).

When we consider the main ingredients of the bureaucratic

model it is not difficult to discern why it became popular. It advocated a hierarchical power structure in which superiors exercised authority over their subordinates. Rational and legal authority was based upon the position of the role occupier in the hierarchy. There was a delineation of power and rewards in the form of monetary compensations. It was also a form of organization which was based on impersonalized work relationships, and individuals, regardless of their position, could be assessed in terms of their technical competence. Those found wanting could be penalized. It was believed that this model could function as an instrument of the efficiency which was sorely needed by large-scale organizations in both Western societies and developing countries.

This approach to organizations was based on scientific rationality. The prescription was that organizations must be approached as if they were rational phenomena. This was supported by the methodological presupposition that, 'there is a hard concrete reality which can be systematically investigated' (Burrell and Morgan 1979: 128). One fundamental implication is that it should be possible to subject organizations to total control. This was not only thought to be applicable to the behaviour of the organizations in relation to the achievement of their stated goals, it also had implications for the behaviour of those who worked for the organization.

From the classical theory perspective people in organizations are regarded as, 'Rational economic [beings whose] feelings were irrational and their activities had to be carefully circumscribed and controlled to ensure that it would not interfere with the effective performance of the organisational task' (Eldridge and Crombie 1974: 116). Therefore, it is hardly surprising that a commitment to efficiency and the optimum way of doing things was seen to be critical to the role of management (Mangham 1979).

Amongst the many criticisms which the prescriptive style of management has received is that, for example, it promotes a simplistic and naïve approach to the management of organizations and that its principles are primarily constructed upon a 'mechanistic model' (March and Simon 1958). It is also criticized because it offers too narrow a perception of the managerial role and regards organizations as being 'without its people' (Bennis 1966). Of course, this should not be taken too

237

literally, people *were* seen as parts of an organization, but only as cogs in a machine.

Despite these criticisms, the principles of the classical theory of management flourished, first in the Western world and then inevitably in less developed countries. This led to the importation of knowledge and technology. Indeed 'in most developing countries socio-economic development involves a massive transfer of technology from industrialised countries. Such a transfer indeed requires increased competence and high qualification levels of workers' (Naymark 1983: 87). However, it has also been questioned whether such transfers of organizational designs or management skills are useful to the process of development and whether they enhance the quality of life of the population of recipient countries (Mansfield and Zeffane 1983).

DESCRIBING A ROLE FOR THE PROJECT MANAGER

The tendency of classical theorists, including microeconomists, has been to regard an enterprise in the context of a 'closed mechanical system' and to pay scant regard to the external environment (Morgan 1986). Equally, people within the organization are regarded as machines which are mainly responsive to their immediate environment. As they are also thought to be economic creatures they were more often than not seen and treated as units of cost. The role of managers was to maintain the organization in such a way that it remained cost effective and economically viable. This philosophy is in operation in most developing countries, especially when it concerns the management of development programmes and activities. As Kast and Rosenzweig aptly summarize, 'Micro-economics as a normative theory attempts to prescribe what [the manager] should do in order to maximise profit' (Kast and Rosenzweig 1974: 72).

The management of development projects was developed against this deterministic background of prescribing the best way of doing things to achieve rapid national development. Baum's (1978) early writing on the 'project cycle' was a general introduction to the World Bank procedure and exemplifies the widespread preoccupation with classical principles of organization and management theory. The early management administration theorists such as Fayol (1916), Mooney and Reiley (1931), and Koontz and O'Donnel (1968) viewed organizations as simple 'input–process–output' mechanisms. They also viewed organizations as being static and in isolation from the environment in which they exist. They have evidently been very influential in affecting the perspective of the external funding agencies towards development projects as this is precisely how these bodies appear to view development projects (Analoui 1989b). From this perspective the role of a project manager is primarily seen to be that of an 'implementor', as somebody who is simply carrying out instructions received from above.

The contention of this chapter is that the failure of many projects can be traced back to the application of prescriptive managerial philosphy with its desire for predictable outcome. It has almost become a rule that a project will begin, start to founder and then become eligible for the next, virtually inevitable stage: that of rehabilitation.

When a project fails to achieve some or all of its objectives, it is regarded as a dysfunctional mechanical structure; the 'wornout' or 'defective' parts are replaced with new ones. The outcry is that more financial input is required in order to revitalize and thus restore the project to its previous condition. Rehabilitation in this context may even involve restructuring the project organization and a complete or partial change of the management team. This is done in the hope that this time it may succeed. Often the rehabilitated project fails again, simply because the role of management in monitoring the unpredictable and ever-changing external factors is underestimated.

THE DEVELOPMENT AND THE NEED FOR MANAGEMENT OF PLANNED CHANGE

In the late 1960s views concerning the structure of organizations and the ways in which their activities could be managed began to change. This was partly due to the fact that the shortcomings of the prescriptive philosophy had become increasingly evident, both in Western societies and in developing countries. Bureaucracy as a model for organization and management can be held responsible, to a greater or lesser extent, for the failure of many development projects. Inappropriate organization structure and inadequate management were held by many to be the main contributors to the high failure rate. Rondinelli criticizes the key actors involved in the realization of the development programmes, asserting that 'The World Bank appraisers give the problems of managing projects little attention, instead they concentrate on financial, economic and technical feasibility' (Rondinelli 1980: 21).

Arguably, with the work of Goodman and Love (1980) the need to move away from a static approach towards a more dynamic conception of the management of development projects has become increasingly evident. Unlike the advocates of the prescriptive philosophy, they view development programmes as essential means for the realization of planned change, albeit within a specific socio-economic context. In this way development is viewed as, 'Related to selected planned changes in social and economic structures of the society in an effort to reach predetermined objectives acceptable to society as a whole' (Goodman and Love 1980: 3).

It could be argued that development programmes should be viewed as deliberate intervention schemes. A realistic position for project management is to describe the art of effectively managing the realization of desirable planned changes within a dynamic environmental context (Analoui 1989a). This view of management takes the role of the project managers beyond the conventional boundaries where predictability and control is overemphasized. In other words, in accordance with Sayles (1964: 258–9) 'Only managers who can deal with uncertainty, with ambiguities and with battles that are never won, but only fought well, can hope to succeed.'

However, it is not only the environmental context in which the development project is operating which is subject to change. The organization's activity itself can experience unpredictable changes due to gradual or sudden changes in the behaviour of its members. Moreover, the perception and the needs of the beneficiaries of a development project could change. This factor is often underplayed when the success or failure of a particular project is discussed.

The implications of this for the management of development programmes and projects, whether a manufacturing plant or an agricultural scheme, are basically threefold. First, it is evident that the managers of planned change activities ought to possess the necessary qualities to facilitate the process of transmuting a 'given' state to that of a 'desired' one; second, a development project once it has achieved the 'desired' state should ideally become capable of being a self-maintaining entity. However, this would only be possible if managers are capable of being flexible – that is, they should be able to change and adjust in direct relationship to the ever-changing demands of the external environment and internal world of the development project (Analoui 1989a). Third, not only must development project managers react to what is happening in the external environment, but, in return, they must also inevitably act on other organizations and institutions within their immediate environment and beyond. That is, development projects individually and collectively contribute to energizing those processes involved in perpetual development and change. These implications will be fully explored below.

Phases in the management of development projects

First, in order to explore the ramifications of these three points in relation to development activities, a methodology for the carrying out of effective intervention needs to be worked out. Such a methodology must also have the potential to be used as a diagnostic tool in order that a project's activities can be explained, irrespective of its objectives, size, location, or sector in the context of planned change.

As illustrated in Figure 12.1, development projects can best be regarded as the means by which a desired change can be realized. That is, they can be seen to bridge the gap between the original and the desired state. For example, in an agricultural project, the aim might be to increase the annual crop yield by 30 per cent. A project in which pesticides were to be used could then be seen to bridge the gap between the original and desired state. In a further example, the objective may be to increase the output of a power plant from 130 megawatts to 200 megawatts. The installation of another turbo-charged generator may well be seen as the means by which the gap between the original and desired state could be bridged. Planned change can also be concerned with human performance. For example, in order to render the senior

241

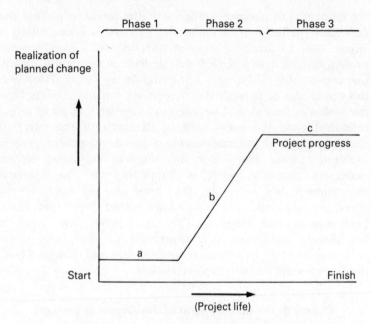

Figure 12.1 Development in the context of intervention and change

Notes: Phase 1, Identification and preparation;
Phase 2, Implementation; Phase 3, Operation and maintenance.
a = actual state; b = development gap; c = desired state.

managers of a credit organization more efficient, their training needs could first be identified and a training programme devised to achieve that desired efficiency. Smith *et al.* (1982) put forward a similar view of organizational change. That is, we can intervene in order to achieve a desired change in an organization. However, these authors, like so many who deal with the subject of change, tend to assume that the circumstances prior to and after intervention may remain unchanged. Smith *et al.* view the process of planned change as the unfreezing of the old state in order to create yet another frozen state. Arguably, as stated earlier, in the field of development although the completion of a project marks the achievement of the desired state, it does not guarantee that that particular state will remain desirable. Unfortunately, the traditional prescriptive philosphy has generated a situation where projects are viewed as a disjointed series of activities. It is often assumed that the task is complete when implementation has been successfully achieved (Iglesias 1976). This itself accounts for many project failures. Therefore, while the impression commonly given by some writers is that project management should primarily be concerned with the implementation of a project phase, it is quite clear that pre- and post-implementation phases are crucially important. These phases should also be included in the range of responsibilities which are assigned to the managers of development projects.

Descriptive management of development projects may consist of the following three interrelated phases:

1 identification and preparation;
2 implementation and transformation;
3 operations and maintenance.

These broad phases also correspond to those employed in the process of managing planned change. These are:

1 the identification of the gap between the present and the desired state, and the preparation of the ground to achieve the desired state;
2 the transformation of the present to the desired state;
3 The realization and maintenance of the changed state.

In this way the maintenance of a successfully implemented project is as much a part of the project management's responsibility as is ensuring that, for example, the feasibility studies made prior to embarking upon the implementation activities are accurate.

Thus, project management is viewed as the art of managing organized activities which are aimed at the achievement of development through the realization of planned intervention schemes. To achieve its goals and objectives the organization needs to be equipped with inbuilt continuous self-performance monitoring and feedback systems to ensure its continued sustainability. In this way, the principle role of management would be to ensure the realization and integration of the three phases identified above. It is to these three phases that we now turn.

THE IDENTIFICATION AND PREPARATION PHASE

The first and principal concern of those involved needs to be with accurately identifying the need for change. However, simply perceiving where the need for change may lie, will obviously not be sufficient to merit embarking upon the preparation for that change. The preparation for change which is clearly a crucial phase in the project's activities needs to be based on well informed technical specialists' views. Alternatively, the use of an elaborate survey of the current situation could spell out what exactly needs to be done. It is of the utmost importance that every effort is made to identify the gap between the actual and the desired stage as accurately as possible.

Another significant issue which is often neglected is the notion of commitment. It is frequently observed that projects fail to achieve their objectives simply because of a considerable lack of commitment on the part of its beneficiaries, funding agencies, project members and/or management. Arguably, this could partly result from a lack of involvement on the part of those involved, particularly the beneficiaries, in the decision-making process – that is, the process of identifying where the need for change lies and deciding on the best possible course of action. Logically, it may help to ensure the success of an intervention scheme if those with a vested interest are involved from the outset.

Other activities which would be included in this phase are feasibility studies, the securing of financial assistance, and ensuring the availability of the supporting facilities such as communication, infrastructure, and power supply. Finally, the recruitment and selection of the project's personnel, including the managers, those who are to train them and the administrative staff, also constitute crucial aspects of this first phase.

The implementation and transformation phase

This phase of the project's life constitutes the most visible and high risk period in almost any development programme. It is usually concerned with the carrying out of one or more series of coordinated activities which are aimed at transforming the actual state to the desired one. As shown in Figure 12.1 'implementation' is an umbrella term for the many activities by which the gap between the two states is filled.

The degree to which these implementing activities will be successful will depend, to a large extent, on how accurately the need for change was identified and how the process of transformation is to be managed. Therefore, it is equally important to recognize that the project manager's role as a 'change agent' is a crucial one. The project manager in this context, unlike his predecessors, will not passively follow pre-ordained procedures as an implementor. Rather he would be charged with the responsibility of managing change. In this capacity he would be simultaneously involved in an ongoing process of dealing with factors both inside and outside the project. To be able to do this successfully, to facilitate the transformation process, project managers need to be flexible and proactive (Pedler *et al.* 1986). As Gittinger argues, 'Circumstances will change and project managers must be able to respond intelligibly to these changes' (Gittinger 1982: 24). Changes in economic or structural factors tend to affect the transformation process. The fact that a proactive project manager is required imposes certain conditions on the training and development of these change agents. He or she needs to possess many attributes apart from those abilities and skills required for the carrying out of tasks of a technical nature. This new breed of project manager would need to acquire the kind of attributes, skills and knowledge which would enable effectively dealing with other people – that is, those within the project organization and those who are either directly or indirectly associated with it (Austen and Neale 1984). This could well prove to be a major determinant of the project's success or failure. 'The project manager's task is [therefore] a complex one requiring him or her to steer the project through many obstacles' (Goodman and Love 1980: 15). These include varied responsibilities such as supervision and control, completion and handover.

The process of completion itself is a crucial and time-consuming one. It is often seen as having been reached once the desired state has been achieved. However, as we argued earlier a project which has successfully passed through the transformation phase has not been concluded unless a link is made between this and the operational and maintenance phase. In the case of a manufacturing plant, for example, commissioning is required to ensure that a plant continues to be operable, when for example, it is being scaled down or dismantled and transferred to a new administration.

A project's activities may not necessarily all come under the ambit of one manager. Indeed the person who manages the implementation and transformation phase may be one of a team of managers, with the team as a whole working together to oversee and coordinate the three phases. The fact that we would now have a 'management team' rather than a set of managers working as individuals, has one important implication (Taylor and Watling 1973). When it comes to evaluating the development project it should now be seen as an ongoing process, rather than single sets of project cycles. Under this type of management this process could be planned from the outset and carried out periodically during and after the completion of each phase. Continual monitoring of the circumstances in which a project is being implemented and transformed should provide the project management team, and therefore the project manager in charge of this particular phase, with sufficient information to make any necessary changes. In this way they should be able to negotiate their way round what would previously have been unforeseen difficulties.

The operations and maintenance phase

From a prescriptive viewpoint, project evaluation as an activity represents the final stage of the project cycle. It is suggested that, 'Project evaluation is one of the last tasks in the project cycle. As in every cycle the later steps are inexorably linked to the earlier ones. Thus, evaluation leads to policy which leads to planning which leads to further implementation' (Goodman and Love 1980: 230). Traditionally, the principal role of the project manager is to ensure that the desired state is achieved. Once this is done the responsibility for the maintenance and upkeep of the 'desired state' is handed over to an operations manager or an individual in a similar role. This discontinuity has serious implications in relation to the enterprise's ability to survive. For example, the manager of the operations and maintenance phase may not necessarily possess the same degree of commitment as the managers of the previous phase.

Indeed, this phase is so fraught with unforeseen problems and difficulties that it is not unusual for apparently completed projects to be rendered in need of rehabilitation at this stage. It is typical for financial shortages to be blamed for the failure, or for host countries to be accused of not being sufficiently assiduous in relation to the enterprise. This attitude of holding host countries to be culpable in the event of failure can be seen to be a direct outcome of the traditional doctor–patient prescriptive approach. When rehabilitation does take place it usually only means that the project is restored to its previous condition. Attempts to ensure that the project may be able to maintain itself again in the operations and maintenance phase are not necessarily made.

CONCLUSION

When we are faced with issues such as reconstruction and rehabilitation, the question of why so many projects fail to achieve their development objectives, and whether or not to restore a project to its previous state, gain significance. While it must be acknowledged that poor and ineffective management constitutes one of the major factors which may contribute to the failure of many projects, it is equally important to observe the parallel which has existed between the development of the art of project management and the ways in which development projects have hitherto been managed. The traditional approach to the management of projects has been preoccupied with the maintenance of the *status quo* and the desire for ultimate predictability and control. When faced with unplanned and unpredictable circumstances efforts have been confined to monitoring and evaluating the setbacks rather than overcoming the real obstacle, which is the fundamental approach. This approach does not view development in the context of planned change and thus does not require the managers of such projects to learn how to deal with uncertain, unpredictable, changing situations.

The world within which project organizations have to survive is characterized by rapid change. No longer can the management of development projects rely on the application of the methods and procedures of yesterday. Since a substantial number of projects needing rehabilitation have failed to survive the operational phase of their life cycle, it is deemed imperative to adopt the kind of managerial policy which, on a continuous and uninterrupted basis, can initiate and deal with change. This also calls for a different type of development project manager. They should be able to function successfully in relation to the fluctuating socio-economic, cultural and political environment in which the development gap is correctly identified and transformed and the desired state achieved. This lays down the basis for developing a preventative management philosophy which is capable of reducing the need for the further reconstruction and rehabilitation of development projects by maximizing their survivability within an ever-changing environment.

REFERENCES

Alfred, P.S. (1965) *My Years with General Motors*, London: Sidgwick & Jackson.

Analoui, F. (1989a) *Organisational structure, environment and the need for the management of change*, Discussion Paper no. 5 (new series), Development and Project Planning Centre, University of Bradford.

—— (1989b) 'Project manager's role: towards a descriptive approach', *Project Appraisal*, vol. 4, no. 1, pp. 32–8.

Ashley, D.B., Lurie, C.S. and Yeselskie, E.J. (1987) 'Determinants of construction project success', *Project Management Journal*, vol. 6, pp. 36–42.

Austen, A.D. and Neale, R.H. (1984) *Managing Construction Projects*, Geneva: International Labour Office.

Baum, W.C. (1978) 'The World Bank project cycle', *Finance and Development*, vol. 15, no. 4, December.

Bennis, W.G. (1966) *Changing Organizations*, New York: MacGraw-Hill.

Braverman, H. (1974) *Labour and Monopoly Capital*, New York and London: Monthly Review Press.

Burrell, G., and Morgan, G. (1979) *Sociological Paradigms and Organisational Analysis*, London: Heinemann.

Cyert, R.M. and March, J.G. (1963) *A Behavioural Theory of the Firm*, New York: Prentice-Hall.

Drucker, P.F. (1970) *Technology, Management and Society*, New York: Harper & Row.

Duffy, P.J. and Thomas, R.D. (1988) *Project Planning and Management: An Integrated Approach*, New York: Pergamon Press.

Eldridge, J.E.T. and Crombie, A.D. (1974) *A Sociology of Organisations*, London: George Allen & Unwin.

Fayol, H. (1916) *General and Industrial Management* (translated by C. Storr) London: Pitman.

Gittinger, J.P. (1982) *The Economic Analysis of Agricultural Projects*, 2nd edn, London and Baltimore: Johns Hopkins University Press for the World Bank.

Goodman, J.L. and Love, N.R. (1980) *Project Planning and Management: An Integrated Approach*, New York: Pergamon Press.

Iglesias, G.U. (1976) *Implementation: The Problem of Achieving Results*, Manila: EROPA.

Kast, E.F. and Rosenzweig, E.J. (1974) *Organisation and Management: A System Approach*, Tokyo: MacGraw-Hill.

Koontz, H. and O'Donnel, C. (1968) *Principles of Management*, 4th edn, New York: MacGraw-Hill.

Mangham, L. (1979) *The Political Organisational Change*, New York: Associated Business Press.

Mansfield, R. and Zeffane, R. (1983) *Organisational Structure and National Contingencies*, Aldershot: Gower.

March, R.K. and Simon, A.H. (1958) *Organisations*, New York: John Wiley & Sons.

Mooney, D.J. and Reiley, C.A. (1931) *Onward Industry*, New York: Harper & Row.

Morgan, G. (1986) *Images of Organisations*, London: Sage.

Naymark, J. (1983) 'Training, education and culture: observations on the theory and practice of training in developing countries', in F. Blackler (ed.) *Social Psychology and Developing Countries*, New York: John Wiley & Sons.

Overseas Development Administration (1988) *Appraisal of Projects in Developing Countries: A Guide for Economists*, 3rd edn, London: ODA.

Pedler, M., Burgoyne, J. and Boydell, T. (1986) *A Manager's Guide to Self-Development*, London: MacGraw-Hill.

Pugh, D.S., Hickson, D.J. and Ginings, C.R. (1976) *Writers On Organisations*, 2nd edn, Harmondsworth: Penguin.

Rondinelli, D. (1980) 'International assistance policy and development project administrations: the impact of impervious rationality', *Journal of International Organisation*, reprinted in J.L. Goodman and N.R. Love, *Project Planning and Management: An Integrated Approach*, New York: Pergamon Press.

Sayles, L. (1964) *Managerial Behaviour*, New York: MacGraw-Hill.

Silverman, D. (1970) *The Theory of Organisations*, London: Heinemann.

Simon, H.A. (1965) *The Shape of Automation for Men and Management*, New York: Harper & Row.

Smith, M., Beck, J., Cooper, C.L., Cox, C., Ottaway, D. and Talbot, R. (1982) *Introducing Organizational Behaviour*, London: Macmillan.

Taylor, F. (1911) *The Principles of Scientific Management*, New York: Harper & Row.

Taylor, W.F. and Watling, T.F. (1973) *Practical Project Management*, New York: Halstead Press.

Waterston, A. (1974) *Development Planning Lessons from Experience*, Baltimore: Johns Hopkins University Press.

Weber, M. (1947) *The Theory of Social and Economic Organization*, Oxford: Oxford University Press.

BIBLIOGRAPHY

African, Caribbean and Pacific States/European Economic Community, (1986) *Towards 2000: People-Centred Development*, report prepared by Mr C. Jackson for ACP/EEC Joint Assembly, 1986–7, Brussels: EEC.

Alfred, P.S. (1965) *My Years with General Motors*, London: Sidgwick & Jackson.

Analoui, F. (1989) *Organisational Structure, Environment and the Need for the Management of Change*, Discussion Paper, no. 5 (new series), Development and Project Planning Centre, University of Bradford.

—— (1989a) 'Project manager's role: towards a descriptive approach', *Project Appraisal*, vol. 4, no. 1, pp. 32–8.

Asante S.K.B. and Date-Bah S.K. (1980) 'From concession to joint venture agreement: restructuring mineral agreements – a case study from Ghana' (based on a report prepared for the UN Centre for Transnational Corporations).

Ascher, K. (1984) *The Politics of Privatisation: Contracting Out Public Services*, London: Macmillan Education.

Ascher, W. (1982) 'Political forecasting and development policy', *Vierteljahresbericht*, no. 90, December.

Ashley, D.B., Lurie, C.S. and Yeselskie, E.J. (1987) 'Determinants of construction project success', *Project Management Journal*, vol. 6, pp. 36–42.

Asian Development Bank (1984) *Rural Development in Asia and the Pacific*, vol. 1, Papers and Proceedings of the ADB Regional Seminar on Rural Development, vols I and II, Manila, Philippines: ADB.

Austen, A.D. and Neale, R.H. (1984) *Managing Construction Projects*, Geneva: International Labour Office.

Ayub, M. and Hegstad, S. (1987) 'Management of public industrial enterprises' *World Bank Research Observer*, vol. 2, no. 1, pp. 79–101.

Bagadion, B.U. (1985) 'Developing irrigators' organisations: a learning process approach', in M.M. Cenea (ed.), *Putting People First: Sociological Variables in Rural Development*, Oxford: Oxford University Press.

Baum, W.C. (1978) 'The World Bank project cycle', *Finance and Development*, vol. 15, no. 4, December.

Baum, W.C. and Tolbert, S.M. (1985) *Investing in Development: Lessons of World Bank Experience*, New York: Oxford University Press for the World Bank.

Baumol, W. and Willig, R. (1986) 'Contestability: developments since the book', *Oxford Economic Papers*, vol. 38 supplement, pp. 9–36.

Bennis, W.G. (1966) *Changing Organisations*, New York: MacGraw-Hill.

Berg, E. (1982) 'Changing the public–private mix: a survey of some recent experiences in LDCs', DM/83/10, IMF: Washington DC.

Blackwell, M. and Nocera, S. (1988) 'The impact of debt to equity conversion', *Finance and Development*, June.

Blejer, M. and Khan, M. (1984) 'Government policy and private investment in developing countries', *IMF Staff Papers*, vol. 31.

Bolton, D. (1985) *Nationalization: A Road to Socialism?*, London: Zed Press.

Braverman, H. (1974) *Labour and Monopoly Capital*, New York and London: Monthly Review Press.

Brealey, R. and Myers, S. (1984) *Principles of Corporate Finance*, 2nd edn, London: MacGraw-Hill.

Brett, E.A. (1988) 'States, markets and private power: problems and possibilities', in P. Cook and C. Kirkpatrick (eds), *Privatisation in Less Developed Countries*, Brighton: Wheatsheaf Books.

—— (1988) 'Adjustment and the state: the problems of administrative reform', *IDS Bulletin*, vol. 19, no. 4, pp. 1–11.

Bridger, G. (1986) 'Rapid project appraisal', *Project Appraisal*, vol. 1, no. 4, December.

Burrell, G. and Morgan, G. (1979) *Sociological Paradigms and Organisational Analysis*, London: Heinemann.

Burton, M.A. and Franks, T.R. (1989) 'Successful Rehabilitation: can old habits be changed?', Paper given at Asian Regional Symposium on the Modernization and Rehabilitation of Irrigation and Drainage Schemes, Philippines, February.

Burton, M.A. and Smout, I.K. (1986) 'Training programmes for irrigation staff and farmers', ODI/IIMI Irrigation Management Network Papers 86/1d and 86/1e, London: Overseas Development Institute.

Chenery, H.B. (1986) 'Growth and transformation', in H. Chenery, S. Robinson and M. Synquin (eds), *Industrialization and Growth: A Comparative Study*, London: Oxford University Press.

Cherns, A. (1983) 'Social psychology and development', in F. Blackler (ed.), *Social Psychology and Developing Countries*, New York: John Wiley & Sons.

Choksi, A. and Papageorgiou, D. (eds) (1985) *Economic Liberalisation in Developing Countries*, Oxford: Basil Blackwell.

Cole, S. (1987) 'The economic costs of plant closure', *Project Appraisal*, vol. 2, no. 1, March.

Collins, P. (1987) 'Implementing administrative reforms in international development organisations', *Public Administration and Development*, vol. 7, pp. 125–42.

Cook, P. (1988) *Economic Liberalisation, Privatisation and State Enterprise Efficiency in Less Developed Countries*, Report to British Council/Overseas Development Administration, September.

Cook, P. and Kirkpatrick, C. (eds) (1988) *Privatisation in Less Developed Countries*, Brighton: Wheatsheaf Books.

Corden, W.M. (1989) 'Macroeconomic adjustment in developing countries', *World Bank Research Observer*, vol. 4, no. 1.

Craig, J. (1988) 'Privatisation in Malaysia: present trends and future prospects', in P. Cook and C. Kirkpatrick (eds), *Privatisation in Less Developed Countries*, Brighton: Wheatsheaf Books.

Cyert, R.M. and March, J.G. (1963) *A Behavioural Theory of the Firm*, New York: Prentice-Hall.

Development Assistance Committee, (1982) *Guidelines on Aid for Maintenance and Strengthening of Existing Services and Facilities* (Addendum to DAC Guidelines on Local and Recurrent Cost Financing, 1979), Paris: OECD.

Dornbusch, R. (1980) *Open Economy Macro-Economics*, New York: Basic Books.

Drucker, P.F. (1970) *Technology, Management and Society*, New York: Harper & Row.

—— (1986) 'The changed world economy', *Foreign Affairs*, vol. 64, no. 4, pp. 768–91.

Duffy, P.J. and Thomas, R.D. (1988) *Project Planning and Management: An Integrated Approach*, New York: Pergamon Press.

Easterly, W.R. (1989) 'Policy distortions, size of government and growth' PPR Working Papers no. 344, World Bank, December.

Economic Development Institute (1987) 'Management training and research for African development', *EDI Policy Seminar Report Series*, no. 5, January, Washington, DC.

Eldridge, J.E.T. and Crombie, A.D. (1974) *A Sociology of Organisations*, London: George Allen & Unwin.

European Economic Community (1978) *Integrated Rural Development Projects Carried out in Black Africa with EDF Aid: Evaluation and Outlook for the Future*, H. Dupriez, Brussels: EEC.

European Investment Bank (1986) *Annual Report*, Luxembourg.

Fayol, H. (1916) *General and Industrial Management*, (translated by C. Storr), London: Pitman.

Federal Republic of Germany (1986) *Learning from Mistakes: Nine Years of*

Evaluating Project Reality, Findings and Conclusions, Ministry of Economic Cooperation, Bonn.

Food and Agriculture Organisation (FAO) (1990) *The Design of Agricultural Investment Projects: Lessons from Experience*, Investment Centre Technical Paper no. 6, Rome.

Francis, H.R.H. and Hinton J., (1987) *Minor Canal Management in the Gezira Irrigation Scheme, Sudan*, Interim Report, ODU Research Report, OD/93, Hydraulics Research Ltd, Wallingford, UK.

Franks, T.R. (1986) 'Water management on the Rice Canal System, Pakistan', *Irrigation and Drainage Systems*, vol. 1, pp. 5–18.

—— (1989) 'Bureaucracy, organisation culture and development', *Public Administration and Development*, vol. 9, pp. 357–68.

Franks, T.R., Broyles, J.E., and Carleton, W.T. (1985) *Corporate Finance: Concepts and Applications*, Boston: Kent.

Fransman, M. (ed.) (1982) *Industry and Accumulation in Africa*, London: Macmillan.

Furubotn, E. and Pejovich, S. (1972) 'Property rights and economic theory: a survey of recent literature', *Journal of Economic Literature*, vol. X, no. 4, pp. 1137–62.

Gasper, D. (1985) 'Bargaining in project appraisal and evaluation', Project Planning Centre Discussion Paper no. 116, (old series), University of Bradford.

Ghana, Republic of (1985) *Progress of the Economic Recovery Programme 1984–1986 and Policy Framework 1986–1988*, Accra.

—— (1987) *Public Investment Programme 1986–1988*, vol. 1 – Main Report, Accra.

Gittinger, J.P. (1982) *The Economic Analysis of Agricultural Projects*, 2nd edn, London and Baltimore: Johns Hopkins University Press for the Economic Development Institute.

Goodman, J.L. and Love, N.R. (1980) *Project Planning and Management: An Integrated Approach*, New York: Pergamon Press.

Government of Ghana (1983) 'A principled approach to designing a tax regime for mining in Ghana', Accra.

Government of Tanzania, Marketing Development Bureau (1981) *Price Policy Recommendations for the 1982–3 Agricultural Price Review*.

—— Marketing Development Bureau (1986) *Annual Review of Agriculture*.

—— Marketing Development Bureau (1986) *Annual Review of Sugar Cane*.

—— Marketing Development Bureau (1986) *Annual Review of Coffee*.

—— Marketing Development Bureau (1986) *Annual Review of Tea*.

—— Marketing Development Bureau (1986) *Annual Review of Tobacco*.

—— Ministry of Agriculture and Livestock Development (1983) *The Agricultural Policy of Tanzania*

—— Ministry of Finance, Planning and Economic Affairs (1988) *Hali ya Uchumi wa Taifa Katika Mwaka 1987*.

—— Ministry of Planning and Economic Affairs (1982) *Structural Adjustment Programme*.

—— Project Preparation and Monitoring Bureau (1984) *Export Crop Packages – A Framework for Action*.

—— Project Preparation and Monitoring Bureau, (1984) *National Sisal Programme*.

—— Project Preparation and Monitoring Bureau, (1984) *National Tea Programme*.

—— Project Preparation and Monitoring Bureau, (1988) *Coffee Expansion Programme*.

Grindle, M.S. (1984) *Politics and Policy Implementation in the Third World*, Princeton, NJ: Princeton University Press.

Harding, T.M. and Franks, T.R. (1988) 'The matrix management of irrigation projects: integrated management of major irrigation schemes in Sri Lanka', *Agricultural Administration and Extension*, vol. 28, pp. 133–46.

Hillebrandt, P.M. and Meikle, J.L. (1989) 'Construction project rehabilitation: policies for improved resource use and performance', in M.A. Tribe (ed.), *Proceedings of the Conference on Project Rehabilitation in Developing Countries*, Development and Project Planning Centre, University of Bradford.

Hirschman, A.O. (1970) *Exit, Voice and Loyalty: Responses to Decline in Firms, Organisations and States*, Cambridge, Mass.: Harvard University Press.

Hood, C. (1979) *The Limits of Administration*, London: John Wiley.

Huq, M.M. (1989) *The Economy of Ghana: The First 25 Years Since Independence*, London: Macmillan.

Iglesias, G.U. (1976) *Implementation: The Problem of Achieving Results*, Manila: EROPA.

International Bank for Reconstruction and Development (1983) *Ghana: The Cocoa Sector*, IBRD Working Paper, western Africa Programs, Dept 1, Div. B., Adjustment Report no. 4702–GH, October.

International Fund of Agricultural Development (1986) *Rural Development and the Peasant Farmer*, A Statement by Bahman Mansuri, ✓ Director, Africa Division, IFAD, at EDF Seminar 'Rural development: how can we make it work?', Brussels.

International Institute for Land Reclamation and Improvement (1982) 'Evaluation of irrigation projects sponsored by the EEC', Synthesis report, London.

International Labour Organization (1987) 'Privatisation – its impact on labour relations in ASEAN', ASEAN Tripartite Symposium on Privatisation, Chiang Mai, Thailand, February.

International Monetary Fund (1986) *World Economic Outlook*, Washington, DC.

—— (1988) *World Economic Outlook*, Washington, DC.

Israel, Arturo (1987) *Institutional Development – Incentives to Performance*, Baltimore: Johns Hopkins University Press for the World Bank.

Kast, E.F. and Rosenzweig, E.J. (1974) *Organisation and Management: A System Approach*, Tokyo: MacGraw-Hill.

Killick, T. (1976) 'The possibilities of development planning', *Oxford Economic Papers*, vol. 28, no. 2, pp. 161–84.

—— (ed.) (1984) *The IMF and Stabilisation: Developing Country Experiences*, London: Heinemann Educational Books, with the Overseas Development Institute.

—— and Commander, S. (1988) 'State divestiture as a policy instrument in developing countries', *World Development*, vol. 16, no. 12, pp. 1465–80.

Kitchen, R.L., (1986) *Finance for the Developing Countries*, Chichester: Wiley.

—— (1987) 'Project rehabilitation and capital restructuring: principles and practice', *Project Appraisal*, vol. 2, no. 3, September.

Koontz, H.and O'Donnel, C.(1968) *Principles of Management*, 4th edn, New York: MacGraw-Hill.

Krugman, P. and Taylor, L. (1978) 'Contractionary effects of devaluation', *Journal of International Economics*, vol. 8, November.

Lawrence, P.R. (1975) 'How to deal with resistance to change', *Harvard Business Review on Management*, New York: Harper & Row.

Lonsdale, J. (1985) 'Political accountability in African history', in Patrick Chabal (ed.), *Political Domination in Africa*, Cambridge: Cambridge University Press.

McCulloch, M. (1986) 'Project frameworks – a logical development for more effective aid', in *British Overseas Aid in 1985*, London: HMSO/Overseas Development Administration.

Mangham, L.(1979) *The Political Organisational Change*, New York: Associated Business Press.

Mansfield, R. and Zeffane, R. (1983) *Organisational Structure and National Contingencies*, Aldershot: Gower.

March, R.K. and Simon, A.H. (1958) *Organisations*, New York: John Wiley & Sons.

Meikle, F.S. (1989) 'Tools for the analysis of project performance with findings from an example of their use in reviewing a number of Egyptian projects', in M.A. Tribe (ed.), *Proceedings of the Conference on Project Rehabilitation in Developing Countries*, Development and Project Planning Centre, University of Bradford.

Merrey, D.J. and Jinapala, K. (1988) 'On physical remodelling and institutional strengthening: an evaluation of the implications of the pilot field channel experience for the rehabilitation project at Uda Walawe, Sri Lanka', International Irrigation Management Institute. Working Paper no. 7.

Millward, R. (1988) 'Measured sources of inefficiency in the performance of private and public enterprises in LDCs', in P. Cook and C. Kirkpatrick (eds), *Privatisation in Less Developed Countries*, Brighton: Wheatsheaf Books.

Minogue, M. and O'Grady, J. (1985) 'Contracting out local authority services in Britain', *Local Government Studies*, May–June, pp. 35–50.

Mitchell, T.F. (1978) *People in Organisations: Understanding Their Behavior*, New York: McGraw-Hill.

Mooney, D.J. and Reiley, C.A. (1931) *Onward Industry*, New York: Harper & Row.

Moore, M.P. (1981) 'The sociology of irrigation management in Sri Lanka', *Water Supply and Management*, vol. 5, part 1, pp. 117–33.

Morgan, G. (1986) *Images of Organisations*, London: Sage.

Morley, R. (1988) *The Macroeconomics of Open Economies*, Aldershot: Edward Elgar.

Mosley, P. (1987) 'Conditionality as bargaining process: structural adjustment lending, 1980–86', *Princeton Essays in International Finance*, no. 168, October.

—— (1988) 'Privatisation, public-based lending and World Bank behaviour', in P. Cook and C. Kirkpatrick (eds), *Privatisation in Less Developed Countries*, Brighton: Wheatsheaf Books.

Myrdal, G. (1968) *Asian Drama*, London: Penguin Books.

Naymark, J. (1983) 'Training, education and culture: observations on the theory and practice of training in developing countries', in F. Blackler (ed.), *Social Psychology and Developing Countries*, New York: John Wiley & Sons.

Nellis, J. (1986) 'Public enterprises in sub-Saharan Africa', mimeo, Washington, DC: World Bank.

Nelson, J. (1984) 'The political economy of stabilisation: commitment, capacity and public response', *World Development*, vol. 12, no. 10, pp. 983–1006.

NIPEP (1985) *Aspects of the Black Economy in India*, Delhi: The National Institute of Public Finance and Policy.

Nixson, F. and Leeson, P.F. (1988) 'Development economics and the state', in P.F. Leeson and M.M. Minogue (eds), *Perspectives on Development: Cross-Disciplinary Themes in Development Studies*, Manchester: Manchester University Press.

Overseas Development Administration, (1974) *Wadi Dhuleil, Jordan: an ex-post evaluation*, London.

—— (1981) *An Evaluation of ODA financed projects to assist Malawi Railways*, London.

—— (1983) *A review of ODA's experience with hospital projects*, London.

—— (1984) *The evaluation of aid projects and programmes*, London.

—— (1985) *Major issues in grain storage; an overview of evaluations*, London.

—— (1985) *An Evaluation of the UK/Bangladesh grain storage rehabilitation project*, London.

—— (1988) *Appraisal of Projects in Developing Countries: A Guide for Economists*, 3rd edn, London: ODA.

Overseas Development Institute (1986) *Privatisation: The Developing Country Experience*, Overseas Development Institute Briefing Paper, London: ODI.

Pack, H. (1988) 'Industrialization and trade', in H. Chenery and T.N. Srinivasan (eds), *Handbook of Development Economics*, vol. 1, Amsterdam: Elsevier.

Papps, I. (1987) 'Techniques of project appraisal', in N. Gemmell (ed.), *Surveys in Development Economics*, Oxford: Basil Blackwell.

Park, Y. (1986) 'A system for evaluating the performance of government-invested enterprises in the Republic of Korea', *World Bank Discussion Papers*, no. 3, November.

Pedler, M., Burgoyne, J. and Boydell, T. (1986) *A Manager's Guide to Self-Development*, London: MacGraw-Hill.

Pendse, D.R. (1988) *Privatisation: Myths and Realities*, Project for Economic Education, Bombay.

Pfefferman, G.P. and Madarassy, A. (1989) 'Trends in private investment in thirty developing countries', *International Finance Corporation Discussion Paper no. 6*, Washington, DC.

Please, S. and Amoako, K.Y. (1986) 'OAU, ECA and the World Bank: do they really disagree?', in J Ravenhill (ed.), *Africa in Economic Crisis*, London: Macmillan.

Porter, L.W., Lawler, E.E. and Hackman, J.R. (1987) *Behaviour in Organisations*, New York: McGraw-Hill.

Potts, D. (1989) *Rehabilitation of Export-Oriented Agriculture in Tanzania – Same Again or Something Different?*, mimeo, Development and Project Planning Centre, University of Bradford.

Pugh, D.S., Hickson, D.J. and Ginings, C.R. (1976) *Writers On Organisations*, 2nd edn, Harmondsworth: Penguin.

Raikes, P. (1986) 'Eating the carrot and wielding the stick: the agricultural sector in Tanzania', in J. Boesen and K.J. Havnevik, *Tanzania – Crisis and Struggle for Survival*, Uppsala, Scandinavian Institute of African Studies.

Ravenhill, J. (1986) 'Africa's continuing crises: the elusiveness of development', in J. Ravenhill (ed.), *Africa in Economic Crisis*, London: Macmillan.

—— (1988) 'Adjustment with growth: a fragile consensus', *Journal of Modern African Studies*, vol. 26, no. 2.

Roberts, J. (1989) 'Liberalising foreign exchange rates in Sub-Saharan Africa', *Development Policy Review*, vol. 7, January.

Rondinelli, D. (1980) 'International assistance policy and development project administrations: the impact of impervious rationality', *Journal of International Organisation*, Reprinted in J.L. Goodman and N.R. Love, *Project Planning and Management*, New York: Pergamon Press.

Rothstein, R. (1976) 'Politics and policymaking in the Third World: does a reform strategy make sense?', *World Development*, vol. 4, no. 8, pp. 695–708.

Sandbrook, R. (1988) 'Patrimonialism and the failing of parastatals: Africa in comparative perspective', in P. Cook and C. Kirkpatrick (eds), *Privatisation in Less Developed Countries*, Brighton: Wheatsheaf Books.

Sauermann, H. (1979) 'On the economic and financial rehabilitation of West Germany 1945–1949', *Zeitschrift für die Gesamte Staatswissenschaft*, vol. 135, no. 3, September.

Sayles, L. (1964) *Managerial Behaviour*, New York: MacGraw-Hill.

SEDES, (1986) 'Evaluation of the Iringa region (Tanzania) agricultural development project, phase II, interim report'.

Seers, D. and Belshaw, D.G.R. (eds) (1979) *The Rehabilitation of the Economy of Uganda*, 2 vols, Commonwealth Fund for Technical Cooperation, London: Commonwealth Secretariat.

Shackleton, J.R. (1987) 'The political economy of privatisation in less developed countries', Unpublished paper to UK Development Studies Association Annual Conference, September.

Short, R. (1984) 'The role of public enterprises: an international statistical comparison', in R. Floyd, C. Gray, and R. Short, *Public Enterprise in Mixed Economies*, Washington, DC: IMF.

Silverman, D. (1970) *The Theory of Organisations*, London: Heinemann.

Simon, H.A. (1965) *The Shape of Automation for Men and Management*, New York: Harper & Row.

Sinha, D. (1983) 'Applied social psychology and problems of national development', in F. Blackler (ed.), *Social Psychology and Developing Countries*, New York: John Wiley & Sons.

Smith, M., Beck, J., Cooper, C.L., Cox, C., Ottaway, D. and Talbot, R. (1982) *Introducing Organisational Behaviour*, London: Macmillan.

Squire, L. and van der Tak, H.G. (1975) *Economic Analysis of Projects*, Baltimore: Johns Hopkins University Press for World Bank.

Taylor, F. (1911) *The Principles of Scientific Management*, New York: Harper & Row.

Taylor, L. (1988) *Varieties of Stabilisation Experience*, Oxford: Clarendon Press.

Taylor, W.F. and Watling, T.F. (1973) *Practical Project Management*, New York: Halstead Press.

Tribe, M.A. (1989) 'The planning and economic analysis of rehabilitation projects', in M.A. Tribe (ed.), *Proceedings of the Conference on Project Rehabilitation in Developing Countries*, Development and Project Planning Centre, University of Bradford.

—— (1989) 'Project rehabilitation in Ghana's Economic Recovery Programme', mimeo, DPPC Discussion Papers (new series), no. 14.

Tribe, M.A. and Yaffey, M.J.H. (1988) 'The planning and appraisal of rehabilitation projects', 2 vols, Development and Project Planning Centre, University of Bradford (training materials in private circulation).

UNIDO (1985) *Handbook of Industrial Statistics 1984*, New York: UN.

—— (1988) *UNIDO Policy on Industrial Rehabilitation*, Vienna, February.

—— (1988) 'Regenerating African manufacturing industry: country briefs' (PPD. 97), *Studies on the Rehabilitation of African Industry*, no. 2, Vienna, November.

—— (1988) 'The agro-based industries in Zambia and Angola: key characteristics and rehabilitation issues' (PPD.102 and PPD. 103), *Studies on the Rehabilitation of African Industry*, no. 4 and no. 5, Vienna, December.

—— (1988) *Industry and Development: Global Report 1988–89* (ID/360), Vienna.

—— (1989) Draft report on Round-Table Meeting on Industrial Rehabilitation, Lusaka, Zambia, 8–10 March 1989 (PPD. 120), *Studies on the Rehabilitation of African Industry*, no. 6, Vienna, June.

Uphoff, N. (1986) 'Activating community capacity for water management: experience from Gal Oya, Sri Lanka', in D.C. Korten (ed.), *Community Management: Asian Experiences and Perspectives*, Connecticut, USA: Kumarian Press.

US Agency for International Development (1982) *Aid Policy Paper: Recurrent Costs*, Washington, DC.

—— (1983) *Irrigation in AID's Experience: A Consideration Based on Evaluations*, Washington, DC.

Waterston, A. (1974) *Development Planning Lessons from Experience*, Baltimore: Johns Hopkins Press.

Weber, M. (1947) *The Theory of Social and Economic Organisation*, Oxford: Oxford University Press.

Weiss J. (1989) *Industrial Policy in Jamaica in the 1980s*, Development and Project Planning Centre, Occasional Paper no. 13, University of Bradford.

Wood, D.J. (1986) 'The World Bank of tomorrow: policies and operations', in *Recovery in the Developing World: The London Symposium on the World Bank's Role*, Washington, DC: The World Bank.

World Bank (1981) *Accelerated Development in Sub-Saharan Africa: An Agenda for Action*, Washington, DC: World Bank.

—— (1981) *Water Management in Bank Supported Irrigation Project Systems: An Analysis of Past Experience*, Washington, DC.

—— (1982) *IDA in Retrospect*, Oxford: Oxford University Press for the World Bank.

—— (1983) *World Development Report,* London and New York: Oxford University Press for the World Bank.

—— (1984) *Institutional Development in Africa: A review of World Bank Project Experiences,* two vols, Washington, DC.

—— (1984) *Towards Sustained Development in Sub-Saharan Africa,* Washington, DC: World Bank.

—— (1985) *Tenth Annual Review of Project Performance Audit Results,* Operations Evaluation Department, World Bank, Washington, DC.

—— (1985) *Sustainability of Projects: Final Review of Experience,* Operations Evaluation Department, June 14 (restricted distribution).

—— (1986) *Financing Adjustment with Growth in Sub-Saharan Africa, 1986–1990,* Washington, DC.

—— (1988) *World Development Report,* Washington, DC. and London: Oxford University Press for the World Bank.

—— (1989) *Africa's Adjustment and Growth in the 1980s,* Washington: World Bank and UNDP.

—— (1989) *World Development Report,* London: Oxford University Press for the World Bank.

—— (1989) *Project Performance Results for 1987,* Operations Evaluation Department, World Bank, Washington, DC.

—— (1989) *Industrial Restructuring: Policy and Practice,* Industry Development Division, World Bank, Washington, DC, March.

Yaffey, M.J.H. (1989) 'Financial analysis: project or portfolio', Chapter 6 in this volume.

Youker, R. (1977) 'Organisation alternatives for project managers', *Harvard Management Review,* vol. 5, pp. 112–21.

INDEX

acceptance criteria 32, 145–6,
147–8, 150–1, 152, 153
ACP (African, Caribbean and
Pacific Countries) 26, 51
Adedeji, A. 19
adjustment 211; Africa 9, 178–80;
commitment needed 13–14;
economic analysis and
149–50; lending 5–6, 10;
long-term view 11–12
adoption rates 67–8, 68
Africa 26, 39; debt 19, 106;
economic situation 104–6;
planning process 11; roads
42; 'state' 13; sub-Saharan *see*
sub-Saharan Africa; *see also
under individual countries*
agricultural projects 54–74;
improving design *see* design;
performance 54–6; problems
in implementation 56–7
agriculture 105; estate *see*
Tanzania; manufacturing
rehabilitation and 111, 192–3
Alfred, P.S. 236
Amboni Group 78, 80, 86, 91;
survival strategies 88–9, 89
Amoako, K.Y. 194
Analoui, F. 239, 240, 241
Angola 103, 191; industrial
rehabilitation 113, 114–15, 117
animal health projects 40
annual operating planning
(AOP) 60

appraisal *see* economic appraisal
Arab countries 17
arbitrage pricing theory (APT)
131–2, 138
Arusha Declaration 77
Ascher, K. 202
Ascher, W. 202
Ashanti Goldfields 166–71,
173–4; rehabilitation
programme 169–71
Ashanti Goldfields Corporation
(AGC) 166, 167, 169, 170, 174
Ashley, D.B. 234
Asia 17, 24, 25; *see also under
individual countries*
Asian Development Bank (ADB)
40, 41, 50, 51, 55
assets: institutional change and
fixed 215–16, 224, 230, 231;
valuation of existing 148, 171
Austen, A.D. 245
axle limit restrictions 42
Ayub, M. 197

Bagadion, B.U. 229
Bangladesh 47; Grain Storage
43, 48
Baum, W.C. 18, 154; definition
of a project 3, 140–1; project
cycle 238; sunk costs 143,
144–5
Baumol, W. 198
Belshaw, D.G.R. 154
beneficiary participation 70, 244